Kaplan Publishing are constantly finding new ways to make a difference to your studies and our exciting online resources really do offer something different to students looking for exam success.

This book comes with free MyKaplan online resources so that you can study anytime, anywhere. **This free online resource is not sold separately and is included in the price of the book.**

Having purchased this book, you have access to the following online study materials:

CONTENT	AAT	
	Text	Kit
iPaper version of the book	✓	✓
Progress tests with instant answers	✓	
Mock assessments online	✓	✓
Material updates	✓	✓

D1390350

How to access your online resources

Kaplan Financial students will already have a MyKaplan account and these extra resources will be available to you online. You do not need to register again, as this process was completed when you enrolled. If you are having problems accessing or line materials, please ask your course administrator.

If you are already a registered MyKaplan user go to www.MyKaplan.co.uk and log in. Select the 'add a book' feature and enter the ISBN number of this book and the unique pass key at the bottom of this card. Then click 'finished' or 'add another book'. You may add as many books as you have purchased from this screen.

If you purchased through Kaplan Flexible Learning or via the Kaplan Publishing website you will automatically receive an e-mail invitation to MyKaplan. Please register your details using this email to gain access to your content. If you do not receive the e-mail or book content, please contact Kaplan Flexible Learning.

If you are a new user register at www.MyKaplan.co.uk and click on the link contained in the email we sent you to activate your account. Then select the 'add a book' feature, enter the ISBN number of this book and the unique pass key at the bottom of this card. Then click 'finished' or 'add another book'.

Your Code and Information

This code can only be used once for the registration of one book online. This registration and your online content will expire when the final sittings for the examinations covered by this book have taken place. Please allow one hour from the time you submit your book details for us to process your request.

Please scratch the film to access your MyKaplan code.

Please be aware that this code is case-sensitive and you will need to include the dashes within the passcode, but not when entering the ISBN. For further technical support, please visit www.MyKaplan.co.uk

MANAGEMENT ACCOUNTING: COSTING

STUDY TEXT

Qualifications and Credit Framework

AQ2016

This Study Text supports study for the following AAT qualifications:

AAT Advanced Diploma in Accounting – Level 3

AAT Advanced Certificate in Bookkeeping – Level 3

AAT Advanced Diploma in Accounting at SCQF Level 6

British Library Cataloguing-in-Publication Data

A catalogue record for this book is available from the British Library.

Published by
Kaplan Publishing UK
Unit 2, The Business Centre
Molly Millars Lane
Wokingham
Berkshire
RG41 2QZ

ISBN: 978-1-78415-626-8

This Product includes content from the International Auditing and Assurance Standards Board (IAASB) and the International Ethics Standards Board for Accountants (IESBA), published by the International Federation of Accountants (IFAC) in 2015 and is used with permission of IFAC.

CONTENTS

	Page number
Introduction	P.5
Unit guide	P.7
The assessment	P.16
Unit link to synoptic assessment	P.17
Study skills	P.18

STUDY TEXT

Chapter

1	Management accounting	1
2	Cost classification	11
3	Inventory	41
4	Labour	89
5	Expenses	119
6	Overheads	127
7	Basic variance analysis	183
8	Job, batch and service costing	203
9	Process costing	213
10	Marginal costing	263
11	Short-term decision making	283
12	Long-term decision making	321
Mock Assessment Questions		367
Mock Assessment Answers		383
Glossary		391
Index		I.1

INTRODUCTION

HOW TO USE THESE MATERIALS

These Kaplan Publishing learning materials have been carefully designed to make your learning experience as easy as possible and to give you the best chance of success in your AAT assessments.

They contain a number of features to help you in the study process.

The sections on the Unit Guide, the Assessment and Study Skills should be read before you commence your studies.

They are designed to familiarise you with the nature and content of the assessment and to give you tips on how best to approach your studies.

STUDY TEXT

This Study Text has been specially prepared for the revised AAT qualification introduced in September 2016.

It is written in a practical and interactive style:

- Key terms and concepts are clearly defined.

- All topics are illustrated with practical examples with clearly worked solutions based on sample tasks provided by the AAT in the new examining style.

- Frequent practice activities throughout the chapters ensure that what you have learnt is regularly reinforced.

- 'Pitfalls' and 'examination tips' help you avoid commonly made mistakes and help you focus on what is required to perform well in your examination.

ICONS

The chapters include the following icons throughout.

They are designed to assist you in your studies by identifying key definitions and the points at which you can test yourself on the knowledge gained.

 Definition

These sections explain important areas of Knowledge which must be understood and reproduced in an assessment.

 Example

The illustrative examples can be used to help develop an understanding of topics before attempting the activity exercises.

 Test your understanding

These are exercises which give the opportunity to assess your understanding of all the assessment areas.

Quality and accuracy are of the utmost importance to us so if you spot an error in any of our products, please send an email to mykaplanreporting@kaplan.com with full details.

Our Quality Co-ordinator will work with our technical team to verify the error and take action to ensure it is corrected in future editions.

UNIT GUIDE

Introduction

Management Accounting: Costing provides students with the knowledge and skills needed to understand the role of cost and management accounting in an organisation, and how organisations use such information to aid management decision making. This unit takes students from Elements of Costing at Foundation level and gets them ready to prepare organisational budgets and report on performance at Professional level.

On successful completion of this unit, students should be able to carry out costing procedures in an organisation's accounting department with minimal supervision. They will be able to gather, analyse and report cost and revenue information to support managerial planning, control and decision making.

Students will develop a deeper understanding of the fundamental principles that underpin management accounting methodology and techniques, how costs are handled in organisations, and why different organisations treat costs in different ways. They will be able to recognise different approaches to management accounting and provide informed and reasoned judgements to guide management. They will also learn how to apply these principles and appreciate why effective cost accounting is crucial to any organisation.

Students will learn the techniques required for dealing with direct costs and revenues, and with the treatment of short-term overhead costs. These include: inventory control methods; direct labour costing; allocation and apportionment of indirect costs to responsibility centres; calculation of overhead absorption rates, including under absorptions and over absorptions; and prime, marginal and absorption costing calculations.

They will also learn the techniques required for decision making, using both short-term and long-term estimates of costs and revenues. These include: estimating changes in unit costs and profit as activity levels change; segmented profit or loss by products; break-even (cost volume profit – CVP) analysis; limiting factor decision making; job, batch, unit, process and service costing; reconciling budgeted and actual costs and revenues by means of flexible or fixed budgets; and capital investment appraisal techniques.

This unit builds on the knowledge and skills that students develop at Foundation level in Elements of Costing and prepares them for the Professional level units, Management Accounting: Budgeting and Management Accounting: Decision and Control. Together, these units give students an underpinning understanding of cost and management accounting principles and the ability to apply relevant techniques.

Management Accounting: Costing is a **mandatory** unit in this qualification.

Learning outcomes

On completion of this unit the learner will be able to:

- Understand the purpose and use of management accounting within an organisation.

- Apply techniques required for dealing with costs.

- Apportion costs according to organisational requirements.

- Analyse and review deviations from budget and report these to management.

- Apply management accounting techniques to support decision making.

Scope of content

To perform this unit effectively you will need to know and understand the following:

Chapter

1 **Understand the purpose and use of management accounting within an organisation**

1.1 **Demonstrate an understanding of internal reporting**   1, 10

Students need to know:

- The purpose of internal reporting and providing accurate information to management.

- How to calculate:

  - Costs, contribution and reported profits for an organisation.

  - Segmented costs, contribution and reported profits by product.

1.2 **Demonstrate an understanding of ethical principles in management accounting**   1

Students need to know:

- The need for integrity in preparing management accounts.

- That third parties (such as banks) may also be users of management accounts.

1.3 **Critically compare different types of responsibility centres**   1

Student need to know:

- The differences in cost and revenue reporting between responsibility centres, which are:

  - cost centres

  - profit centres

  - investment centres

Chapter

1.4 Explain and demonstrate the difference between marginal and absorption costing

1, 6, 10

Students need to know:

- How to calculate prime, marginal and full absorption costs.

- The difference between product and period costs.

- The impact on reported performance of marginal vs full absorption costing in both the short run and long run.

- Ethical considerations regarding manipulation profits.

- When each method is appropriate.

2 Record and analyse cost information

2.1 Record and calculate materials, labour and overhead costs

3, 4, 6

Students need to be able to:

- Prepare and interpret inventory records.

- Calculate direct labour costs per unit of production or service.

- Calculate overtime premiums and bonuses.

- Complete timesheets and pay calculations (including overtime and bonus).

- Account for overheads.

- Calculate direct labour cost per equivalent finished production.

2.2 Analyse and use appropriate cost information

3, 4, 6

Students need to be able to:

- Analyse cost information for materials, labour and overheads in accordance with the organisation's costing procedures.

- Prepare cost accounting journal entries for direct material or indirect materials; direct or indirect labour; or overhead costs.

KAPLAN PUBLISHING

Chapter

2.3   Apply inventory control methods   3

Students need to know:

- Inventory control measures, including different valuation methods. These include:

    - Inventory buffers, lead times, minimum/maximum order quantities.

    - The concept of economic order quantity.

    - Compliance with inventory control policies.

    - The effect on reported profits of choice of method.

Students need to be able to:

- Account for inventories using FIFO, LIFO (for internal reporting) and AVCO methods.

- Analyse closing inventory balances.

- Make calculation for the inventory control measure listed above.

2.4   Differentiate between cost classifications for different purposes   2

Students need to know:

- The implications of different cost classifications for cost analysis, decision making and reporting. These are:

    - Fixed costs.

    - Variable costs.

    - Semi-variable costs.

    - Stepped costs.

Chapter

2.5 **Differentiate between and apply different costing systems**   1, 8, 9

Students need to know:

- The appropriate choice of costing system for different business sectors and individual organisations.

- How to record cost information, using different costing systems. These are:

  – Job costing.

  – Batch costing.

  – Unit costing.

  – Process costing.

  – Service costing.

3 **Apportion costs according to organisational requirements**

3.1 **Calculate and use overhead costs**   6

Students need to know:

- The concept of activity based costing, including appropriate cost drivers.

- Different method of indirect cost allocation, apportionment or absorption.

Students need to be able to:

- Attribute overhead costs to production and service cost centres:

  – Allocation versus apportionment.

  – Direct method.

  – Step-down method.

Chapter

3.2 Calculate overhead recovery rates using traditional methods   6

Students need to be able to:

- Calculate overhead recovery rates in accordance with suitable bases of absorption. These are:

  - For a manufacturer: machine hours or direct labour hours.

  - For a service business: suitable basis for the specific business.

3.3 Calculate overhead recovery rates using activity based costing   6

Students need to be able to:

- Calculate overhead recovery rates using appropriate cost drivers.

3.4 Demonstrate understanding of the under or over recovery of overheads   6

Students need to be able to:

- Account for under or over recovered overhead costs in accordance with established procedures. These include:

  - Making under or over absorption calculations.

  - Making cost journal postings.

  - Interpreting the significance of under or over recoveries of overhead costs.

4   Analyse and review deviations from budget and report these to management

4.1 Calculate variances   7

Students need to able to:

- Compare budget/standard vs actual costs and revenues, and calculate variances using:

  - Fixed budgets.

  - Flexible budgets.

Chapter

4.2   Analyse and investigate variance   7

Students need to be able to:

- Determine the cause and effects of variances.

- Investigate any significant variance, and draw conclusions for remedial action.

4.3   Report on variances   7

Students need to be able to:

- Identify and explain key variances.

- Produce management reports in an appropriate format.

5   Apply management accounting techniques to support decision-making

5.1   Estimate and use short-term future income and costs   11, 12

Students need to know:

- The importance of profession competence in estimating income and costs.

Student need to be able to:

- Use estimates of relevant future income and costs for short-term decision making.

- Use CVP analysis

  – Break-even analysis (both by calculation and by linear break-even chart).

  – Margin of safety and margin of safety %.

  – Target profit.

  – Profit-volume analysis.

- Use limiting factor decision making.

Chapter

5.2 Assess and estimate the effect of changing activity levels

2

Students need to know:

- The effect of changing activity levels on unit costs and profits.

Student need to be able to:

- Calculate changes in forecast unit costs and profits.

- Explain such effects.

5.3 Use long-term future income and costs

12

Students need to know:

- The appropriate choice of technique for long-term decision making:
  - Payback.
  - Net present value.
  - Internal rate of return.

Students need to be able to:

- Interpret the results from a capital investment appraisal (using the techniques above).

Delivering this unit

Unit Name	Content links	Suggested order of delivery
Final Accounts Preparation	Management Accounting: Costing builds on the knowledge and understanding of management accounting as a whole, and also links with Final Accounts Preparation.	N/A

THE ASSESSMENT

Test specification for this unit assessment

Assessment type

Computer based unit assessment

Marking type

Computer marked

Duration of exam

2 hours 30 minutes

Learning outcomes		Weighting
1	Understand the purpose and use of management accounting within an organisation	15%
2	Apply techniques required for dealing with costs	35%
3	Apportion costs according to organisational requirements	19%
4	Analyse and review deviations from budget and report these to management	10%
5	Apply management accounting techniques to support decision making	21%
Total		100%

UNIT LINK TO SYNOPTIC ASSESSMENT

AAT AQ16 introduces a Synoptic Assessment, which students must complete if they are to achieve the appropriate qualification upon completion of a qualification. In the case of the Advanced Diploma in Accounting, students must pass all of the mandatory assessments and the Synoptic Assessment to achieve the qualification.

As a Synoptic Assessment is attempted following completion of individual units, it draws upon knowledge and understanding from those units. It may be appropriate for students to retain their study materials for individual units until they have successfully completed the Synoptic Assessment for that qualification.

With specific reference to this unit, the following learning objectives are also relevant to the Advanced Diploma in Accounting Synoptic Assessment

LO1 Understand the purpose and use of management accounting within an organisation.

LO2 Apply techniques for dealing with costs.

LO3 Apportion costs according to organisational requirements.

LO4 Analyse and review deviations from budget and report these to management.

LO5 Apply management accounting techniques to support decision making.

STUDY SKILLS

Preparing to study

Devise a study plan

Determine which times of the week you will study.

Split these times into sessions of at least one hour for study of new material. Any shorter periods could be used for revision or practice.

Put the times you plan to study onto a study plan for the weeks from now until the assessment and set yourself targets for each period of study – in your sessions make sure you cover the whole course, activities and the associated Test your knowledge activities.

If you are studying more than one unit at a time, try to vary your subjects as this can help to keep you interested and see subjects as part of wider knowledge.

When working through your course, compare your progress with your plan and, if necessary, re-plan your work (perhaps including extra sessions) or, if you are ahead, do some extra revision/practice questions.

Effective studying

Active reading

You are not expected to learn the text by rote, rather, you must understand what you are reading and be able to use it to pass the assessment and develop good practice.

A good technique is to use SQ3Rs – Survey, Question, Read, Recall, Review:

1   **Survey the chapter**

    Look at the headings and read the introduction, knowledge, skills and content, so as to get an overview of what the chapter deals with.

2   **Question**

    Whilst undertaking the survey ask yourself the questions you hope the chapter will answer for you.

KAPLAN PUBLISHING

3   Read

Read through the chapter thoroughly working through the activities and, at the end, making sure that you can meet the learning objectives highlighted on the first page.

4   Recall

At the end of each section and at the end of the chapter, try to recall the main ideas of the section/chapter without referring to the text. This is best done after short break of a couple of minutes after the reading stage.

5   Review

Check that your recall notes are correct.

You may also find it helpful to re-read the chapter to try and see the topic(s) it deals with as a whole.

Note taking

Taking notes is a useful way of learning, but do not simply copy out the text.

The notes must:

- be in your own words
- be concise
- cover the key points
- be well organised
- be modified as you study further chapters in this text or in related ones.

Trying to summarise a chapter without referring to the text can be a useful way of determining which areas you know and which you don't.

Three ways of taking notes

1   Summarise the key points of a chapter

2   Make linear notes

A list of headings, subdivided with sub-headings, listing the key points.

If you use linear notes, you can use different colours to highlight key points and keep topic areas together.

Use plenty of space to make your notes easy to use.

3   Try a diagrammatic form

The most common of which is a mind map.

To make a mind map, put the main heading in the centre of the paper and put a circle around it.

Draw lines radiating from this to the main sub-headings which again have circles around them.

Continue the process from the sub-headings to sub-sub-headings.

Highlighting and underlining

You may find it useful to underline or highlight key points in your study text – but do be selective.

You may also wish to make notes in the margins.

Revision phase

Kaplan has produced material specifically designed for your final examination preparation for this unit.

These include pocket revision notes and a bank of revision questions specifically in the style of the new syllabus.

Further guidance on how to approach the final stage of your studies is given in these materials.

Further reading

In addition to this text, you should also read the 'Accounting Technician' magazine every month to keep abreast of any guidance from the examiners.

Management accounting

1

Introduction

This chapter considers the basic principles of management accounting and management information. It contains fundamental principles that the rest of the course is built on.

ASSESSMENT CRITERIA

Demonstrate an understanding of internal reporting (1.1)

Demonstrate an understanding of ethical principles in management accounting (1.2)

Critically compare different types of responsibility centres (1.3)

Differentiate between and apply different costing systems (2.5):

– unit

CONTENTS

1 Management accounting
2 Terminology
3 The cost card

1 Management accounting

1.1 Introduction

The primary purpose of **Management accounting** is to provide information for use within an organisation. **Internal users**, such as departmental managers, will require a variety of information to ensure the smooth running of their department.

It is also possible that some **external users**, such as banks, may also review the management accounts of a business.

1.2 The aims of management accounting

The aim of management accounting is to assist management in the following areas of running a business:

- **Decision making**

  Management accountants use management information to make informed decisions about the future.

- **Planning**

  Management accountants provide the information for the creation of short, medium and long term plans; for example, a short term plan is the preparation of annual budgets.

- **Co-ordinating**

  Planning enables all departments to be co-ordinated and to work together.

- **Controlling**

  The comparison of actual results with the budget helps to identify areas where operations are not running according to plan. Investigating the causes, and acting on the results of that investigation, helps to control the activities of the business.

- **Communicating**

  Preparing plans that are then distributed to departmental managers helps to communicate the aims of the business to those managers.

- **Motivating**

  Plans and budgets should include targets to motivate managers (and staff) and improve their performance. If the target is too difficult, however, it is likely to demotivate and the target is unlikely to be achieved.

1.3 Management information

A management accountant's main objective is to provide information to managers to enable the correct decisions to be made. The information provided may be the same as that required for financial accounting but there are no regulations that need to be applied.

Management information needs to have the attributes of good information. It needs to be:

- **Fit for purpose** – management information needs to be **accurate**, **relevant** and **complete**. The reason the information is required will determine how accurate it needs to be. For example, if the cost of a single item is required then pounds and pence will be needed for accuracy but the costs for a division or department of an organisation may be accurate to the nearest thousand pounds. Information needs to be complete enough to enable managers to make informed decisions. Ensuring that information is complete does not mean that all information should be provided to all managers. Managers only require information that will be relevant to their decisions.

- **Cost-effective** – the benefits obtainable from the information must also exceed the cost of acquiring it

- **Timely** – information should be available when it is required. To improve timeliness Management Information Systems can be installed into organisations. These are computer packages that allow reports to be produced and data to be extracted with ease. Information which is not available until after a decision is made will be useful only for comparisons and long term control

1.4 Cost accounting

Cost accounting is usually a large part of management accounting. As its name suggests, it is concerned with **establishing costs**. It developed within manufacturing businesses.

Cost accounting is primarily directed at enabling management to perform the functions of **planning, control** and **decision making:**

(a) determining costs and profits during a control period

(b) valuing inventory of raw materials, work in progress and finished goods, and controlling inventory levels

(c) preparing budgets, forecasts and other control data for a forthcoming control period

(d) creating a reporting system which enables managers to take corrective action where necessary to control costs

(e) providing information for decision-making such as pricing.

Items (a) and (b) are traditional **cost accounting roles**; (c) to (e) extend into management accounting.

Cost accounting is not confined to the environment of manufacturing, although it is in this area that it is most fully developed. **Service industries, central and local government, and accountancy and legal practices** make use of cost accounting information. Furthermore, it is not restricted purely to manufacturing and operating costs, but also to administration, selling and distribution and research and development.

1.5 Ethical principles in management accounting

A management accountant's responsibility is not just to satisfy the needs of an individual client or employer. It should also be to act in the public interest. In acting in the public interest a management accountant should observe and comply with the fundamental ethical requirements shown in the IFAC Code.

Management accountants are expected to present information fully, honestly and professionally and so that it will be understood in its context.

Integrity means that a member must be straightforward and honest in all professional and business relationships. Integrity also implies fair dealing and truthfulness.

To maintain integrity a management accountant has the following responsibilities:

- Communicate unfavourable as well as favourable information

- Avoid activities that affect their ability to perform

- Avoid conflicts of interest and advise others of potential conflicts

- Recognise and communicate personal and professional limitations

- Refrain from activities that could discredit the profession

- Refuse gifts or favours that might influence behaviour

- Do not subvert the company's legitimate objectives

2 Terminology

2.1 Introduction

This section looks at some of the basic terminology you will encounter whilst working through this unit.

2.2 Cost object

A **cost object** is anything for which costs can be ascertained. Cost units and cost centres, described below, are types of cost object.

2.3 Cost units

A **cost unit** is a unit of product or service in relation to which costs are ascertained.

To help with planning, control and decision making, businesses often need to calculate a cost per unit of output.

A key question, however, is what exactly we mean by a 'unit of output', or '**cost unit**'. This will mean different things to different businesses but we always looks at what the business produces.

- A car manufacturer will want to determine the cost of each car and probably different components as well.

- In a printing firm, the cost unit could be the specific customer order.

- For a paint manufacturer, the unit could be a litre of paint.

- An accountancy firm will want to know the costs incurred for each client. To help with this it is common to calculate the cost per hour of chargeable time spent by staff.

- A hospital might wish to calculate the cost per patient treated; the cost of providing a bed for each day or the cost of an operation.

2.4 Responsibility centres

 Definition

A **responsibility centre** is an individual part of a business whose manager has personal responsibility for its performance.

The main responsibility centres are:

- Cost centre
- Profit centre
- Investment centre

A **cost centre** is a production or service location, function, activity or item of equipment whose costs are identified and recorded. A **cost centre** is a part of a business for which costs are determined.

- For a paint manufacturer cost centres might be: mixing department, packaging department, administration, or marketing departments.

- For an accountancy firm, the cost centres might be: audit, taxation, accountancy, word processing, administration, and canteen. Alternatively, they might be the various geographical locations, e.g. the London office, the Cardiff office, the Plymouth office.

- Cost centre managers need to have information about costs that are incurred and charged to their cost centres. The performance of a cost centre manager is judged on the extent to which cost targets have been achieved.

A **profit centre** is a part of the business for which both the costs incurred and the revenues earned are identified.

- Profit centres are often found in large organisations with a divisionalised structure, and each division is treated as a profit centre.

- Within each profit centre, there could be several costs centres and revenue centres.

- The performance of a profit centre manager is measured in terms of the profit made by the centre.

- The manager must therefore be responsible for both costs and revenues and in a position to plan and control both.

- Data and information relating to both costs and revenues must be collected and allocated to the relevant profit centres.

Managers of **investment centres** are responsible for investment decisions as well as decisions affecting costs and revenues.

- Investment centre managers are therefore accountable for the performance of capital employed as well as profits (costs and revenues).

- The performance of investment centres is measured in terms of the profit earned relative to the capital invested (employed).

> 📝 **Test your understanding 1**
>
> A cost centre is defined as:
>
> A   A unit of product or service for which costs are accumulated
>
> B   A production or service location, function, activity or item of equipment for which costs are accumulated
>
> C   Costs that relate directly to a unit
>
> D   Costs that contain both a fixed and a variable element

2.5   Product and period costs

A product cost is a cost that relates to the product or service being produced or provided e.g. raw materials

A period cost is a cost that relates to a time period e.g. monthly rent, annual salaries.

2.6   The purpose of internal reporting

Management information can be produced in **any format** that is useful to the business and tends to be produced frequently, for instance **every month.**

To provide information as a basis for informed decision making the types of report that you may come across include:

- Budgeted financial reports – budgeted statement of profit or loss, budgeted statement of financial position

- Segmented reports – reports that are produced for different segments, products or services, of the business

- Variance reports – reports that are produced comparing what the business did (actual results) with what they had planned to do at the start of the period (flexed budget)

- Cash flow forecasts – reports that aim to forecast cash flow into and out of the business

- Cost cards – see next section

Reports are usually intended to initiate a decision or an action.

If a report describes what happened in the past, a control action may be taken in an attempt to prevent a repeat of this behaviour.

Reports may advise on a certain course of action and recommend what decision should be taken.

3 The cost card

3.1 Cost cards

A cost card is used to show the breakdown of the costs of producing output based on the classification of each cost.

A cost card can be produced for one unit or a planned level of production. The cost card below is an example of a cost card for a planned level of production i.e. in total.

The following chapters are aimed at being able to build up the total or unit cost.

	£
Direct costs	
Direct materials	250,000
Direct labour	120,000
Direct expenses	10,000
Prime cost (*total of direct costs*)	380,000
Variable production overheads	15,000
Marginal production cost (*total of direct and variable costs*)	395,000
Fixed production overheads	35,000
Absorption cost (*total production cost*)	430,000
Non-production overheads (e.g. administration overhead; selling overhead)	20,000
Total cost	450,000

Note: The terminology in this cost card will be explained during your studies.

4 Summary

In this introductory chapter we looked at some of the basic principles and terminology used in cost and management accounting.

You need to be aware of the difference between **cost units** (individual units of a product or service for which costs can be separately ascertained) and **cost centres** (locations or functions in respect of which costs are accumulated).

Test your understanding answers

 Test your understanding 1

A cost centre is defined as:

B   A production or service location, function, activity or item of equipment for which costs are accumulated.

Cost classification

2

Introduction

This chapter considers how costs can be classified and the various uses of classification in management accounting.

ASSESSMENT CRITERIA

Differentiate between cost classifications for different purposes (2.4):

- fixed costs
- variable costs
- semi-variable costs
- stepped costs

Differentiate between and apply different costing systems (2.5):

- unit

Assess and estimate the effects of changing activity levels (5.2)

CONTENTS

1 Cost classification
2 Classification by element
3 Classification by function
4 Classification by nature
5 Classification by behaviour
6 Changing activity levels
7 The high-low method

1 Cost classification

1.1 Purpose of cost classification

Costs can be **classified** (collected into logical groups) in many ways. The particular classification selected will depend upon the purpose for which the resulting analysed data will be used, for example:

Classification	Purpose
By element – materials, labour and expenses	Cost control
By function – production (cost of sales), and non-production (distribution costs, administrative expenses).	Financial accounts
By nature – direct and indirect	Cost accounts
By behaviour – fixed, variable, stepped fixed and semi-variable	Budgeting, decision making

Classification of costs will also be determined by the **type of business** that is being run. For example fuel for a taxi firm is required for the service they provide whereas fuel for a delivery vehicle for a manufacturing company is not part of the product they produce.

2 Classification by element

2.1 Cost classification by element

Classification by element involves stating costs according to what the cost is as follows:

- **Materials** – includes raw materials for a manufacturer or alternatively the cost of goods that are to be resold in a retail organisation

- **Labour** – consists of basic pay and also overtime, commissions and bonuses as well.

- **Expenses** – includes electricity, depreciation and rent.

✍ Test your understanding 1

Classify the following costs for a clothes retailer by element.

Cost	Materials	Labour	Expenses
Designer skirts	☐	☐	☐
Heating costs	☐	☐	☐
Depreciation of fixtures and fittings	☐	☐	☐
Cashier staff salaries	☐	☐	☐

---

3 Classification by function

3.1 Cost classification by function

For financial accounting purposes costs are split into the following categories:

Production (Operating costs)

- **Cost of sales** – also known as **production** costs. This category could include production labour, materials, supervisor salaries and factory rent.

Non-production (non-operating costs)

- **Distribution** – this includes selling and distribution costs such as sales team commission and delivery costs.

- **Administrative costs** – this includes head office costs, IT support and HR support.

Depreciation

Depreciation is a measure of how much a non-current asset is wearing out or being used up. The classification will depend on which asset is being depreciated. For example:

- Cost of sales – depreciation on a machine in the production line

- Distribution – depreciation of a delivery van

- Administration – depreciation of a computer in the accounts department

---

Depreciation can be calculated in two ways:

- The diminishing (reducing) balance method of depreciation allows a higher amount of depreciation to be charged in the early years of an asset's life compared to the later years. This reflects the increased levels of usage of such assets in the earlier periods of their lives.

- The straight line method calculates a consistent amount of depreciation over the life of the asset.

Test your understanding 2

George plc makes stationery. Classify the following costs by function in the table below.

Cost	Production	Administration	Distribution
Purchases of plastic to make pens	☐	☐	☐
Managing director's bonus	☐	☐	☐
Depreciation of factory machinery	☐	☐	☐
Salaries of factory workers	☐	☐	☐
Insurance of sales team cars	☐	☐	☐

4 Classification by nature

4.1 Cost classification by nature

To be able to account for costs incurred it is necessary to know which costs are associated with the final product/service and which are incurred whilst producing the product/service. Classification by nature is how this is done:

- A **direct cost** is an item of cost that is traceable directly to a cost unit. An example of direct costs for a toy maker producing teddy bears might be:

  Direct material – fur fabric, stuffing

  Direct labour – employee stuffing the bear

  Direct expenses – patent for bear design

The **total** of all **direct** costs is known as the **prime cost** per unit.

- An **indirect** cost is a cost that cannot be identified with any one finished unit. An example of indirect costs for a toy maker producing a teddy bear might be:

  Indirect material – cleaning products

  Indirect labour – the production line supervisor

  Indirect expenses – rent, rates, electricity

These costs are incurred as a result of running the business but cannot necessarily be identified to an individual teddy bear.

Indirect costs are often referred to as **overheads**.

📝 Test your understanding 3

Camberwell runs a construction company. Classify the following costs by nature (direct or indirect) in the table below.

Cost	Direct	Indirect
Bricks	☐	☐
Plant hire for long term contract	☐	☐
Builders' wages	☐	☐
Accountants' wages	☐	☐

Test your understanding 4

Direct costs are:

A   A unit of product or service for which costs are accumulated

B   A production or service location, function, activity or item of equipment for which costs are accumulated

C   Costs that relate directly to a unit

D   Costs that contain both a fixed and a variable element

Test your understanding 5

P Harrington is a golf ball manufacturer. Classify the following costs by nature (direct or indirect) in the table below.

Cost	Direct	Indirect
Machine operators wages	☐	☐
Supervisors wages	☐	☐
Resin for golf balls	☐	☐
Salesmen's salaries	☐	☐

5   Classification by behaviour

5.1   Cost classification by behaviour

For **short term** budgeting purposes, management needs to be able to predict **how costs will vary with differing levels of activity** (i.e. the number of units being produced).

For example, if a furniture manufacturer expected to produce 1,000 chairs in a particular month, what should he budget for the costs of wood, labour, selling costs, factory heat and light, manager's salaries, etc? How would these costs differ (if at all) if he expected to produce 2,000 chairs?

To make short term budgeting and forecasting easier, costs are split into the following categories:

- Variable
- Fixed
- Stepped
- Semi-variable

5.2 Variable costs

Variable costs are costs that vary with changes in level of activity. Variable costs are **constant per unit** of output and increase in direct proportion to activity.

For example, if you make twice the number of units then the amount (and hence the cost) of raw material used would double.

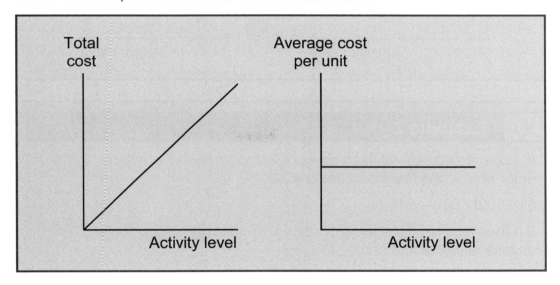

☀ Example 1

If a business has total variable costs of £10,000 when it produces 1,000 units what is the variable cost per unit?

£10,000/1,000 = £10

What would be the total variable cost if the activity increased to 2,000 units?

£10 × 2,000 = £20,000

5.3 Fixed costs

Fixed costs are costs that, in the short term, are not affected by changes in activity level. The total cost stays constant as activity levels change. This leads to a decrease in the cost per unit of output as activity levels increase.

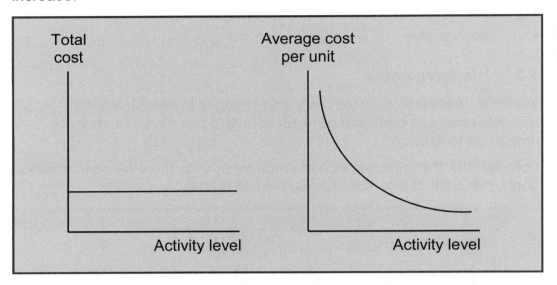

:O: Example 2

If a business has total fixed costs of £15,000 when it produces 1,000 units what is the fixed cost per unit?

£15,000/1,000 = £15

If a business has total fixed costs of £15,000 when it produces 3,000 units what is the fixed cost per unit?

£15,000/3,000 = £5

What would be the total fixed cost if the activity increased to 5,000 units?

£15,000

Test your understanding 6

Which of the following best describes a 'pure' fixed cost?

A cost which:

A represents a fixed proportion of total costs

B remains at the same level up to a particular level of output

C has a direct relationship with output

D remains at the same level whenever output changes

5.4 Stepped costs

Stepped fixed costs are costs that remain fixed up to a particular level of activity, but which rise to a higher (fixed) level if activity goes beyond that range.

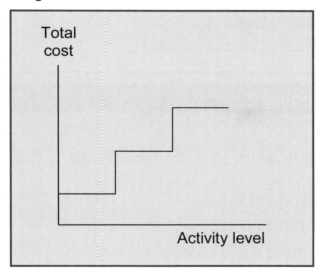

 Example 3

A business has total fixed costs of £20,000 when it produces 1,000 units but if it goes above this level fixed costs increase by 50%. What would the fixed costs be if the business produced 2,000 units?

£20,000 × 1.5 = £30,000

5.5 Semi-variable costs

Semi-variable costs are those that have a fixed element and a variable element:

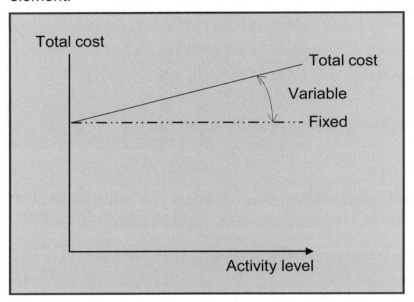

Test your understanding 7

A semi-variable cost is:

A A unit of product or service for which costs are accumulated

B A production or service location, function, activity or item of equipment for which costs are accumulated

C A cost that relate directly to a unit

D A cost that contains both a fixed and a variable element

Test your understanding 8

Gilbert plc is a furniture manufacturer. Classify the following costs by their behaviour in the table below.

Cost	Fixed	Variable	Semi-variable
Director's salary	☐	☐	☐
Wood	☐	☐	☐
Rent of factory	☐	☐	☐
Phone bill – includes a line rental	☐	☐	☐
Factory workers wage	☐	☐	☐

Test your understanding 9

Identify the following statements as either true or false.

	True	False
Stepped costs have a fixed and variable element	☐	☐
Fixed costs vary directly with changes in activity	☐	☐
Variable costs have a constant cost per unit.	☐	☐

5.6 Cost behaviour assumptions

To be able to use cost behaviours to produce budgets there are some assumptions that are made:

* Any **change** in cost is only due to change in **activity levels**
* Costs are assumed to be either **fixed** or **variable**, or at least **separable into these elements**.
* Total fixed costs remain fixed throughout the activity range (unless told otherwise).
* Total variable costs change in direct proportion to volume.
* Economies or diseconomies of scale are ignored; this ensures that **the variable cost per unit is constant**.
* Efficiency and productivity do not change with volume.
* If a cost is **direct** it will have a **variable** cost behaviour

Note: The use of cost behaviour to classify costs only holds in the short term, **in the long term** (by definition) **all costs are variable**.

6 Changing activity levels

6.1 Introduction

The **behavioural characteristics** of costs are used when planning or forecasting costs at different levels of production or activity.

When producing a forecast it may be necessary to identify the type of behaviour a cost is exhibiting. It is useful to remember the following:

- Fixed costs are constant in total

- Variable costs are constant per unit

- Semi-variable costs are neither constant in total nor constant per unit.

Example 4

A company has a mix of variable, semi variable and fixed costs. Identify the behaviour for each of the costs shown below:

Cost	1,000 units £	3,000 units £
1	4,500	7,500
2	1,830	5,490
3	5,000	5,000
4	12,250	36,750

Workings:

Cost	1,000 units		3,000 units	
	Total £	Per unit £	Total £	Per unit £
1	4,500	4.50	7,500	2.50
2	1,830	1.83	5,490	1.83
3	5,000	5.00	5,000	1.67
4	12,250	12.25	36,750	12.25

- **Cost 1** must be a **semi-variable cost** as the total cost changes when activity level change and the cost per unit also changes at the different activity levels

- **Cost 2** is a **variable cost** as the cost per unit is constant at each activity level

- **Cost 3** is a **fixed cost** as the total cost does not change as activity level changes

- **Cost 4** is a **variable cost** as the cost per unit is constant at each activity level

---

 Test your understanding 10

Identify if the following costs are variable, fixed or semi-variable.

	1,500 units	**2,500 units**
Material	£7,500	£12,500
Labour	£12,000	£20,000
Rent	£17,000	£17,000
Electricity	£16,750	£21,250

6.2   Stepped fixed costs

If a forecast has a stepped fixed cost included then information will have to be provided as to when the step up in cost would occur and by how much.

 Example 5

A manufacturing business has variable production costs of £3 per unit and fixed costs of £60,000. A further cost is the salary of the factory supervisor of £18,000 per annum. If more than 100,000 units of the product are made then an additional factory supervisor must be employed at the same salary.

What is the total cost of production and the cost per unit at the following production levels:

(i)   60,000 units

(ii)   90,000 units

(iii)   120,000 units

	Production level		
	60,000 units £	90,000 units £	120,000 units £
Variable production costs			
60,000 × £3	180,000		
90,000 × £3		270,000	
120,000 × £3			360,000
Fixed costs	60,000	60,000	60,000
Supervisor's salary (stepped)	18,000	18,000	36,000
Total production cost	258,000	348,000	456,000
Cost per unit	£4.30	£3.87	£3.80

The total costs are made up of both fixed and variable costs but the cost per unit falls as the production quantity increases. This is because the fixed costs are spread over a higher number of units of production

6.3 Semi-variable costs

Changes in activity level may also require the separation of the fixed and variable element of a semi-variable cost. The total fixed cost will remain constant as activity changes but the total variable cost will change in proportion to the activity changes.

The splitting or separating of a semi-variable cost is done by using the high-low method.

7 The high-low method

7.1 High-low method

If a semi-variable cost is incurred, it is often necessary to estimate the fixed element and the variable element of the cost for the purposes of budgeting. This can be done using the high-low method.

Remember:

Total cost = Fixed cost + (Variable cost per unit × Activity level)

Example 6

A factory has incurred the following power costs in the last six months with different levels of production in each month:

	Production units	Power costs £
January	20,000	18,000
February	16,000	16,500
March	18,000	17,200
April	24,000	20,500
May	22,000	19,400
June	19,000	17,600

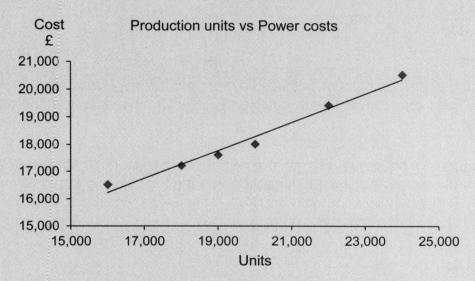

What are the fixed and variable elements of the power cost?

Step 1

Find the highest and lowest levels of production (activity) and their related costs.

		Units	Cost £
High	April	24,000	20,500
Low	February	16,000	16,500

Step 2

Find the variable cost element by determining the increased power cost per unit between highest and lowest production levels.

		Units	Cost £
High	April	24,000	20,500
Low	February	16,000	16,500
	Difference	8,000	4,000

The power cost has increased by £4,000 for an increase in 8,000 units of production. The variable power cost is therefore:

$$\frac{£4,000}{8,000} = £0.50 \text{ per unit}$$

Step 3

Using either the highest or the lowest production level (from step 1) find the fixed cost element by deducting the total variable cost from the total cost.

		£
April	Total cost	20,500
	Total variable cost 24,000 × 0.5	(12,000)
		8,500

		£
February	Total cost	16,500
	Total variable cost 16,000 × 0.5	(8,000)
		8,500

If production levels of 30,000 units are anticipated next month, what is the expected power cost?

The semi-variable power cost consists of the fixed cost (£8,500) and a variable cost per unit (£0.50). Therefore for an activity level of 30,000 units the total cost is predicted to be:

	£
Variable cost 30,000 × 0.50	15,000
Fixed cost	8,500
Total cost	23,500

Test your understanding 11

C Ling has a contract with a customer to produce 4,000, 5,000 or 6,000 units of product.

Revenues and costs for 4,000 units are shown below. Fixed overheads remain constant for the range charted but indirect labour will increase by £2,000 when production reaches 5,500 units.

Possible production level	4,000 units
	£
Sales revenue	50,000
Variable costs:	
Material	2,000
Labour	4,000
Overheads	6,000
Fixed costs:	
Indirect labour	12,000
Overheads	8,000
Total cost	32,000
Total profit	18,000
Profit per unit	4.50

Calculate:

- The sales revenue per unit if the contract is for 4,000 units.

- The variable cost per unit if the contract is for 4,000 units.

- The fixed cost per unit if the contract is for 4,000 units.

- The total cost if the contract is for 6,000 units.

- The total profit if the contract is for 6,000 units.

Test your understanding 12

Biscuit Making Company

The general manager has given you the task of supplying cost data for the manufacture of a specific brand of chocolate biscuit for 20X9 on the basis of projected costs. A cost clerk has given you data on variable and fixed costs, which is relevant over the range of production.

Complete the budgeted cost schedule for the different levels of production.

BUDGETED COST SCHEDULE		YEAR 20X9			
		ACTIVITY (Packets)			
		150,000	**175,000**	**200,000**	**225,000**
Description	£	£	£	£	
Variable costs:					
Direct material	12,000				
Direct labour	9,000				
Packing costs	1,500				
Fixed costs:					
Depreciation costs	12,000				
Rent and rates	26,000				
Supervisory costs	12,000				
Administration costs	8,000				
Total costs	80,500				
Cost per packet (2 decimal places)	0.54				

The cost per packet has *increased/decreased** because the fixed cost per unit has *increased/decreased**

*delete as appropriate

Test your understanding 13

The electricity used in a factory has a semi-variable cost behaviour. The manager wants to know how much electricity to budget for if he was to make 75 units.

Units	Total cost £
10	120
50	200
100	300

A £150

B £100

C £250

D £137.50

 Test your understanding 14

The total production cost for making 10,000 units was £12,000 and the total production cost for making 25,000 was £21,000. What is the full production cost for making 40,000 units?

A cost which:

A 6,000

B 24,000

C 30,000

D 72,667

Test your understanding 15

Charlie Ltd is preparing its budget for the next quarter and it needs to consider different production levels.

The semi-variable costs should be calculated using the high-low method. If 3,000 batches are produced then the semi-variable cost will be £8,500.

Complete the table below and calculate the estimated profit per batch at the different activity levels.

Units sold and produced	1,000	1,500	2,000
Sales revenue	25,000		
Variable cost			
Direct materials	5,000		
Direct labour	2,400		
Overheads	3,600		
Semi-variable costs	4,500		
Variable element			
Fixed element			
Fixed cost	3,500		
Total cost	19,000		
Total profit	6,000		
Profit per batch (to 2 decimal places)	6.00		

KAPLAN PUBLISHING

Test your understanding 16

Wendy Sheds is preparing its budget for the next quarter and it needs to consider different production levels.

The semi-variable costs should be calculated using the high-low method. If 300 batches are produced then the semi-variable cost will be £600.

Complete the table below and calculate the estimated profit per shed at the different activity levels.

Sheds sold and produced	500	750	1,000
Sales revenue	8,000		
Variable cost			
Direct materials	800		
Direct labour	760		
Overheads	1,440		
Semi-variable costs	900		
Variable element			
Fixed element			
Fixed cost	700		
Total cost	4,600		
Total profit	3,400		
Profit per shed (to 2 decimal places)	6.80		

Test your understanding 17

A manufacturing business has variable production costs of £3 per unit and fixed costs of £50,000. These include rent of £18,000 per annum. If more than 50,000 units of the product are made, then additional floor space must be rented at a cost of £20,000 per annum.

What is the total cost of production and the cost per unit at the 60,000 units?

	Total	Per unit
A	£230,000	£3.83
B	£250,000	£4.17
C	£268,000	£4.47
D	£88,000	£1.47

8 Summary

Costs can be classified in a variety of different ways for different purposes. The basic classification is into **materials, labour and expenses**, each of which will be dealt with in detail in the following chapters. A further method of classification of costs is between **direct and indirect** costs.

For decision-making and budgeting purposes, it is useful to distinguish costs according to their **behaviour** as production levels change. The basic classifications according to behaviour are **fixed** and **variable** costs although there are also **stepped** costs and **semi-variable** costs. The fixed and variable elements of semi-variable costs can be isolated using the **high/low method**.

Test your understanding answers

Test your understanding 1

Cost	Materials	Labour	Expenses
Designer skirts	☑	☐	☐
Heating costs	☐	☐	☑
Depreciation of fixtures and fittings	☐	☐	☑
Cashier staff salaries	☐	☑	☐

Test your understanding 2

Cost	Production	Administration	Distribution
Purchases of plastic to make pens	☑	☐	☐
Managing director's bonus	☐	☑	☐
Depreciation of factory machinery	☑	☐	☐
Salaries of factory workers	☑	☐	☐
Insurance of sales team cars	☐	☐	☑

Test your understanding 3

Cost	Direct	Indirect
Bricks	☑	☐
Plant hire for long term contract	☑	☐
Builders' wages	☑	☐
Accountants' wages	☐	☑

Test your understanding 4

Direct costs are:

C Costs that relate directly to a unit.

Test your understanding 5

Cost	Direct	Indirect
Machine operators wages	☑	☐
Supervisors wages	☐	☑
Resin for golf balls	☑	☐
Salesmen's salaries	☐	☑

Test your understanding 6

D Pure fixed costs remain exactly the same in total regardless of the activity level.

Test your understanding 7

A semi-variable cost is:

D A cost that contains both a fixed and a variable element

KAPLAN PUBLISHING

Test your understanding 8

Cost	Fixed	Variable	Semi-variable
Director's salary	☑	☐	☐
Wood	☐	☑	☐
Rent of factory	☑	☐	☐
Phone bill – includes a line rental	☐	☐	☑
Factory workers wage	☐	☑	☐

Test your understanding 9

	True	False
Stepped costs have a fixed and variable element	☐	☑
Fixed costs vary directly with changes in activity	☐	☑
Variable costs have a constant cost per unit.	☑	☐

Test your understanding 10

To identify cost behaviours it is necessary to look at the total costs and the cost per unit.

A **fixed cost** will be constant in total as activity changes – **Rent** is a fixed cost as it stays at £17,000.

A **variable cost** will be constant per unit as activity changes – **Material** (£5 per unit) and **Labour** (£8 per unit) are variable costs

A **semi-variable cost** will be neither constant in total nor constant per unit as activity changes – **Electricity** is a semi-variable cost. The total cost changes and so does the cost per unit (£11.17 per unit for 1,500 units and £8.50 per unit for 2,500 units).

Test your understanding 11

- The sales revenue per unit if the contract is for 4,000 units

    50,000/4,000 = £12.50

- The variable cost per unit if the contract is for 4,000 units

    (2,000 + 4,000 + 6,000)/4,000 = £3.00

- The fixed cost per unit if the contract is for 4,000 units

    (12,000 + 8,000)/4,000 = £5.00

- The total cost if the contract is for 6,000 units

    (£3.00 × 6,000) + (12,000 + 2,000) + (8,000) = £40,000

- The total profit if the contract is for 6,000 units

    (£12.50 × 6,000) − £40,000 = £35,000

 Test your understanding 12

BUDGETED COST SCHEDULE		YEAR 20X9		
		ACTIVITY (Packets)		
	150,000	175,000	200,000	225,000
Description	£	£	£	£
Variable costs:				
Direct material	12,000	14,000	16,000	18,000
Direct labour	9,000	10,500	12,000	13,500
Packing costs	1,500	1,750	2,000	2,250
Fixed costs:				
Depreciation costs	12,000	12,000	12,000	12,000
Rent and rates	26,000	26,000	26,000	26,000
Supervisory costs	12,000	12,000	12,000	12,000
Administration costs	8,000	8,000	8,000	8,000
Total costs	80,500	84,250	88,000	91,750
Cost per packet (2 decimal places)	0.54	0.48	0.44	0.41

The cost per packet has **decreased** because the fixed cost per unit has **decreased**.

Test your understanding 13

The cost for the electricity for 75 units is:

C   £250

Variable cost

$$\frac{300 - 120}{100 - 10} = £2$$

Fixed cost

$300 - (100 \times 2) = £100$

Cost for 75 units

$100 + (75 \times 2) = £250$

 Test your understanding 14

C

	£
Cost of 25,000 units	21,000
Less cost of 10,000 units	12,000
Difference = variable cost of 15,000 units	9,000

$$\text{Variable cost per unit} = \frac{£9,000}{15,000} = 60\text{p each}$$

Fixed costs = total cost − variable costs

Fixed costs = £21,000 − £(25,000 × 0.6) = £6,000

Therefore total cost for 40,000

	£
Variable (40,000 × 0.6)	24,000
Fixed	6,000
	30,000

Test your understanding 15

Units sold and produced	1,000	1,500	2,000
Sales revenue	25,000	37,500	50,000
Variable cost			
Direct materials	5,000	7,500	10,000
Direct labour	2,400	3,600	4,800
Overheads	3,600	5,400	7,200
Semi-variable costs	4,500		
Variable element		3,000	4,000
Fixed element		2,500	2,500
Fixed cost	3,500	3,500	3,500
Total cost	19,000	25,500	32,000
Total profit	6,000	12,000	18,000
Profit per batch (to 2 decimal places)	6.00	8.00	9.00

Splitting the semi-variable cost:

$$\frac{8,500 - 4,500}{3,000 - 1,000} = £2 \text{ per unit}$$

Variable cost (at 3,000 units) = 3,000 × £2 = £6,000

Fixed cost = £8,500 − £6,000 = £2,500

Test your understanding 16

Sheds sold and produced	500	750	1,000
Sales revenue	8,000	12,000	16,000
Variable cost			
Direct materials	800	1,200	1,600
Direct labour	760	1,140	1,520
Overheads	1,440	2,160	2,880
Semi-variable costs	900		
Variable element		1,125	1,500
Fixed element		150	150
Fixed cost	700	700	700
Total cost	4,600	6,475	8,350
Total profit	3,400	5,525	7,650
Profit per shed (to 2 decimal places)	6.80	7.37	7.65

Test your understanding 17

B

	60,000 units
	£
Variable production costs	
60,000 × £3	180,000
Fixed costs	50,000
Additional rentals	20,000
Total production cost	250,000
Cost per unit	£4.17

Inventory

Introduction

This chapter looks at the procedures that a business should have in place to ensure that records of inventory (materials) are kept accurate and up to date. In particular it looks at the purchasing of inventory, the valuation of inventory and inventory control.

ASSESSMENT CRITERIA

Record and calculate material costs (2.1):

– prepare and interpret inventory records

Analyse cost information for material in accordance with the organisation's costing procedures (2.2)

Prepare costing accounting journal entries for direct material or indirect materials (2.2)

Apply inventory control measures (2.3):

– economic order quantity (EOQ)
– first in first out (FIFO)
– last in first out (LIFO)
– Average cost (AVCO)

CONTENTS

1 Inventory control cycle
2 Materials documentation
3 The stores department
4 Cost of having inventory
5 Systems of inventory control
6 Pricing issues of raw materials
7 Integrated bookkeeping – materials

1 Inventory control cycle

1.1 Introduction

Inventory often forms the **largest single item of cost** for a business so it is essential that the inventory purchased is the most suitable for the intended purpose.

Inventory includes:

- raw materials or components to be used in the manufacture of products

- items bought to be sold on (retailer or wholesaler)

- items that will be used for general day to day running of the business

1.2 Control of purchasing

When goods are purchased they must be ordered, received by the stores department, recorded, issued to the manufacturing department that requires them and eventually paid for. This process needs a great deal of paperwork and strict internal controls.

Internal control consists of full documentation and appropriate authorisation of all transactions, movements of inventory and of all requisitions, orders, receipts and payments.

If control is to be maintained over purchasing, it is necessary to ensure that:

- only necessary items are purchased

- orders are placed with the most appropriate supplier after considering price and delivery details

- the goods that are actually received are the goods that were ordered and in the correct quantity/quality

- the price paid for the goods is correct (i.e. what was agreed when the order was placed).

To ensure that all of this takes place requires a reliable system of checking and control.

KAPLAN PUBLISHING

1.3 Overview of procedures

It is useful to have an overview of the purchasing process.

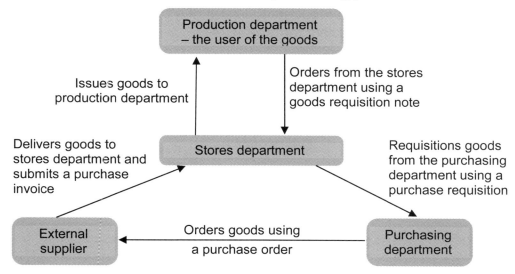

There are many variations of the above system in practice, but it is a fairly typical system and does provide good control over the purchasing and issuing process. Details about the documentation mentioned in the diagram above follows.

2 Materials documentation

2.1 Goods requisition note (also called 'materials requisition')

The user department (e.g. a production department) will notify the stores department that it requires certain goods using a 'goods requisition note'. This note will be authorised by the departmental manager.

Example 1

The production department requires 400 litres of a particular oil coded L04 from the stores department for product A.

GOODS REQUISITION NOTE		
Requiring department: *Production*	**Number:** *4027*	
Required for: *Product A*	**Date:** *14 April 20X4*	
Code	Description	Quantity
L04	*Oil*	*400 litres*
Authorised by: *Factory Manager* **Received by:**		

2.2 Purchase requisition

It is important that an organisation **controls** the goods that are ordered from suppliers. Only goods that are genuinely necessary should be ordered. Therefore, before any order for goods is placed, a purchase requisition must be completed.

Each purchase requisition must be **authorised** by the appropriate person. This will usually be the storekeeper or store manager.

When the purchase requisition has been completed it is sent to the purchasing department so that the purchase order is prepared.

Example 2

The storekeeper completes the requisition to order the 400 litres of oil for production. The code for the type of oil that is to be purchased is L04. Delivery is to be made directly to the stores department by 2 May.

PURCHASE REQUISITION

Date: 15 April 20X4   **Number:** 6843

Purpose: General machinery maintenance

Goods requisition note (if any): 4027

Quantity	Material code	Job code	Delivery details		Purchase order details
			Date	Place	
400 litres	L04	–	2 May 20X4	Stores	

Origination department: Stores

Authorisation: Storekeeper

Note that the purchase requisition must have the following elements:

- Be dated.
- Be consecutively numbered.
- Include the purpose for which the materials are required, showing any relevant job code where necessary.
- Include a detailed description of the precise materials required.
- Show when and where the goods are required.
- Include space to record the eventual purchase order details.
- Be authorised by the appropriate person in the department placing the purchase requisition.

2.3   Purchase order

The person placing the order must first check that the purchase requisition has been authorised by the appropriate person in the organisation.

Once the supplier of the goods has been chosen depending on price, delivery and quality, the price is entered on the purchase order together with details of the goods being ordered. The purchase order is then be authorised by the appropriate person in the organisation and dispatched to the supplier.

A copy of the purchase order is sent to the stores department so they know that goods are due and can alert appropriate management if they are not received and to the accounts department to be matched to the supplier's invoice.

An example purchase order is shown below.

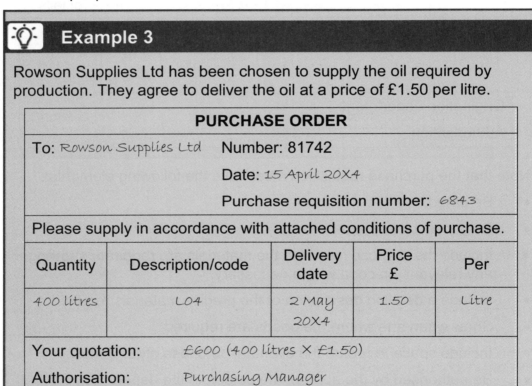

Example 3

Rowson Supplies Ltd has been chosen to supply the oil required by production. They agree to deliver the oil at a price of £1.50 per litre.

PURCHASE ORDER

To: *Rowson Supplies Ltd*   Number: 81742

Date: *15 April 20X4*

Purchase requisition number: *6843*

Please supply in accordance with attached conditions of purchase.

Quantity	Description/code	Delivery date	Price £	Per
400 litres	*L04*	*2 May 20X4*	*1.50*	*Litre*

Your quotation: *£600 (400 litres × £1.50)*

Authorisation: *Purchasing Manager*

2.4   Delivery note

A delivery note is sent by the supplier to the stores with the goods being delivered. This will include a description of the goods being delivered along with the quantity. The contents and quality of the items delivered should be checked against the delivery note and this is then signed by the person receiving the goods as evidence that the goods arrived.

Any concerns about the goods (for example, too few, too many, the wrong colour, or the wrong size) should be referred immediately to the appropriate manager before accepting the goods.

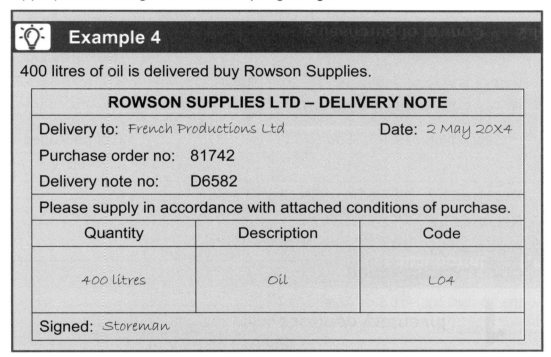

Example 4

400 litres of oil is delivered buy Rowson Supplies.

ROWSON SUPPLIES LTD – DELIVERY NOTE		
Delivery to: *French Productions Ltd*		Date: *2 May 20X4*
Purchase order no: 81742		
Delivery note no: D6582		
Please supply in accordance with attached conditions of purchase.		
Quantity	Description	Code
400 litres	*Oil*	*L04*
Signed: *Storeman*		

2.5   Goods received note

When goods are received by the organisation they will be taken to the stores department rather than being delivered directly to the department that will use the goods. This enables the receipt of goods to be controlled. When the goods are received, the stores department will check:

(a)   that the goods that arrive agree in **all** detail to those ordered on the purchase order

(b)   that the details of the delivery note agree with the actual goods delivered.

When the stores department are satisfied with all of the details of the delivery, the details are recorded on a goods received note (GRN).

The GRN is evidence that the goods that were ordered have been received and therefore should be, and can be, paid for. The GRN will, therefore, be sent to the accounts department to be matched with the supplier's invoice.

As evidence of the actual receipt of the goods the GRN is also used for entering receipts of materials in the stores records.

Example 5

FRENCH PRODUCTIONS LTD
GOODS RECEIVED NOTE

No: GRN 272

SUPPLIER: Rowson Supplies Ltd   DATE: 2 May 20X4

PURCHASE ORDER NO: 81742

Description	Code	Qty	No of packages
Oil	LO4	400 litres	1

Received by: STORES – FINISHING AREA

Required by: PRODUCTION

Accepted by: STORES SUPERVISOR

QUALITY ASSURANCE

Inspected by: SIG: ....Storeman...

Qty passed: 400   Qty rejected: Nil

2.6   Issues to the user department (production department)

The circle is completed when the stores department issues the goods to the production department. The goods must agree with the original goods requisition note.

2.7   Purchase invoice

The purchase invoice for goods details the amount that the receiver of the goods must pay for them and the date that payment is due. The purchase invoice might be included when the goods themselves are delivered, or might be sent after delivery.

The person responsible for payment must check that the details of the purchase invoice agree to the goods received note, the delivery note and the purchase order. This is to ensure that:

- what was ordered was received

- what was received is what is being paid for

- the price charged is that agreed.

Once it is certain that the purchase invoice agrees with the goods that were actually received then the invoice can be authorised for payment by the appropriate person in the organisation.

Example 6

ROWSON SUPPLIES LTD – PURCHASE INVOICE		
To: *Ronson Supplies Ltd*	Date:	*2 May 20X4*
Purchase order no: 81742		
Invoice no: 16582		
		£
For supply and delivery of:		
400 litres of oil L04 @ £1.50 per litre		600.00
Payment due in 30 days		

2.8 Goods returned note

If goods are damaged or are not as ordered, they will be returned to the supplier. A goods returned note will be used, authorised by the stores department's manager.

When unused materials are returned from user departments to the stores, the transaction will be recorded on a document similar to the materials requisition but usually printed in a different colour. It will be completed by the user department that is returning the goods and signed by the storekeeper as evidence that the goods were returned to stores.

When the goods are returned the details on the goods returned note must be checked to the actual goods themselves.

2.9 Credit note

If goods have been returned to the supplier, or there is some fault with the invoice (e.g. incorrect price or discount), a credit note will be requested from the supplier.

✏️ Test your understanding 1

Which of the following documents would be completed in each situation?

	Material Requisition	Purchase Requisition	Goods received note	Goods returned note
Material returned to stores from production	☐	☐	☐	☐
Form completed by the stores department detailing inventory requirements	☐	☐	☐	☐
Materials returned to supplier	☐	☐	☐	☐
Form completed by stores on receipt of goods	☐	☐	☐	☐
Form completed by production detailing inventory requirements.	☐	☐	☐	☐

Test your understanding 2

Match the document with the correct situation.

Goods received note	Form completed by the purchasing department to order supplies
Purchase order	Form completed by the stores department detailing inventory requirements
Purchase requisition	Details the amount due to be paid and the date payment is due by
Stores record card	Form received with goods on delivery
Delivery note	Document completed to show the movement of inventory
Purchase invoice	Document completed by stores on receipt of goods

3 The stores department

3.1 Function of the stores department

The stores or inventory department is responsible for the receipt, storage, issue and recording of the raw materials used in the production process.

3.2 Receipt of goods

When raw materials are received from suppliers they will normally be delivered to the stores department. The stores personnel must check that the goods delivered are the ones that have been ordered, in the correct quantity, of the correct quality and in good condition using the goods received note and the purchase requisition or purchase order.

3.3 Storage of materials

Once the materials have been received they must be stored until required by the production departments.

Storage of materials must be appropriate to their type. For example, foodstuffs must be stored at the correct temperature and wood must be stored in dry conditions. Storage should also be laid out in such a manner that the correct materials can be accessed easily either manually or by machinery.

3.4 Issue of materials

When the production departments require raw materials for production, it is essential that the stores department can provide the correct quantity and quality of materials at the time they are required. This will require careful attention to inventory control policies to ensure that the most efficient levels of inventories of raw materials are kept. Inventory control policies are discussed in a later section.

3.5 Recording of receipts and issues

In many organisations the stores department is also responsible for the recording of the quantities of raw materials that are received from suppliers and issued to the production departments. This normally takes place on the bin cards or the stores/inventory record card.

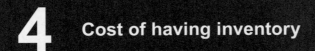

4 Cost of having inventory

4.1 Introduction

Most businesses, whatever their size, will be concerned with the problem of which items to have in inventory and how much of each item should be kept.

There are three forms that inventory can exist in:

* **Raw material** – items that are to be used in the manufacture of products

* **Work in progress** – items that are part way through the manufacturing process

* **Finished goods** – items that have completed the manufacturing process and are ready to be sold

4.2   Functions of inventory

The principal reasons why a business needs to hold inventory are as follows:

(a)   It acts as a buffer in times when there is an unusually high rate of consumption.

(b)   It enables the business to take advantage of quantity discounts by buying in bulk.

(c)   The business can take advantage of seasonal and other price fluctuations (e.g. buying coal in the summer when it is cheaper).

(d)   To prevent any delay in production caused by a lack of raw material so production processes will flow smoothly and efficiently.

(e)   It may be necessary to hold inventory for a technical reason: for example, whisky must be matured.

4.3   Costs of having inventory

Holding inventory costs money and the principal 'trade-off' in an inventory holding situation is between the costs of acquiring and storing inventories on the one hand and the level of service that the company wishes to provide on the other.

The **total cost of having inventory** consists of the following:

(a)   **Purchase price**

(b)   **Holding costs**:

    (i)   the opportunity cost of capital tied up

    (ii)   insurance

    (iii)   deterioration

    (iv)   obsolescence

    (v)   damage and pilferage

    (vi)   warehouse upkeep

    (vii)   stores labour and administration costs.

(c)   **Ordering costs**:

    (i)   clerical and administrative expenses

    (ii)   transport costs.

(d)   **Stock-out costs** (items of required inventory are not available):

    (i)   loss of sales, therefore lost contribution

    (ii)   long-term damage to the business through loss of goodwill

(iii) production stoppages caused by a shortage of raw materials

(iv) extra costs caused by the need for emergency orders.

(e) **Inventory recording systems costs:**

(i) maintaining the stores record card

4.4 Disadvantages of low inventory levels

To keep the holding costs low it may be possible to reduce the volume of inventory that is kept but this can cause some problems:

- Customer demand cannot always be satisfied; this may lead to loss of business if customers become dissatisfied.

- In order to fulfil commitments to important customers, costly emergency procedures (e.g. special production runs) may become necessary in an attempt to maintain customer goodwill.

- It will be necessary to place replenishment orders more frequently than if higher inventories were held, in order to maintain a reasonable service. This will result in higher ordering costs being incurred.

4.5 Disadvantages of high inventory levels

To reduce the problems mentioned above management may consider holding high levels of inventory but again this can have issues:

- Storage or holding costs are very high; such costs will usually include rates, rent, labour, heating, deterioration, etc.

- The cost of the capital tied up in inventories, i.e. the cash spent to buy the inventory, is not available to pay other bills.

- If the stored product becomes obsolete, a large inventory holding of that item could, at worst, represent a large capital investment in an unsaleable product whose cash value is only that of scrap.

- If a great deal of capital is invested in inventories, there will be proportionately less money available for other requirements such as improvement of existing production facilities, or the introduction of new products.

- If there is a sudden drop in the price of a raw material after a high level of inventory has already been purchased, then the extra spent over the new lower price represents the opportunity cost of purchasing in advance. It follows that it would seem sensible to hold higher inventories during an inflationary period and lower inventories during a period of deflation.

5 Systems of inventory control

5.1 Inventory control

Inventory control is 'the method of ensuring that the right **quantity** of the right **quality** of the relevant inventory is available at the right **time** and right **place**.

Inventory control is maintained through the use of the inventory record cards and by carrying out inventory checks on a regular basis.

5.2 Inventory control levels

Many inventory control systems will incorporate some or all of four inventory control levels that assist in keeping costs of inventory holding and ordering down, whilst minimising the chances of stock-outs. The four control levels are:

- re-order level – the level to which the inventory will be allowed to fall before an order is placed

- economic order quantity (EOQ) – the most economic quantity of inventory to be ordered to minimise the total of the cost having inventory.

- maximum inventory level – the highest quantity of inventory that should be held

- minimum inventory level – the lowest quantity of inventory that should be held (also known as buffer inventory).

5.3 Re-order level

This level will be determined with reference to the time it will take to receive the order (the lead time) and the possible inventory requirements during that time.

If it is possible to estimate the **maximum possible lead time** and the **maximum usage rate**, then a 'safe' re-order level, that will almost certainly avoid stock-outs, will be given by:

Re-order level = Maximum usage × Maximum lead time

If a company keeps some buffer inventory then the re-order level would be calculated as:

Re-order level = (Maximum usage × Maximum lead time) + buffer

5.4 Economic order quantity (EOQ)

Once the re-order level is reached, an order will be placed. The size of the order will affect:

(a) average inventory levels (the larger the order, the higher the inventory levels will be throughout the year)

(b) frequency of orders placed in the year (the larger the order, the longer it will take for inventories to fall to the re-order level, and thus the fewer the orders placed in the year).

Increasing the order size will have two conflicting effects on costs: increased holding costs through higher inventory levels and decreased re-ordering costs due to fewer orders placed in the year.

Under certain 'ideal' conditions (including constant rates of usage and constant lead times) a mathematical model can be used to determine the optimum (economic) order quantity (EOQ) that will minimise the total of these two costs – see graph.

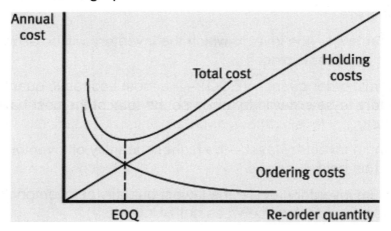

The formula for the economic order quantity is:

$$EOQ = \sqrt{\frac{2 \times C_o \times D}{C_h}}$$

where: C_o = cost of placing each order (note this is not the cost of the materials purchased but the administrative cost of placing the order).

D = annual demand/usage in units

C_h = cost of holding **one** unit of inventory for **one** year

Assumptions of the economic order quantity:

• Demand and lead time are constant and known

• Purchase price is constant

• No buffer inventory is held

Example 7

The demand for a particular product is expected be 25 units a day. Each time an order is placed, administrative costs of £15 are incurred and one unit of inventory held for one year incurs £0.10 of holding costs.

The company operates a 300-day year.

Calculate the economic order quantity.

Solution

$$EOQ = \sqrt{\frac{2 \times C_o \times D}{C_h}}$$

$$EOQ = \sqrt{\frac{[2 \times £15 \times 7{,}500\,(W)]}{£0.10}} = 1{,}500 \text{ units}$$

Working:

Annual demand D = days in year × usage per day

D = 300 × 25 = 7,500

5.5 Maximum and minimum inventory levels

Many inventory systems will also incorporate maximum and minimum inventory 'warning' levels, above or below which (respectively) inventory should not be allowed to rise/fall.

In practice, the maximum inventory level is fixed by taking into account:

(a) rate of consumption of the material

(b) time needed to obtain new supplies

(c) financial considerations due to high inventories tying up capital

(d) storage space with regard to the provision of space and maintenance costs

(e) extent to which price fluctuates

(f) risks of changing specifications

(g) possibility of loss by evaporation, deterioration, etc

(h) seasonal considerations as to both price and availability

(i) economic order quantities.

The minimum inventory level is fixed by taking into account:

(a)   rate of consumption

(b)   time needed to obtain delivery of supplies

(c)   the costs and other consequences of stock-outs.

A simplified method of determining these control levels is by reference to the re-order level, re-order quantity (EOQ) and estimates of possible lead times and usage rates, as follows:

Minimum level = Re-order level – (Average usage × Average lead time)

Maximum level = Re-order level + Re-order quantity – (Minimum usage × Minimum lead time)

If at any time inventories **fall below the minimum level**, this is a warning that **usage or lead time are above average**. Thus the storekeeper will need to keep an eye on inventory levels and be prepared to place an emergency order if inventories get too low.

If inventories **rise above the maximum level** then **usage or lead time have actually been lower** than the expected minimum. If it is usage, this may indicate a general decline in the demand for the inventory and the order quantity (and possibly the re-order level) should be reviewed to avoid holding excess inventory with associated holding costs.

 Example 8

The demand for a particular product is expected to vary between 10 and 50 per day. Lead time is, on average, 5 days, although it has been as short as 3 days and as long as 10 days. The company orders 1,500 units at a time. The company operates a 300-day year.

Calculate the re-order, maximum and minimum inventory levels.

Solution

Re-order level	=	Maximum usage × Maximum lead time
	=	50 per day × 10 days = 500 units
Minimum level	=	Re-order level – (Average usage × Average lead time)
	=	500 – (30 per day (W1) ×5 days) = 350 units
Maximum level	=	Re-order level + re-order quantity – (Minimum usage × Minimum lead time)
	=	500 + 1,500 – (10 per day × 3 days)
	=	1,970 units

Working 1:

$$\text{Average usage} = \frac{\text{minimum usage} + \text{maximum usage}}{2}$$

$$= \frac{10 + 50}{2}$$

$$= \text{30 units per day}$$

 Test your understanding 3

Given below is information about one inventory line that a business holds:

Daily usage (units)   20

Lead time (days)   5

The business operates for 250 days a year and keeps 50 units of inventory as buffer inventory.

The cost of placing each order is £20 and it costs £0.20 to hold an item of inventory for one year.

Calculate:

(i)   the re-order level

(ii)   the economic order quantity

After further investigation of usage and delivery times it has been discovered that usage can vary from 15 units a day to 25 units a day and lead time can be as short as 2 days but at the most 8 days. Calculate the maximum and minimum inventory levels based on this information and your calculations above.

(iii) the minimum inventory level

(iv) the maximum inventory level

Test your understanding 4

Ravenscar Engineering uses a standard component XZ7.

It estimates the following information regarding this unit:

Weekly usage	50 units
Delivery period	5 weeks

The working year is 50 weeks

Ordering costs are £50.63 per order

It costs £5 per unit per year to store the component.

Ravenscar Engineering always keeps a buffer inventory of 20 units.

Calculate:

(i)   Reorder level

(ii)   Economic order quantity

After further investigation of usage and delivery times it has been discovered that usage can vary from 30 units a week to 70 units a week and lead time can be as short as 3 weeks but at the most 7 weeks. Calculate the maximum and minimum inventory levels based on this information and your calculations above.

(iii)   Maximum inventory level

(iv)   Minimum inventory level

5.6   Inventory control systems

There are two main types of inventory control systems:

(a)   re-order level (two-bin) system

In a **re-order level system**, a replenishment order of fixed size is placed when the inventory level falls to the fixed re-order level. Thus a **fixed quantity** is ordered at **variable intervals of time**. This is the most common system used.

The most common practical implementation of the basic re-order level system is the two-bin system. Here, two bins of the inventory item are used and a replenishment order is placed when the first bin becomes empty; inventory is then drawn from the second bin until the order is received. When the order arrives, the second bin is filled up to its original level and the remainder goes into the first (empty) bin. Thus the amount of inventory held in the second bin gives the re-order level.

(b)   periodic (cyclical) review system

In a **periodic review system**, the inventory levels are reviewed at fixed points in time, when the quantity to be ordered is decided. By this method **variable quantities** are ordered at **fixed time intervals**.

Although this may increase the chances of a stock-out (between review times), it has the advantage of being easier to plan the scheduling of inventory counts and orders in advance.

6 Pricing issues of raw materials

6.1   Introduction

The cost of materials purchased will normally be derived from suppliers' invoices but, where many purchases have been made at differing prices, a decision has to be taken as to which cost is used when inventory is issued to the user department (cost centre).

6.2   Methods of pricing

Various methods exist including:

(a)   FIFO (first in, first out)

(b)   LIFO (last in, first out)

(c)   Weighted average (AVCO)

The choice of method will not only affect the charge to the user department for which the material is required, but also the value of the inventory left in stores.

6.3 FIFO, LIFO and AVCO methods

These systems attempt to reflect the movements of individual units in and out of inventory under different assumptions.

- **FIFO** – assumes that issues will be made from the oldest inventory available, leaving the latest purchases in inventory. This means that transfers from stores to production will be made at the oldest prices and the newest prices will be used to value the remaining inventory.

   FIFO could be used when products are perishable e.g. milk

- **LIFO** – assumes that issues will be made from the newest inventory available, leaving the earliest purchases in inventory. This means that transfers from stores to production will be made at the newest prices and the older prices will be used to value the remaining inventory.

   LIFO could be used when products are not perishable e.g. stationery

- **AVCO** – assumes that the issues into production will be made at an average price. This price is derived from taking the total value of the inventory and dividing it by the total units in inventory thus finding the average price per unit. A new average cost is calculated before each issue to production.

   AVCO could be used when individual units of material are indefinable e.g. sand at a builders merchants

6.4 The stores record card

It is usual to record quantities of an inventory item (and often inventory values as well) on a **stores record card**. One such card is maintained for each different inventory item, showing receipts of new inventory from suppliers, issues of inventory to production, and balance of inventory remaining on hand.

Example 9

Sid makes the following purchases of Component X.

Date	Quantity	Unit price £	Total cost £
10 January	50	1.00	50
20 January	60	1.10	66
30 January	40	1.25	50

On 25 January Sid issues 70 units for use in production.

On 31 January Sid issues 60 units for use in production.

No inventory was held at the beginning of the month.

Calculate the value of closing inventory and the cost of inventory issued to production using:

(a) a FIFO basis

(b) a LIFO basis

(c) an AVCO basis (round the average price per unit to 2 decimal places)

Solution

(a) **FIFO basis**

Stores Record Card

Material description: Component X

Code: X100

Date	Receipts			Issues			Balance	
	Quantity	Unit price £	Total £	Quantity	Unit price £	Total £	Quantity	Total £
10 Jan	50	1.00	50				50	50
20 Jan	60	1.10	66				50	50
							60	66
							110	116
25 Jan				50	1	50		
				20	1.10	22	40	44
				70		77		

Date	Quantity	Unit price £	Total £	Quantity	Unit price £	Total £	Quantity	Total £
30 Jan	40	1.25	50				40	44
							40	50
							——	——
							80	94
31 Jan				40	1.10	44		
				20	1.25	25	20	25
				——		——		
				60		69	20	25

(b) LIFO basis

Stores Record Card

Material description: Component X

Code: X100

	Receipts			Issues			Balance	
Date	Quantity	Unit price £	Total £	Quantity	Unit price £	Total £	Quantity	Total £
10 Jan	50	1.00	50				50	50
20 Jan	60	1.10	66				50	50
							60	66
							——	——
							110	116
25 Jan				60	1.10	66		
				10	1.00	10	40	40
				——		——		
				70		76		
30 Jan	40	1.25	50				40	40
							40	50
							——	——
							80	90
31 Jan				40	1.25	50		
				20	1.00	20	20	20
				——		——		
				60		70	20	20

(c) AVCO basis

Stores Record Card

Material description: Component X

Code: X100

Date	Receipts Quantity	Receipts Unit price £	Receipts Total £	Issues Quantity	Issues Unit price £	Issues Total £	Balance Quantity	Balance Total £
10 Jan	50	1.00	50				50	50
20 Jan	60	1.10	66				50	50
							60	66
							110	116
25 Jan				70	1.05	74	40	42
30 Jan	40	1.25	50				40	42
							40	50
							80	92
31 Jan				60	1.15	69	20	23
							20	25

Note: The average cost per unit is calculated based on what is in stores before the issue occurs. For example:

25 Jan £42 ÷ 40 units = £1.05 therefore the valuation of the issue is 70 units × £1.05 = £74 (rounded to the nearest whole number)

In the exam you will be told how many decimal places the 'per unit' figure and total figure need to be.

Test your understanding 5

Amp plc is a printing company specialising in producing accounting manuals. No formal stores accounting system is in operation at present.

Complete the following inventory entries using:

FIFO, LIFO and AVCO (weighted average cost per unit to two decimal places of a £).

Material:	Paper – Code 1564A
Opening inventory:	10,000 sheets – value £3,000

Purchases			Issues		
3 May	4,000 sheets	£1,600	6 May	7,000 sheets	
12 May	10,000 sheets	£3,100	15 May	6,000 sheets	
			22 May	7,200 sheets	

Stores Record Card FIFO

Material: Paper   Code: 1564A

Date	Details	Receipts		Issues			Inventory	
		Sheets	£	Sheets	Price	£	Sheets	£
1.5	Opening inventory							
3.5	Receipt							
6.5	Issue							
12.5	Receipt							
15.5	Issue							
22.5	Issue							

Stores Record Card LIFO

Material: Paper   Code: 1564A

Date	Details	Receipts		Issues			Inventory	
		Sheets	£	Sheets	Price	£	Sheets	£
1.5	Opening inventory							
3.5	Receipt							
6.5	Issue							
12.5	Receipt							
15.5	Issue							
22.5	Issue							

Stores Record Card AVCO

Material: Paper   Code: 1564A

Date	Details	Receipts		Issues			Inventory	
		Sheets	£	Sheets	Price	£	Sheets	£
1.5	Opening inventory							
3.5	Receipt							
6.5	Issue							
12.5	Receipt							
15.5	Issue							
22.5	Issue							

Test your understanding 6

Cavernelli runs a pizza house. The inventory and usage of pizza bases for December was:

		Units	Value (£)
Opening inventory	1 Dec	200	180
Purchases	3 Dec	800	800
Purchases	20 Dec	1,200	1,140
Usage	w/e 7 Dec	400	
	w/e 14 Dec	350	
	w/e 21 Dec	410	
	w/e 28 Dec	475	

Calculate the value of issues and the closing inventory using the FIFO method of pricing (show figures to the nearest £).

The issues are priced at the end of each week.

Stores Record Card FIFO

Material: Pizza

Code: 1626

Date	Details	Receipts		Issues			Inventory	
		Units	£	Units	Price	£	Units	£

Test your understanding 7

Kiveton Cleaning Services supplies its employees with protective clothing. One such item is protective gloves.

Records from the stores department for January showed:

1 Jan	Opening inventory 150 pairs @ £2 each
7 Jan	Purchases 40 pairs @ £1.90
15 Jan	Issues 30 pairs
29 Jan	Issues 35 pairs

Calculate the value of the issues and the closing inventory if the LIFO method is used to price the usage.

Stores Record Card LIFO

Material: Protective gloves

Code: 1607

Date	Details	Receipts		Issues			Inventory	
		Pairs	£	Pairs	Price	£	Pairs	£

Test your understanding 8

Crescent Engineering use a standard component AB3 and the inventory, receipts and issues for the month of September were:

Opening inventory 75 units @ £40 = £3,000.

Date	Receipts (units)	Unit cost £	Issues to production (units)
1 Sept	100	40	
10 Sept	75	42	
15 Sept			60
20 Sept			55
23 Sept	45	42	
30 Sept			50

The company uses the weighted average cost method for pricing issues and valuing inventory. Calculate the total usage for the month and the value of closing inventory (round per unit figures to 2 decimal places and total figures to the nearest £1).

Stores Record Card AVCO

Material: Component AB3

Code: 010203

Date	Receipts			Issues			Inventory	
	Units	Cost	£	Units	Cost	£	Units	£

Test your understanding 9

Navneet Ltd

Identify the method of inventory valuation and complete the stores record card shown below for steel component Magic, for the month of May 20Y0.

Note: Figures in the total columns should be shown to the nearest £. The company's policy is to round prices per unit to two decimal places.

STORES RECORD CARD FOR STEEL COMPONENT MAGIC
Inventory valuation method:

Date 20Y0	Receipts			Issues			Balance	
	Quantity kg	Cost per kg (£)	Total cost (£)	Quantity kg	Cost per kg (£)	Total cost (£)	Quantity kg	£
Balance as at 1 May							25,000	50,000
9 May	30,000	2.30	69,000				55,000	119,000
12 May				40,000		84,500		
18 May	20,000	2.50	50,000					
27 May				10,000				

 Test your understanding 10

Dennis plc has the following kg of raw material in inventory:

Date purchased	Quantity	Cost per kg (£)	Total cost (£)
April 24	500	1.20	600
April 26	450	1.30	585
April 30	600	1.50	900

Calculate the cost of issuing 1,000kg on 1 May and the value of the closing inventory (to the nearest £) using:

- FIFO
- LIFO
- AVCO

6.5 Features of the different methods

FIFO has the following features:

- In times of rapidly increasing prices, material may be **issued** at an early and unrealistically low price, resulting in the particular job showing an unusually large profit.

- Two jobs started on the same day may show a different cost for the same quantity of the same material.

- In times of rapidly increasing prices FIFO will give a higher profit figure than LIFO or AVCO.

- FIFO can be used in the production of financial accounts as it is **acceptable to HMRC and adheres to IAS 2 Inventories**

LIFO has the following features:

- **Closing inventories** will be shown at the earliest prices which mean that in times of rapidly increasing or decreasing prices the inventory figure bears little resemblance to the current cost of replacement therefore **does not adhere to IAS 2** and should not be used for financial reporting of inventory values. LIFO should only be **used within an organisation**.

- As with FIFO, two jobs started on the same day may show a different cost for the same quantity of the same material.

- The LIFO method uses the latest prices for issues to production and therefore the cost obtained is more likely to be in line with other costs and selling prices.

- In times of rapidly increasing prices LIFO will give a lower profit figure than FIFO and AVCO.

AVCO is a compromise on valuation of inventory and issues and the average price rarely reflects the actual purchase price of the material.

6.6 Inventory valuation method and profit

As stated above FIFO will return a higher profit than LIFO if prices are increasing over a time period. If prices are declining LIFO then returns a higher profit. This is due to the valuation of closing inventory and its application in a statement of profit or loss.

Example 10

Charlie has the following extract from their inventory card and was wondering which method of inventory valuation would give him the highest profit.

- 1 July Received 100 units at £10 per unit

- 2 July Received 100 units at £11 per unit

- 3 July Issued 150 units to production.

There is no opening inventory.

Date	Receipts			Issues			Balance	
	Qty	Per unit	Total	Qty	Per unit	Total	Qty	Total
1 July	100	10	1,000				100	1,000
2 July	100	11	1,100				100	1,000
							100	1,100
							—	—
							200	2,100
3 July (FIFO)				100	10	1,000		
				50	11	550	50	550
				—		—		
				150		1,550		

OR

Date	Receipts			Issues			Balance	
3 July (LIFO)				100	11	1,100	50	500
				50	10	500		
				—		—		
				150		1,600		

If we now use the above data to produce a statement of profit or loss for the first few days in July:

FIFO

The closing inventory is valued at the most recent prices therefore the higher prices.

		£
Sales *(illustrative figure)*		2,000
Less: Cost of sales		
Opening inventory	0	
Purchases *(from receipts)*	2,100	
Less: closing inventory	(550)	
	_____	
		(1,550)
		_____
Gross profit		450

LIFO

The closing inventory is valued at the oldest prices therefore the lower prices

		£
Sales *(illustrative figure)*		2,000
Less: Cost of sales		
Opening inventory	0	
Purchases *(from receipts)*	2,100	
Less: closing inventory	(500)	
	_____	
		(1,600)
		_____
Gross profit		400

We can see that FIFO has a higher value of closing inventory (£550) therefore a lower cost of sales (£1,550) which leads to a higher profit. AVCO would return a profit in between FIFO and LIFO.

Test your understanding 11

If raw material prices are subject to inflation, which method of valuing inventories will give the lowest profit?

A   FIFO

B   LIFO

C   AVCO

7 Integrated bookkeeping – materials

7.1 Introduction

The costs of a business have to be recorded in a bookkeeping system. Many businesses use an **integrated bookkeeping system** where the ledger accounts kept provide the necessary **information for both costing and financial accounting**.

7.2 Stores record card (bin card)

Every line of inventory, e.g. component X and material Y, will have a record card showing precisely how much of this item is in inventory. Therefore each time a receipt of a material arrives from a supplier then the stores record card must be updated.

7.3 Stores department entries

In many management accounting systems only the quantity of the materials is entered by the stores department as that is the only information that they have.

7.4 Accounts department entries

Once the stores record card reaches the accounts department then the correct price of the materials, taken from the purchase invoice will be entered.

The stores record card is an important document that helps to control the movement of materials and assess inventory levels.

7.5   Inventory ledger account

The accounting for material is dealt with through a stores ledger account (or the material cost account). This is maintained by the accounting department, the physical inventory shown on these accounts is reconciled with the stores record card. The materials cost account is where the movement of the costs associated with the materials are recorded.

💡 Example 11

Materials cost account

	£		£
Opening balance (1)		Issues to production (4)	
Purchases (2)		Returns to suppliers (5)	
Returns to stores (3)		Production overheads (6)	
		Statement of profit and loss (7)	
		Closing balance (8)	
	———		———
	———		———

(1)   The **opening balance** of materials held in stores at the beginning of a period is shown as a **debit** in the material cost account.

(2)   Materials **purchased** on credit are **debited** to the material cost account. Materials purchased for cash would also be a debit.

(3)   Materials **returned to stores** cause inventory to increase and so are **debited** to the material cost account.

(4)   **Direct materials** used in production are transferred to the **production** account, which is also known as the **Work-In-Progress.** This is recorded by crediting the material cost account.

(5)   Materials **returned to suppliers** cause inventory levels to fall and are therefore '**credited** out' of the materials cost account.

(6)   **Indirect materials** are not a direct cost of manufacture and are treated as **overheads**. They are therefore transferred to the production overhead account by way of a **credit** to the materials cost account.

(7)   Any material **write-offs** are '**credited** out' of the material cost account and transferred to the statement of profit or loss where they are written off.

(8)   The **balancing figure** on the materials cost account is the **closing balance** of material at the end of a period. It is also the opening balance at the beginning of the next period.

Test your understanding 12

What are the correct journal entries the following accounting transactions:

1   Receipt of material into stores paying on credit:

A   Dr Bank, Cr Materials

B   Dr Trade Payables Control, Cr Materials

C   Dr Materials, Cr Bank

D   Dr Materials, Cr Trade Payables Control

2   Issue of material from inventory to production.

A   Dr Bank, Cr Materials

B   Dr Materials, Cr Bank

C   Dr Materials, Cr Production

D   Dr Production, Cr Materials

3   Receipt of material into stores paying immediately by BACS.

A   Dr Bank, Cr Materials

B   Dr Trade Payables Control, Cr Materials

C   Dr Materials, Cr Bank

D   Dr Materials, Cr Trade Payables Control

4   Return of material from production to stores.

A   Dr Materials, Cr Bank

B   Dr Materials, Cr Trade Payables Control

C   Dr Materials, Cr Production

D   Dr Production, Cr Materials

Test your understanding 13

Retail Store Company

Issues are costed from the warehouse and transport department using the weighted average method.

Complete the stores ledger card below for an item of inventory in the clothing department for the month of May 20X8 using the weighted average method for costing issues and valuing inventory.

Note: Figures in the total columns should be shown to the nearest £.

The company's policy is to round prices per unit to three decimal places.

Stores Record Card								
Department:							**Month:**	
	Receipts			**Issues**			**Balance**	
Date	Quantity	Price £	Total £	Quantity	Price £	Total £	Quantity	Total £
1/5 Balance							2,420	12,584
7/5	2,950	5.500	16,226					
11/5	3,200	5.700	18,239					
14/5				4,105				
21/5	1,535	5.400	8,289					
27/5				1,800				
30/5				2,600				

What is the double entry for the issue on the 27th May?

A   Dr Bank, Cr Materials

B   Dr Materials, Cr Bank

C   Dr Materials, Cr Production

D   Dr Production, Cr Materials

8 Summary

Pricing issues of raw materials and valuing inventories are two of the most important techniques that you need to know about in the topic of materials. We have looked at three main methods of pricing issues and valuing inventories: FIFO, LIFO, and Weighted Average Cost. A common examination task is to ask you to record receipts and issues of materials onto a stores ledger card using one of these methods.

We have also looked at the **documents** involved in the process of purchasing materials and the different inventory control systems (re-order level (two-bin) system and the periodic review system.

Another important part of the topic of materials is that of **inventory control** levels – these assist in keeping the costs of inventory holding and inventory ordering at a minimum, whilst minimising stock-outs at the same time. Make sure that you can calculate the re-order level, the EOQ, the maximum inventory level and the minimum inventory level.

Test your understanding answers

Test your understanding 1

	Material Requisition	Purchase Requisition	Goods received note	Goods returned note
Material returned to stores from production	☐	☐	☐	☑
Form completed by the stores department detailing inventory requirements	☐	☑	☐	☐
Materials returned to supplier	☐	☐	☐	☑
Form completed by stores on receipt of goods	☐	☐	☑	☐
Form completed by production detailing inventory requirements.	☑	☐	☐	☐

Test your understanding 2

Goods received note	Document completed by stores on receipt of goods.
Purchase order	Form completed by the purchasing department to order supplies.
Purchase requisition	Form completed by the stores department detailing inventory requirements.
Stores record card	Document completed to show the movement of inventory.
Delivery note	Form received with goods on delivery
Purchase invoice	Details the amount due to be paid and the date payment is due by

Test your understanding 3

(i) Re-order level = (20 units × 5 days) + 50

= 150 units

(ii) EOQ = $\sqrt{\dfrac{2 \times £20 \times 20 \times 250)}{0.2}}$

= 1,000 units

(iii) Minimum inventory level = Re-order level –
(Average usage × Average lead time)

= 150 – (20 × 5)

= 50 units

(iv) Maximum inventory level = Re-order level + EOQ –
(Minimum usage × Minimum lead time)

= 150 + 1,000 – (15 × 2)

= 1,120 units

Test your understanding 4

(i) Reorder level:

(Maximum usage per period × maximum delivery period) + buffer

(50 × 5) + 20 = 270 units

(ii) Economic order quantity:

√[(2 × 50.63 × 50 × 50)/5] = 225 units

(iii) Maximum inventory level:

Reorder level + Reorder quantity − (minimum usage in minimum delivery period)

= 270 + 225 − (30 × 3) = 405 units

(iv) Minimum inventory level:

Reorder level − (average usage in average reorder period)

= 270 − (50 × 5) = 20 units

 Test your understanding 5

Stores Record Card FIFO
Material: Paper   Code: 1564A

Date	Details	Receipts		Issues			Inventory	
		Sheets	£	Sheets	Price	£	Sheets	£
1.5	Opening inventory						10,000	3,000
3.5	Receipt	4,000	1,600				10,000	3,000
							4,000	1,600
							14,000	4,600
6.5	Issue						3,000	900
				7,000	0.30	2,100	4,000	1,600
				7,000		2,100	7,000	2,500
12.5	Receipt	10,000	3,100				3,000	900
							4,000	1,600
							10,000	3,100
							17,000	5600
15.5	Issue			3,000	0.30	900	1,000	400
				3,000	0.40	1,200	10,000	3,100
				6,000		2,100	11,000	3,500
22.5	Issue			1,000	0.40	400		
				6,200	0.31	1,922	3,800	1,178
				7,200		2,322	3,800	1,178

Stores Record Card LIFO
Material: Paper   Code: 1564A

Date	Details	Receipts		Issues			Inventory	
		Sheets	£	Sheets	Price	£	Sheets	£
1.5	Opening inventory						10,000	3,000
3.5	Receipt	4,000	1,600				10,000	3,000
							4,000	1,600
							14,000	4,600
6.5	Issue			4,000	0.40	1,600		
				3,000	0.30	900	7,000	2,100
				7,000		2,500	7,000	2,100
12.5	Receipt	10,000	3,100				7,000	2,100
							10,000	3,100
							17,000	5,200
15.5	Issue						7,000	2,100
				6,000	0.31	1,860	4,000	1240
				6,000		1,860	11,000	3340
22.5	Issue			4,000	0.31	1,240		
				3,200	0.30	960	3,800	1,140
				7,200		2,200	3,800	1,140

Stores Record Card AVCO
Material: Paper   Code: 1564A

Date	Details	Receipts		Issues			Inventory	
		Sheets	£	Sheets	Price	£	Sheets	£
1.5	Opening inventory						10,000	3,000
3.5	Receipt	4,000	1,600				14,000	4,600
6.5	Issue			7,000	0.33	2,310*	7,000	2,290*
12.5	Receipt	10,000	3,100				17,000	5,390
15.5	Issue			6,000	0.32	1,920	11,000	3,470
22.5	Issue			7,200	0.32	2,304	3,800	1,166

* The difference in these two values is the result of rounding the price p/unit to 33p. A more accurate unit price of 32.86p would have valued them both at £2,300.

Test your understanding 6

Stores Record Card FIFO

Material: Pizza

Code: 1626

Date	Details	Receipts		Issues			Inventory	
		Units	£	Units	Price	£	Units	£
1 Dec	Balance b/f						200	180
3 Dec	Receipt	800	800				200	180
							800	800
							1,000	980
7 Dec	Issue			200	0.9	180		
				200	1.0	200	600	600
				400		380	600	600
14 Dec	Issue			350	1.0	350	250	250
20 Dec	Receipt	1,200	1,140				250	250
							1,200	1,140
							1,450	1,390
21 Dec	Issue			250	1.0	250		
				160	0.95	152	1,040	988
				410		402		
28 Dec	Issue			475	0.95	451	565	537

Test your understanding 7

Stores Record Card LIFO

Material: Protective gloves

Code: 1607

Date	Details	Receipts		Issues			Inventory	
		Pairs	£	Pairs	Price	£	Pairs	£
1 Jan	Balance b/f						150	300
7 Jan	Purchases	40	76				150	300
							40	76
							190	376
15 Jan	Issues			30	1.90	57	150	300
							10	19
							160	319
29 Jan	Issues			10	1.90	19		
				25	2.00	50	125	250
				35		69	125	250

Test your understanding 8

Stores Record Card AVCO

Material: Component AB3

Code: 010203

Date	Receipts			Issues			Inventory	
	Units	Cost	£	Units	Cost	£	Units	£
1 Sept							75	3,000
1 Sept	100	40.00	4,000				175	7,000
10 Sept	75	42.00	3,150				250	10,150
15 Sept				60	40.60	2,436	190	7,714
20 Sept				55	40.60	2,233	135	5,481
23 Sept	45	42.00	1,890				180	7,371
30 Sept				50	40.95	2,048	130	5,323

Weighted average price 10th September = 10,150 ÷ 250 = £40.60 per unit

Value of issues: £2,463 + £2,233 + 2,048 = £6,744

Closing inventory valuation: £5,323

Test your understanding 9

INVENTORY RECORD CARD FOR STEEL COMPONENT MAGIC
Inventory valuation method: FIFO

Date 20Y0	Receipts			Issues			Balance	
	Quantity kg	Cost per kg (£)	Total cost (£)	Quantity kg	Cost per kg (£)	Total cost (£)	Quantity kg	£
Balance as at 1 May							25,000	50,000
9 May	30,000	2.30	69,000				55,000	119,000
12 May				40,000	25,000 @ 2 15,000 @ 2.30	84,500	15,000	34,500
18 May	20,000	2.50	50,000				15,000 20,000 35,000	34,500 50,000 84,500
27 May				10,000	2.30	23,000	5,000 20,000 25,000	11,500 50,000 61,500

 Test your understanding 10

- **FIFO**

  Issue = (500 × 1.20) + (450 × 1.30) + (50 × 1.50) = £1,260

  Closing inventory = (600 + 585 + 900) − £1260 = £825

- **LIFO**

  Issue = (600 × 1.5) + (400 × 1.3) = £1,420

  Closing inventory = (600 + 585 + 900) − £1,420 = £665

- **AVCO**

  Issue = (600 + 585 + 900)/(500 + 450 + 600) × 1,000 = £1,345

  Closing inventory = (600 + 585 + 900) − £1,345 = £740

Test your understanding 11

B   LIFO

Test your understanding 12

1   **D**   Dr Materials, Cr Trade Payables Control
2   **D**   Dr Production, Cr Materials
3   **C**   Dr Materials, Cr Bank
4   **C**   Dr Materials, Cr Production

Test your understanding 13

Stores Record Card

Department: Clothing   **Month:** May 20X8

Date	Receipts			Issues			Balance	
	Quantity	Price £	Total £	Quantity	Price £	Total £	Quantity	Total £
1/5 Balance							2,420	12,584
7/5	2,950	5.500	16,226				5,370	28,810
11/5	3,200	5.700	18,239				8,570	47,049
14/5				4,105	5.490	22,536	4,465	24,513
21/5	1,535	5.400	8,289				6,000	32,802
27/5				1,800	5.467	9,841	4,200	22,961
30/5				2,600	5.467	14,214	1,600	8,747

The double entry for the issue on the 27 May is:

D   Dr Production, Cr Materials

Labour

Introduction

Labour is a large cost for many organisations. The cost of labour will depend on the remuneration (payment) system used by an organisation for example: annual salary, hourly rates and overtime or piecework payments.

ASSESSMENT CRITERIA
Record and calculate labour costs (2.1)
Analyse cost information for labour in accordance with the organisation's costing procedures (2.2)
Prepare cost accounting journal entries for direct or indirect labour (2.2)

CONTENTS

1 Employee records
2 Remuneration systems
3 Direct and indirect labour costs
4 Integrated bookkeeping – labour

1 Employee records

1.1 Personnel record details

When an employee joins an organisation it is necessary to record a number of details about them and the details of their job and pay. The personnel department completes this in the individual employee's personnel record.

The type of details that might be kept about an employee are as follows:

- Full name, address and date of birth.
- Personal details such as marital status and emergency contact name and address.
- National Insurance number.
- Previous employment history.
- Educational details.
- Professional qualifications.
- Date of joining organisation.
- Employee number or code.
- Clock number issued.
- Job title and department.
- Rate of pay agreed.
- Holiday details agreed.
- Bank details if salary is to be paid directly into bank account.
- Amendments to any of the details above (such as increases in agreed rates of pay).
- Date of termination of employment (when this takes place) and reasons for leaving.

Example 1

Jonathan Minor started to be employed by your organisation on 1 July 2001 as an engineer in the maintenance department of the organisation. He was born on 22 January 1983. His employee code and clock number are M36084 and his agreed rate of pay is £375.60 per week. He is to be paid in cash.

Complete the employee personnel record for Jonathan.

Solution

PERSONNEL RECORD CARD			
PERSONAL DETAILS			**EMPLOYMENT DETAILS**
Surname: MINOR Other names: JONATHAN	Address: 24 Hill St Reading	Emergency contact: Jane MINOR 24 Hill St Reading	**Previous Employment History**
Date of birth: 22/1/83	Nationality: British	Sex: M	Employer: Date:
Marital status: Single		Dependents: None	(1)
National Insurance Number: WE 22 41 79 J9			(2)
EDUCATIONAL DETAILS			(3)
			(4)
Degree: –		Btec/HND: Engineering	**TRAINING DETAILS**
A Levels: 2	O Levels: 0	GCSE: 7 CSEs: 0	Course Date: attended:
University attended: – College attended: Reading Schools attended Reading High (with dates): (1994 – 1999) Reading Junior (1987 – 1994)			
JOB DETAILS			**OTHER DETAILS**
Date of joining: 1/7/01	Clock number: M36084		Bank account:
Job title: Engineer	Department: Maintenance		
Rate of pay:	Overtime: 1½ times basic		Date of termination:
Date £	Holiday: 15 days		
1/7/01 375.60 pw	Pension Scheme: Joined: 1/7/01		Reason for leaving:

1.2 Attendance records

In most businesses, **records** are needed of the time spent by each employee in the workplace (attendance time) and time spent on the operations, processes, products or services whilst there (job time). Such timekeeping provides basic data for statutory records, payroll preparation, ascertainment and control of labour costs of an operation or product, overhead distribution (when based on wages or labour hours) and statistical analysis of labour records for determining productivity.

Attendance may be recorded by using a **register**, in which employees note their times of arrival and departure, or by means of a **time recording clock** which stamps the times on a card inserted by each employee. Alternatively, employees may be required to submit periodic **timesheets** showing the amounts of normal and overtime work; these may also include job times.

1.3 Holiday records

An employee will usually have an agreed number of days holiday per year. This will usually be paid holiday for salaried employees but may well be unpaid for employees paid by results or on time rates.

It is important for the employer to keep a record of the number of holiday days taken by the employee to ensure that the agreed number per year is not exceeded.

1.4 Sickness records

The organisation will have its own policies regarding payment for sick leave as well as legal requirements for statutory sick pay. Therefore, it will be necessary to keep a record of the number of days of sick leave each year for each employee.

1.5 Other periods of absence

A record will need to be kept of any other periods of absence by an employee. These might be perfectly genuine such as jury service or training courses or alternatively unexplained periods of absence that must be investigated.

1.6 Source of information

Information about an employee's attendance will come from various sources such as clock cards, time sheets and cost cards.

1.7 Clock cards

A **clock card** is a document on which is recorded the starting and finishing time of an employee for ascertaining total actual attendance time.

A clock card is usually some form of electronic or computerised recording system whereby when the employee's clock card is entered into the machine the time is recorded. This will give the starting and finishing time for the day and also in some systems break times taken as well.

Clock cards are used as a source document in the calculation of the employee's earnings.

Example 2

Example of a clock card:

Works number:				Name:	
			Lunch		
Week ending	In	Out	In	Out	Hours
Monday					
Tuesday					
Wednesday					
Thursday					
Friday					
Saturday					
Sunday					
FOREMAN'S SIGNATURE:					

1.8 Daily timesheets

One of these sheets is filled in by each employee (to indicate the time spent by them on each job) and passed to the cost office each day. The total time on the timesheet should correspond to the time shown on the attendance record. Times are recorded daily meaning there is less risk of times being forgotten or manipulated, but these timesheets create a considerable volume of paperwork. Below is an illustration of a daily timesheet.

Example 3

Name:		Frank Smith			Date:		11/6/X5
Clock number:	3				**Week number:**	31	
Job order number	Description	Time		Hours worked	Rate	£	
		Start	Finish				
349	Servicing Ford Ka Y625 AAB	9.00	11.05	2.05			
372	Repair to Range Rover TC03 XYZ	11.05	16.30	4.25			
Signed:	F Smith	**Certified:** A Foreman				**Office ref:**	

1.9 Weekly timesheets

These are similar to daily timesheets but they are passed to the cost office at the end of the week instead of every day (although entries should be made daily in order to avoid error). Weekly timesheets are particularly suitable where there are few job changes in the course of a week.

2 Remuneration systems

2.1 Introduction

Employees in a business will be remunerated or paid for the work that they do. There are a variety of different ways in which this payment is calculated. The main systems of remuneration are:

- annual salaries
- hourly rates of pay and overtime payments
- piecework payments
- bonus schemes.

Different types of employees within a business may well be paid according to different systems depending upon which is the most appropriate for the type of work that they perform.

2.2 Annual salaries

Annual salaries tend to be paid to management and non-production staff such as administrators, secretaries, accounts staff, etc. The annual salary is simply divided by the 12 months in the year and that is the amount of gross pay for that employee for the month.

 Example 4

The sales manager of a business has an annual salary of £30,000. What is the gross amount of his pay each month?

Solution

Monthly gross pay	=	£30,000/12
	=	£2,500

2.3 Hourly rates and overtime payments

Many production and manual workers will be paid for every hour that they work. Normally hourly paid workers will have a standard number of hours that they work each week. If they work for more than this number of hours then they will have worked overtime, which will usually be paid at more than the basic hourly rate.

Overtime has two terms that you need to be aware of – overtime payment and overtime premium.

* The **overtime payment** is the **total** amount paid for hours worked above the normal number of hours.

* The **overtime premium** is the **extra** paid above the normal rate for those overtime hours. For example, if an employee is paid time and a half for any hours above his/her basic, then the 'half' is the premium.

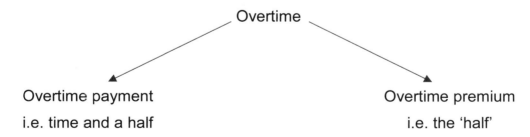

Overtime

Overtime payment
i.e. time and a half

Overtime premium
i.e. the 'half'

This distinction is often necessary for costing purposes, as the premium part of the overtime may be classified separately from the overtime hours at basic rate.

Overtime can be worked for a couple of reasons – **general pressures** in the workplace or to meet the demands of a **specific customer request**. This has an impact on how the overtime is treated in the accounts of a business.

Whether the **overtime premium** is treated as a direct or indirect labour cost will depend upon the reason the overtime was worked:

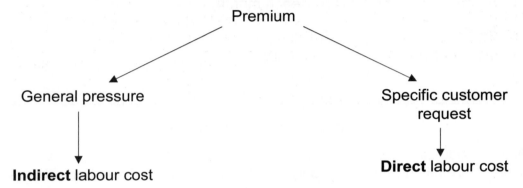

Be careful when answering questions on labour costs – make sure to check what information you are being asked for. Do you need to show the overtime payment or premium? If an exam question asks for the payment then you would split your answer based on normal hours at basic rate and overtime hours at the basic rate plus the premium. If the question asks for premium you would record all the hours worked at a basic rate and then show the premium for the overtime hours separately.

Example 5

An employee works for a standard week of 40 hours at an hourly rate of pay of £8.20. Any overtime hours are paid at time and a half.

In one week he works for 45 hours.

(i)   What is his gross pay, showing the overtime payment?

(ii) What is his gross pay, showing the overtime premium?

Solution

(i)		£
	Basic hours 40 × £8.20	328.00
	Overtime payment 5 × (£8.20 × 1.5)	61.50
		———
	Gross pay	389.50
		———

(ii)		£
	Basic hours 45 × £8.20	369.00
	Overtime premium 5 × (£8.20 × 0.5)	20.50
		———
	Gross pay	389.50
		———

 Test your understanding 1

Below is the weekly timesheet for Thomas Yung (employee number Y4791), who is paid as follows:

- For a basic six-hour shift every day from Monday to Friday – basic pay.

- For any overtime in excess of the basic six hours, on any day from Monday to Friday – the extra hours are paid at time-and-a-half.

- For three contracted hours each Saturday morning – basic pay.

- For any hours in excess of three hours on Saturday – the extra hours are paid at double time.

- For any hours worked on Sunday – paid at double time

Complete the columns headed Basic pay, Overtime premium and Total pay. Zero figures should be entered in cells where appropriate.

Employee's weekly timesheet for week ending 12 December						
Name:	Thomas Yung			**Cost centre:**		Machining
Employee number:	Y4791			**Basic Pay per hour:**		£12
	Hours spent on:		Notes	Basic pay £	Overtime premium £	Total pay £
	Production	Indirect work				
Monday	6	. 2	1 – 3 pm cleaning machinery			
Tuesday	2	4	9 am – 1 pm training course			
Wednesday	8					
Thursday	6					
Friday	6	1	2 – 3 pm health and safety training			
Saturday	6					
Sunday	3					
Total	37	7				

📝 **Test your understanding 2**

An employee's basic week is 40 hours at a rate of pay of £5 per hour. Overtime is paid at 'time and a half'. What is the wage cost of this employee if he works for 45 hours in a week?

A   £225.00

B   £237.50

C   £300.00

D   £337.50

Test your understanding 3

The following information relates to direct labour costs incurred during July 20Y0:

Normal time hours worked	8,000 hours
Overtime at time and a half worked	1,500 hours
Overtime at double time worked	1,000 hours
Total hours worked	10,500 hours
Normal time hourly rate	£7 per hour

Overtime premiums paid are included as part of direct labour costs.

The total cost of direct labour for the month of July 20Y0.

A   £91,000

B   £85,750

C   £70,000

D   £73,500

2.4   Piecework payments

Piecework rates are where the employee is paid per unit of output. The rate will often be based upon the standard (expected) time per unit. This method is an example of 'payment by results'.

Example 6

Graeme MacHue works in the Scottish Highlands producing carved wooden animals for a small company supplying the tourist market. In week 26 he worked 45 hours and his production was:

	Standard time allowed/unit
6 Stags	2.0 hours
5 Otters	1.5 hours
12 Owls	1.0 hour
6 Golden Eagles	2.0 hours

He is paid £5 per standard hour of production (irrespective of actual time worked).

What are his earnings for week 26?

Solution

		£
Stags	6 × 2 × £5	60.00
Otters	5 × 1.5 × £5	37.50
Owls	12 × 1 × £5	60.00
Golden Eagles	6 × 2 × £5	60.00
		————
		217.50
		————

Test your understanding 4

A company operates a piecework system of remuneration. Employees must work for a minimum of 40 hours per week. Joe produces the following output for a particular week:

Product	Quantity	Standard time per item (hours)	Total actual time (hours)
Gaskets	50	0.2	9
Drive belts	200	0.06	14
Sprockets	100	0.1	12
Gears	10	0.7	6
			——
			41
			——

He is paid £6.20 per standard hour worked. What are his earnings for the week?

A   £129.60

B   £254.20

C   £241.80

D   £498.48

Advantages of the piecework system

- It produces a constant labour cost per unit.

- It **encourages efficient work** – an employee taking more than the standard time per unit will only be paid for the standard time. In order for this to motivate, the employee must accept the standard as fair.

To increase motivation, a **differential piecework system** may be implemented, whereby the piece rate is increased for higher output levels.

Disadvantages of the piecework system

- Employees **lack security of income**, so may become demotivated.

- The employee can be **penalised** for low levels of production due to factors that are outside his/her control (e.g. machine breakdown)

2.5 Guaranteed minimum payment

To overcome these disadvantages, the **straight piecework rate** may be accompanied by a **guaranteed minimum payment** (weekly or daily).

Example 7

Standard rate per hour	=	£4.50
Guaranteed minimum per week	=	35 hours

Actual production: 10 units @ 3 hours per unit.

Calculate the weekly pay.

Solution

Standard hours	=	10 × 3 = 30 hours
Pay	=	30 × £4.50 = £135
Subject to guaranteed minimum pay	=	35 × £4.50 = £157.50
Therefore weekly pay	=	£157.50

The employee is paid whichever is the highest value.

Test your understanding 5

Jones is paid £3.00 for every unit that he produces but he has a guaranteed wage of £28.00 per eight-hour day. In a particular week he produces the following number of units:

Monday	12 units
Tuesday	14 units
Wednesday	9 units
Thursday	14 units
Friday	8 units

Jones's wages for the week are:

A   £176

B   £175

C   £172

D   £171

 Test your understanding 6

Continuing with the example of Jones above, what would be his weekly wage if the guarantee were for £140 per week rather than £28 per day?

A   £176

B   £175

C   £172

D   £171

2.6 Bonus schemes

Bonus schemes are a compromise between a day rate and a piecework system. Earnings will comprise:

(a)   a day rate amount, based on hours worked, and

(b)   a bonus based on quantity produced (usually above a certain standard) or on time saved in relation to standard time allowance for the output achieved.

⚬ Example 8

On a particular day, Fred worked for 8.5 hours, producing 15 units. The standard time allowance for each unit is 40 minutes. Fred's basic hourly rate is £4.50 and he is paid a bonus for time saved from standard at 60% of his basic hourly rate.

Calculate Fred's pay for the day.

Solution

		£
Day rate = 8.5 × £4.50		38.25
Bonus		
Standard time 15 × 40/60	10 hours	
Actual time	8.5 hours	
	————	
Time saved	1.5 hours	
	————	
Bonus = 1.5 × £4.50 × 60%		4.05
		————
Total		42.30
		————

2.7 Group bonus schemes

In the case of, for example, an assembly line, where it is impossible for an individual worker on the line to increase productivity without the others also doing so, a group bonus scheme may be used. The bonus is calculated by reference to the output of the group and split between the members of the group (often equally).

 Example 9

Ten employees work as a group. The standard output for the group is 200 units per hour and when this is exceeded each employee in the group is paid a bonus in addition to the hourly wage.

The bonus percentage is calculated as follows:

$$50\% \times \frac{\text{Excess units}}{\text{Standard units}}$$

The percentage is then applied to the standard hourly wage rate of £7.20 to calculate the bonus per hour for each employee:

The following is one week's record of production by the group:

	Hours worked	Production units
Monday	90	24,500
Tuesday	88	20,600
Wednesday	90	24,200
Thursday	84	20,100
Friday	88	20,400
Saturday	40	10,200
	480	120,000

Solution

The standard number of units for the time worked:

480 × 200 = 96,000 units

The number of excess units produced:

120,000 – 96,000 = 24,000 units

The bonus calculation:

24,000/96,000 × 50% = 0.125 = 12.5%

Individual hourly bonus:

£7.20 × 0.125 = £0.90

Group bonus:

480 × £0.90 = £432

If Jones worked for 42 hours and was paid £6.00 per hour as a basic rate what would be his total pay for this week?

Basic	=	42 × £6.00	=	£252
Bonus	=	42 × £0.90	=	£37.80
Total			=	£289.80

📝 Test your understanding 7

Brown and Jones is a firm of joiners. They have a workshop and employ six craftsmen. One of the employees is engaged on the production of standard doors for a local firm of builders.

This employee is paid a bonus based on time saved. The time saved is paid at a rate of 50% of the basic hourly rate.

In addition to the bonus, hours worked over the basic 40 per week are paid at time and a half.

In the week ended 13 February 20X1 the following details were available.

Basic hourly rate	£6.00
Time allowed per standard door	2 hours
Doors produced	25
Time worked	45 hours

The employee's gross pay for the week ended 13 February 20X1 is:

A £270

B £285

C £300

D £315

2.8 Holiday pay

As well as the normal payments of wages and salaries, there are other labour costs which include holiday pay and training time.

Holiday pay is non-productive, but it is nevertheless charged to the cost of production by allocating the full year's holiday pay to overhead and charging it to production for the whole year.

Alternatively, wages may be allocated at **labour rates inflated to include holiday pay** and other non-productive time costs.

2.9 Training time and supervisors' wages

Wages paid during a period of **training** may be charged partly to the job and partly to production overhead. The fact that learners work more slowly than trained employees is offset by the learners' lower rate of pay. Apprentices' remuneration will be charged to a separate account.

Normally, **supervisors' wages** are treated as part of department overhead unless only a particular job is concerned. Where instruction is being given, the remuneration of instructors and supervisors may be included in training time.

2.10 Summary

Different types of employee in an organisation will be paid in different ways. For example, management are normally paid by salary, production workers will be either hourly paid or paid on a piecework basis and the sales team may well be paid according to a bonus scheme.

3 Direct and indirect labour costs

3.1 Recap on direct and indirect costs

- A **direct** cost is an item of cost that is traceable directly to a cost unit.

- An **indirect** cost is a cost that either cannot be identified with any one finished unit. Such costs are often referred to as 'overheads'.

We have seen that there are a variety of different methods of remunerating employees and a number of different elements to this remuneration. For costing purposes the total labour costs must be split between the **direct labour costs**, which can be charged to the units of **production** and any **indirect labour costs**, which are charged as **overheads** to the relevant cost centre.

3.2   Production workers

The wages that are paid to the production workers will **on the whole be direct labour costs** so long as they **relate directly** to the production of output, known as basic rate. The direct labour cost will also include the basic rate for any overtime hours but the **overtime premium** may be treated as an indirect cost.

3.3   Overtime premium

Whether the overtime premium is treated as a direct or indirect labour cost will depend upon the reasons for the overtime:

* If the overtime is worked due to a customer's specific instruction, then the overtime premium will be treated as a direct labour cost.

* If the overtime is due to general pressure of work, then the premium is treated as an indirect labour cost.

3.4   Direct labour cost per unit of production or service

Once the direct labour cost has been identified and calculated it can be related to a unit of product or service:

Direct labour cost per unit = total labour cost ÷ total number of units produced

3.5   Direct labour cost per equivalent finished production

In some time periods the units of product or service may not be fully completed with respect to the labour input when the wages are paid. To ensure that each unit is assigned a fair share of the labour cost incurred in the period the cost per equivalent unit (EU) is calculated.

 Example 10

A direct worker has been working on 70 units. He has fully completed 40 units but 30 units are only 50% complete with regards labour. The direct worker has been paid £165 for the work carried out so far.

Calculate the cost per equivalent unit

40 units that are fully complete = 40 × 100% = 40 EU

30 units that are 50% complete = 30 × 50% = 15 EU.

Total equivalent units = 40 + 15 = 55 EU

Therefore the direct labour cost per equivalent unit
= £165 ÷ 55 = £3 per EU

3.6 Holiday pay

Holiday pay is normally treated as an **indirect** labour cost as **no production** is occurring.

3.7 Training time

The hours paid for the labour force to train are treated as an **indirect** labour cost as **no production** is occurring.

3.8 Idle time

Controllable idle time is treated as an indirect labour cost. Uncontrollable idle time is treated as an expense in the costing income statement.

It should obviously be prevented as far as possible. It is important to analyse the causes of idle time so that necessary corrective action can be taken.

There are three groups of causes of idle time:

(a)   Productive causes (e.g. machine breakdown, power failure or time spent waiting for work, tools, materials or instructions).

(b)   Administrative causes (e.g. surplus capacity, policy changes, unforeseen drop in demand).

(c)   Economic causes (e.g. seasonal fluctuations in demand, cyclical fluctuations in demand, changes in demand because of tax changes).

3.9 Management and supervisors' salaries

Management salaries and supervisors' salaries are all labour costs that are **not related to actual production** of the cost units, therefore they are all treated as **indirect labour costs**.

Test your understanding 8

G Dickson is a football manufacturer. Classify the following costs by nature (direct or indirect) in the table below.

Cost	Direct	Indirect
Basic pay for production workers	☐	☐
Supervisors wages	☐	☐
Bonus for salesman	☐	☐
Production workers overtime premium due to general pressures.	☐	☐
Holiday pay for production workers	☐	☐
Sick pay for supervisors	☐	☐
Time spent by production workers cleaning the machinery	☐	☐

4 Integrated bookkeeping – labour

4.1 Introduction

The costs of a business have to be recorded in a bookkeeping system. Many businesses use an **integrated bookkeeping system** where the ledger accounts kept provide the necessary **information for both costing and financial accounting**.

4.2 Wages control account

Accounting for wages and salaries is based upon two fundamental principles:

- The accounts must reflect the full cost to the employer of employing someone.

- The accounts must show the payable for PAYE and NIC that must be paid over to the HMRC.

There are three accounts to record transactions:

- The wages expense account, which shows the total expense to business i.e. Gross Pay and Employer's NIC.

- The PAYE/NIC account /Trade Union account/Pension account which is used to record the liability owed to HMRC/due to Trade Union/Pension Company.

- The wages and salaries control account is used as a control. One side of each double entry is put through the control account. This account is cleared out each payroll run and there is never a balance brought down.

The **wages and salaries control account** can also be called the **labour cost account** in a management accounting system.

💡 Example 11

Wages and salaries control account

	£		£
Bank (1)		Production (4)	
HMRC liability (2)		Production overheads (5)	
Pension (3)			
	———		———
	———		———

(1) The labour cost **incurred** or **net pay** is paid out of the **bank** to the employees.

(2) The amount of PAYE, Employees and Employers NIC that is owed to the HMRC is recorded in the control account as a debit and in the PAYE/NIC account as a credit or liability.

(3) Pensions, or other payments that are made out of the employees gross wage, will also need to be recorded

(4) **Direct labour costs** are transferred out of the wages control account via a credit entry to the production account. The production account can also be referred to as Work in Progress (WIP).

(5) **Indirect labour costs** are collected in the production overheads account. They are transferred there via a credit entry out of the wages control account and then debited in the production overheads account.

Test your understanding 9

What are the correct journal entries the following accounting transactions:

1   Payment for labour:

A   Dr Bank, Cr Wages Control

B   Dr Trade Payables Control, Cr Wages Control

C   Dr Wages Control, Cr Bank

D   Dr Wages Control, Cr Trade Payables Control

2   Analysis of direct labour:

A   Dr Bank, Cr Wages Control

B   Dr Wages Control, Cr Bank

C   Dr Wages Control, Cr Production

D   Dr Production, Cr Wages Control

3   Analysis of payment for labour relating to overtime premium that was due to a specific customer request:

A   Dr Production, Cr Wages Control

B   Dr Production Overheads, Cr Wages Control

C   Dr Wages Control, Cr Production

D   Dr Wages Control, Cr Production Overheads

4   Analysis of payment for labour relating to overtime premium that was due to general work pressures.

A   Dr Wages Control, Cr Production

B   Dr Wages Control, Cr Production Overheads

C   Dr Production, Cr Wages Control

D   Dr Production Overheads, Cr Wages Control

Test your understanding 10

Below is the weekly timesheet for Ekta Plasm (employee number EP0516), who is paid as follows:

- For a basic six-hour shift every day from Monday to Friday – basic pay.

- For any overtime in excess of the basic six hours, on any day from Monday to Friday – the extra hours are paid at time-and-a-third.

- For three contracted hours each Saturday morning – basic pay.

- For any hours in excess of three hours on Saturday – the extra hours are paid at double time.

- For any hours worked on Sunday – paid at double time

- Any overtime worked is due to general work pressures

Complete the columns headed Basic pay, Overtime premium and Total pay. Zero figures should be entered in cells where appropriate.

Employee's weekly timesheet for week ending 24 April						
Name:		Ekta Plasm		**Cost centre:**		Sewing
Employee number:		EP0516		**Basic Pay per hour:**		£9
	Hours spent on:		Notes	Basic pay £	Overtime premium £	Total pay £
	Production	Indirect work				
Monday	6					
Tuesday	3	3	10 am – 1 pm training course			
Wednesday	8					
Thursday	7					
Friday	6	1	2 – 3 pm health and safety training			
Saturday	5					
Sunday	3					
Total	38	4				

Complete the Wages Control account below from the timesheet above.

Wages control account

	£		£
Bank		Production	
		Production overheads	
	————		————
	————		————

5 Summary

This chapter has considered the **methods of payment** of labour that may be used by organisations. These may be annual salaries, hourly rates of pay, performance related pay (piecework) and profit related pay (bonus schemes). In order to pay the correct amount to employees there must be detailed recording of the time spent at work by each employee on time sheets or by a time clock and clock cards.

The distribution between **direct and indirect labour** costs is an important one.

Direct labour costs including the following:

- production workers' wages (excluding overtime premiums)

- bonus payments for production workers

- overtime premiums where overtime was worked at the specific request of the customer.

Indirect labour costs include the following:

- holiday pay

- training time

- idle time

- supervisors' salaries

- management salaries

- overtime premiums where overtime was due to the general pressure of work.

- production supervisors' wages that cannot be allocated to specific cost units.

Test your understanding answers

Test your understanding 1

Employee's weekly timesheet for week ending 12 December						
Name:		Thomas Yung		**Cost centre:**		Machining
Employee number:		Y4791		**Basic Pay per hour:**		£12
	Hours spent on:		Notes	Basic pay £	Overtime premium £	Total pay £
	Production	Indirect work				
Monday	6	2	1 – 3 pm cleaning machinery	96	12	108
Tuesday	2	4	9 am – 1 pm training course	72	0	72
Wednesday	8			96	12	108
Thursday	6			72	0	72
Friday	6	1	2 – 3 pm health and safety training	84	6	90
Saturday	6			72	36	108
Sunday	3			36	36	72
Total	37	7		528	102	630

Test your understanding 2

B

Basic	= 40 × 5	= £200
Overtime	= 5 × 5 × 1.5	= £37.50
Total pay		= £237.50

Test your understanding 3

B

Basic pay 10,500 hrs @ £7	£73,500
Overtime 1,500 hrs @ 3.5	£5,250
Overtime 1,000 hrs @ £7	£7,000
	£85,750

Test your understanding 4

C   £241.80

Multiply the quantity by the standard time per item for each item to give a standard time of 39 hours. This is multiplied by the rate per standard hour. 39 × £6.20 = £241.80.

Test your understanding 5

A

Total weekly wage:

	£
Monday (12 × £3)	36
Tuesday (14 × £3)	42
Wednesday (guaranteed)	28
Thursday (14 × £3)	42
Friday (guaranteed)	28
	176

Test your understanding 6

D

	£
Monday (12 × £3)	36
Tuesday (14 × £3)	42
Wednesday (9 × £3)	27
Thursday (14 × £3)	42
Friday (8 × £3)	24
	___
	171
	___

As the weekly earnings are above £140, the guaranteed amount is not relevant to the calculations in this instance.

Test your understanding 7

C

Gross wage:

Basic pay – 45 hrs @ £6	£270.00
Overtime – 5 hrs @ £3	£15.00
Bonus:	
25 doors × 2 hours = 50 hours allowed	
Time taken – 45 hours	
Time saved – 5 hours × £3	£15.00
	_____
	£300.00
	_____

Test your understanding 8

Cost	Direct	Indirect
Basic pay for production workers	☑	☐
Supervisors wages	☐	☑
Bonus for salesman	☐	☑
Production workers overtime premium due to general pressures.	☐	☑
Holiday pay for production workers	☐	☑
Sick pay for supervisors	☐	☑
Time spent by production workers cleaning the machinery	☐	☑

Test your understanding 9

1   Payment for labour:

    C   Dr Wages control, Cr Bank

2   Analysis of direct labour:

    D   Dr Production, Cr Wages control

3   Analysis of payment for labour relating to overtime premium that was due to a specific customer request:

    A   Dr Production, Cr Wages control

4   Analysis of payment for labour relating to overtime premium that was due to general work pressures.

    D   Dr Production Overheads, Cr Wages control

Test your understanding 10

Employee's weekly timesheet for week ending 24 April

Name:		Ekta Plasm	Cost centre:		Sewing	
Employee number:		EP0516	Basic Pay per hour:		£9	

	Hours spent on:		Notes	Basic pay £	Overtime premium £	Total pay £
	Production	Indirect work				
Monday	6			54	0	54
Tuesday	3	3	10 am – 1 pm training course	54	0	54
Wednesday	8			72	6	78
Thursday	7			63	3	66
Friday	6	1	2 – 3 pm health and safety training	63	3	66
Saturday	5			45	18	63
Sunday	3			27	27	54
Total	38	4		378	57	435

Wages control account

	£		£
Bank	435	Production	342
		Production overheads	93
	───		───
	435		435
	───		───

Production is **direct** labour cost **only** therefore the cost is:

Basic hours less the time spent on non-production activities

£378 – (4 × 9) = £342

Production overheads are the **indirect costs** (the overtime is worked due to general work pressure so is classed as indirect) therefore the cost is:

57 + (4 × 9) = £93

Expenses

5

Introduction

All other costs that are not material or labour related are known as expenses. This chapter looks at the distinction between different types of expense, how expenses are recorded and the difference between capital and revenue expenditure.

NOTE: In the real world the term 'expenses' could include both direct and indirect components. In the exam, however, expenses are always treated simply as 'overheads' with no separation into direct and indirect elements.

ASSESSMENT CRITERIA
Record and calculate overhead costs (2.1)
Analyse cost information for overheads in accordance with the organisation's costing procedures (2.2)
Prepare cost accounting journal entries for overheads (2.2)

CONTENTS

1 Expenses
2 Direct and indirect expenses
3 Recording expenses
4 Capital and revenue expenditure

1 Expenses

1.1 Introduction

Costs incurred by a business, other than material and labour costs, are known as expenses.

Expenses of a business can cover a wide variety of areas. They might include:

Manufacturing Expenses	Selling and Distribution Expenses	Administration Expenses
Cost of power	Advertising costs	Rent of office buildings
Factory rental	Packaging costs	Telephone bills
Light and heat cost	Costs of delivering goods to the customer	Postage costs
Depreciation of machinery	Warehouse rental for storage of goods	Auditors fees

The list could go on and we will consider many of these later in this chapter and in the next chapters.

2 Direct and indirect expenses

2.1 Introduction

Remember that direct costs are those that can be related directly to a cost unit, whilst indirect costs (overheads) cannot be specifically traced to individual units.

2.2 Direct expenses

Expenses are far more likely to be indirect; however, some examples of direct expenses are given below. Direct expenses can be identified with a specific cost unit and are production costs.

- **Royalty or patent costs** payable for use of a particular component, technique, trade name, etc. in the production or service.

- **Sub-contracted charges**: if the business hires another company or a self-employed person to perform a particular function directly related to the product or service provided, this will be treated as a direct expense.

  For example, a building contractor will very often use sub-contractors to carry out electrical and plumbing work on a particular contract. The charge invoiced to the builder for this work (which will include both labour and materials) will be analysed as a direct expense of the contract.

- Expenses associated with **machinery or equipment** used for a particular job: hire charges, maintenance, power, etc.

2.3 Indirect expenses

Indirect expenses cannot be identified with a specific cost unit. They are far more common and can be categorised in various ways, depending upon the organisational structure of the business and the level of detail required in the cost accounts.

Depending upon their nature, indirect expenses may be:

- production costs (production overheads); or

- non-production costs (non-production overheads).

NOTE: In the real world the term 'expenses' could include both direct and indirect components. In the exam, however, expenses are always treated simply as 'overheads' with no separation into direct and indirect elements.

3 Recording expenses

3.1 Allocation to cost centres

For control purposes, all costs eventually need to be **allocated to cost centres and/or cost units**. For materials and labour costs, this may be achieved by use of coded materials requisitions or analysed timesheets. The same principle will apply to expenses, although the allocation of indirect expenses may be done in stages.

The general approach to expense recording and allocation will be as follows.

3.2 Direct expenses

When the invoice arrives (e.g. from a sub-contractor), the relevant product/job/client will be identified and the invoice **coded** accordingly before being passed to the data processing department for recording in the ledgers.

3.3 Indirect expenses

These, by definition, will not be directly identifiable with a particular cost unit and will therefore initially be charged to an **appropriate cost centre**.

Some expenses will relate solely to **one cost centre**.

For example, advertising invoices will be allocated to the marketing/selling department and petrol bills for delivery vehicles will be charged to distribution. The invoices can therefore be coded to the appropriate centre.

Many expenses will, however, relate to **more than one cost centre** – for example, rent, rates and other buildings costs, where the building is shared by several cost centres.

Ultimately, these costs will generally be coded to a collecting cost centre and then **shared between the appropriate cost** centres using some agreed basis (e.g. floor area occupied). This is known as overhead apportionment and is covered in detail in Chapter 6.

3.4 Documentation

Most expenses will be documented by way of a **supplier's invoice or bill**. The authorisation for payment, codings for posting to the appropriate ledger accounts/cost centres and other internally added information may be attached by way of a standard **ink stamp** with appropriate boxes for manual completion.

4 Capital and revenue expenditure

4.1 Introduction

One particular distinction in expenditure classification is between capital expenditure and revenue expenditure.

4.2 Capital expenditure

 Definition

Capital expenditure is expenditure incurred in:

(a) the acquisition of non-current assets required for use in the business and not for resale

(b) the alteration or improvement of non-current assets for the purpose of increasing their revenue-earning capacity.

4.3 Revenue expenditure

 Definition

Revenue expenditure is expenditure incurred in:

(a) the acquisition of assets acquired for conversion into cash (e.g. goods for resale)

(b) the manufacturing, selling and distribution of goods and the day-to-day administration of the business

(c) the **maintenance** of the revenue-earning capacity of the non-current assets (i.e. repairs, etc).

In practice, there can be some difficulty in clearly distinguishing between alteration/improvement of non-current assets (capital) and their maintenance (revenue). For example, is the installation of a modern heating system to replace an old inefficient system an improvement or maintenance? However, you will not need to make such decisions in your assessment.

Test your understanding 1

RFB plc makes wheels for a variety of uses: wheelbarrows, carts, toys, etc.

Complete the following form by putting a tick for each of the cost items into the appropriate column.

	Capital expenditure	Revenue expenditure
Purchase of a lorry	☐	☐
Electricity and power costs	☐	☐
Purchase of a chair for the office	☐	☐
Road tax for the lorry	☐	☐
Purchase of premises	☐	☐
Repair of a broken window	☐	☐

Test your understanding 2

RFB plc makes wheels for a variety of uses: wheelbarrows, carts, toys, etc.

Complete the following form by putting a tick for each of the cost items into the appropriate column.

	Capital expenditure	Revenue expenditure
Repairs to machinery	☐	☐
Purchase of new delivery vehicle	☐	☐
Depreciation of delivery vehicle	☐	☐
Vehicle tax for new vehicle	☐	☐
Installation of air conditioning unit	☐	☐
Redecoration of office	☐	☐

4.4   The accounting treatments

Capital expenditure is initially shown in the statement of financial position as non-current assets. It is then charged to the statement of profit or loss over a number of periods, via the depreciation charge.

Revenue expenditure is generally charged to the statement of profit or loss for the period in which the expenditure was incurred.

4.5   The relevance of the distinction to cost accounting

Cost accounting is mainly directed towards gathering and analysing cost information to assist management in planning, control and decision-making. In particular:

(a)   the determination of **actual and budgeted costs** and profits for a period and for individual cost centres and cost units

(b)   the valuation of **inventories** (raw materials, finished goods, etc).

Thus **revenue expenditure** is of far greater relevance than capital expenditure. The main impact of capital expenditure on the above will be the depreciation charges that arise and that may be charged as a direct product/service cost (as in the depreciation of machinery or equipment used in production or provision of a service) or as an overhead (depreciation of buildings, motor vehicles, etc).

5   Summary

We have now seen how expenses cover all expenditure that is not related to materials or labour. It is important that you are able to distinguish between **direct and indirect expenses**. Direct expenses are any expenses that can be related specifically to a cost unit. Indirect expenses are far more common and are known as overheads.

The distinction between **capital and revenue expenditure** is also important. You must be able to decide whether an expense is capital or revenue in nature. Revenue expenditure is written off to the statement of profit or loss in the period in which it is incurred, whilst capital expenditure is written off to the statement of profit or loss over a number of accounting periods, via a depreciation charge.

Test your understanding answers

✎ Test your understanding 1

	Capital expenditure	Revenue expenditure
Purchase of a lorry	☑	☐
Electricity and power costs	☐	☑
Purchase of a chair for the office	☐	☑
Road tax for the lorry	☐	☑
Purchase of premises	☑	☐
Repair of a broken window	☐	☑

✎ Test your understanding 2

	Capital expenditure	Revenue expenditure
Repairs to machinery	☐	☑
Purchase of new delivery vehicle	☑	☐
Depreciation of delivery vehicle	☐	☑
Vehicle tax for new vehicle	☐	☑
Installation of air conditioning unit	☑	☐
Redecoration of office	☐	☑

KAPLAN PUBLISHING

Overheads

Introduction

This chapter looks at how **overheads** (indirect expenses) are **allocated** or **apportioned** to cost centres and how overheads are then **absorbed** into the cost of a product via an **overhead absorption rate**. This chapter applies **absorption costing principles.**

ASSESSMENT CRITERIA
Calculate and use overhead costs (3.1):
– allocation and apportionment
– direct
– step down
– activity based costing
Calculate overhead recovery rates using traditional methods (3.2)
Calculate overhead recovery rates using activity based costing (3.3)
Demonstrate understanding of the under or over recovery of overheads (3.4)

CONTENTS

1 Overheads
2 Absorption costing
3 Allocation and apportionment
4 Reapportionment
5 Absorption
6 Under/over absorption of overheads
7 Integrated bookkeeping – overheads
8 Activity based costing

1 Overheads

1.1 Introduction

There are three categories of indirect costs (making up total overheads):

- indirect materials
- indirect labour
- indirect expenses.

1.2 Production and non-production overheads

Production overheads are included in the total production cost of a product. They could include factory rent, rates, insurance, light, heat, power and other factory running cost.

For a **service industry**, it is more difficult to make a clear distinction between production and non-production overheads. For example, there is rarely a building that is devoted entirely to the provision of the service itself (i.e. equivalent to a factory) that does not also house the administrative, financial, selling and other functions of the business. Thus it is common to include most, if not all, of a service industry's expenses under the other functional headings described below.

Non-production overheads can be split into different categories determined by why or how the cost is incurred:

(a) **Administrative costs**

These include the running costs of non-production buildings; staff and other expenses for non-production departments; management salaries and training costs.

(b) **Selling and distribution costs**

These include sales persons' salaries, commissions; running costs of sales showrooms and offices; delivery vehicle expenses; packaging costs; advertising and promotional costs.

(c) **Finance costs**

These include loan and overdraft interest payable; bank charges; lease interest element; cost of irrecoverable debts.

(d) **Legal and professional charges**

These include auditors', accountants', solicitors', financial advisors' fees; professional subscriptions; professional indemnity insurance; licence costs.

The main reason for wanting to calculate full costs are to value inventories of manufactured goods and also to calculate a selling price based on full costs.

2 Absorption costing

2.1 Production overheads

Production overheads of a factory can include the following costs:

- heating the factory
- lighting the factory
- renting the factory.

Production may take place over a number of different cost centres and each centre should be assigned with its fair share of overhead cost. There may also be a number of service cost centres that provide support to the production cost centres.

Examples of production cost centres include:

- Assembly
- Machining
- Finishing.

Examples of production service cost centres include:

- Maintenance
- Canteen
- Stores.

2.2 Absorption costing

Production overheads are recovered by absorbing them into the cost of a product and this process is called absorption costing.

The main aim of absorption costing is to recover overheads in a way that fairly reflects the amount of time and effort that has gone into making a product or service.

Absorption costing involves the following stages:

- allocation and apportionment of overheads to the different cost centres
- reapportionment of service cost centre overheads to the production cost centres
- absorption of overheads into the products.

Absorption costing allows businesses to make decisions about pricing policies and value its inventory in accordance with IAS 2 Inventories which defines cost as comprising: 'all costs of purchase, costs of conversion and other costs incurred in bringing the inventories to their present location and condition'.

Absorption costing values each unit of inventory at the total cost incurred to **produce** the unit. This includes direct materials, direct labour, direct expenses, variable production overheads and fixed production overheads. All these costs would be referred to as **product costs**. **Non-production** costs are considered **period costs** and are not included in the cost of a unit but are deducted in full from the gross profit.

🔍 Definition

Absorption costing is a method of building up a full product cost which adds direct costs and a proportion of production overhead cost by means of one or a number of overhead absorption rates.

The basic layout for calculating the budgeted profit or loss under absorption costing is as follows (with illustrative figures).

	£
Sales revenue (10,000 × £10)	100,000
Cost of sales (at full **production** cost, £8)	(80,000)
	———
Gross profit	20,000
Less: **Non-production** costs	(12,000)
	———
Profit for the period	8,000
	———

Example 1

XYZ plc

XYZ plc manufactures toy horses and has produced a budget for the quarter ended 30 June 20X5 (Quarter 1) as follows.

Sales	190 units @ selling price of £12
Production	200 units
Opening inventory	20 units
Variable production cost per unit	£8
Fixed production cost per unit	£2
Selling and distribution costs	£250

Required:

Draft the statement of profit or loss using absorption costing principles:

Solution

Closing inventory = Opening inventory + production – sales

Closing inventory = 20 + 200 – 190 = 30 units

The cost per unit in the cost of sales includes the variable production cost and the fixed production cost.

	£	£
Sales revenue 190 × £12		2,280
Less: Cost of sales		
Opening inventory 20 × £10	200	
Production costs 200 × £10	2,000	
Closing inventory 30 × £10	(300)	
		1,900
Gross profit		380
Non-production costs		(250)
Profit for the period		130

2.3 Advantages of absorption costing

Absorption costing has a number of advantages:

- The costing technique adheres to the accounting standard for the valuation of inventory (IAS 2) so can be used for **statutory financial reporting**.

- When valuing inventory using absorption costing the total production cost is considered. This means that when deciding on a selling price all production costs should be covered.

- The analysis of under- or over- absorption of overheads is a useful exercise in controlling costs (covered later in this chapter).

This chapter will detail the procedure for assigning production overheads to units of output.

3 Allocation and apportionment

3.1 Allocation, apportionment and absorption

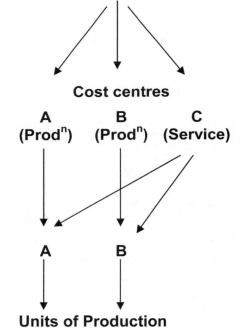

Step 1: Allocation or Apportionment

Step 2: Reapportion

Step 3: Absorb

The purpose of **allocation** and **apportionment** is to attribute production overhead costs to production cost centres.

Where a business has a mix of production and service cost centres any production overheads in the service cost centres are **reapportioned** to the production centres.

The purpose of **absorption** is to assign the production overheads to the units produced by the cost centre.

There are 3 steps to achieving the process:

Step 1: Overheads are allocated or apportioned to cost centres using suitable bases.

Step 2: Any service centre costs are reapportioned to production centres using suitable bases.

Step 3: Overheads are absorbed into units of production using suitable bases.

3.2 Allocation

 Definition

When an overhead relates entirely to one production or service centre it can be **wholly attributed** to that single production or service centre. This is allocation.

Examples of costs that relate to one specific cost centre are given below:

Cost centre	Allocated cost
Accounts	Accounting overhead
Machining department	Insurance of machines
Stores	Stores wages
Canteen	Maintenance of kitchen equipment

3.3 Apportionment

 Definition

When an overhead relates to **more than one** production and/or service centre it is shared over these centres on a fair or suitable basis. This is apportionment.

Examples of bases of apportioning overheads are as follows:

Nature of cost	Possible bases of apportionment
Rent and rates	Floor space (m^2)
Lighting and heating	Usage of electricity (KwH)
Insurance of inventory	Value of inventory
Depreciation	Carrying amount of asset
Supervisors' salaries	Time spent supervising

 Example 2

Example of cost allocation and apportionment

A Ltd has three cost centres: assembly, machining and administration. It has the following budgeted overheads costs for the year to December 20X4:

	£
Oil for machining department	2,000
Salary of assembly department supervisor	20,000
Insurance of machines in machining department	4,000
Rent of factory	16,000
Maintenance salaries	40,000
Canteen costs for factory	15,000
	97,000

Required:

(a) Allocate any costs to the relevant cost centres.

(b) Apportion the costs that cannot be allocated using the information below:

	Assembly	Machining	Maintenance	Total
Area (m^2)	3,000	3,000	2,000	8,000
No of employees	15	10	5	30

Solution

Looking at the overhead costs it is possible to identify 4 costs that are wholly attributable to one centre – Oil for **machining**, supervisors' salary for **assembly**, insurance for the machines in the **machining** department and salaries for the **maintenance** department. These costs are allocated to specific departments.

The remaining costs relate to more than one centre so need to be shared or apportioned across the centres they relate to.

To do this, the calculation is:

$$\frac{\text{Total overhead}}{\text{Total of basis}} \times \text{centre basis}$$

Rent– area

Assembly

$$\frac{16,000}{8,000} \times 3,000 = 6,000$$

Machining

$$\frac{16,000}{8,000} \times 3,000 = 6,000$$

Maintenance

$$\frac{16,000}{8,000} \times 2,000 = 4,000$$

Canteen costs – staff

Assembly

$$\frac{15,000}{30} \times 15 = 7,500$$

Machining

$$\frac{15,000}{30} \times 10 = 5,000$$

Maintenance

$$\frac{15,000}{30} \times 5 = 2,500$$

It is also possible to use percentages or fractions to share the costs over the cost centres. With some information percentages or fractions will be a quicker and easier to use to perform the apportionment and may save you time in the exam.

	Assembly	**Machining**	**Maintenance**	**Total**
Area (m²)	3,000	3,000	2,000	8,000
Area as a %	$\frac{3,000}{8,000}$ × 100 = 37.5%	$\frac{3,000}{8,000}$ × 100 = 37.5%	$\frac{2,000}{8,000}$ ×100 = 25%	$\frac{8,000}{8,000}$ ×100 = 100%
No of employees	15	10	5	30
Employees as fractions	$\frac{15}{30} = \frac{1}{2}$	$\frac{10}{30} = \frac{1}{3}$	$\frac{5}{30} = \frac{1}{6}$	$\frac{30}{30} = 1$

Rent – area

Assembly

16,000 × 37.5% = 6,000

Machining

16,000 × 37.5% = 6,000

Maintenance

16,000 × 25% = 4,000

Canteen costs – staff

Assembly

$$\frac{1}{2} \times 15,000 = 7,500$$

Machining

$$\frac{1}{3} \times 15,000 = 5,000$$

Maintenance

$$\frac{1}{6} \times 15,000 = 2,500$$

Overhead cost	Basis of allocation/ apportionment	Assembly £	Machining £	Maintenance £	Total £
Oil	Allocate		2,000		2,000
Salary (supervisor)	Allocate	20,000			20,000
Insurance	Allocate		4,000		4,000
Rent	Floor area	6,000	6,000	4,000	16,000
Salaries (maintenance)	Allocate			40,000	40,000
Canteen	No of employees	7,500	5,000	2,500	15,000
		33,500	17,000	46,500	97,000

Test your understanding 1

An organisation has four departments Fixing, Mending, Stores and Canteen.

The budgeted overhead costs for the organisation are as follows:

	£
Rent	32,000
Building maintenance costs	5,000
Machinery insurance	2,400
Machinery depreciation	11,000
Machinery running expenses	6,000
Power	7,000

There are specific costs that are to be allocated to each cost centre as follows:

	£
Fixing	5,000
Mending	4,000
Stores	1,000
Canteen	2,000

The following information about the various cost centres is also available:

	Fixing	Mending	Stores	Canteen	Total
Floor space (m²)	15,000	8,000	5,000	2,000	30,000
Power usage %	45	40	5	10	100
Value of machinery (£000)	140	110	–	–	250
Machinery hours (000)	50	30			80
Value of equipment (£000)	–	–	5	15	20
Number of employees	20	15	3	2	40
Value of stores requisitions (£000)	100	50	–	–	150

Task

Allocate and apportion the costs to the four departments.

Overhead cost	Basis	Fixing £	Mending £	Stores £	Canteen £	Total £
Specific overheads						12,000
Rent						32,000
Building maintenance						5,000
Machinery insurance						2,400
Machinery depreciation						11,000
Machinery running cost						6,000
Power						7,000
						75,400

Test your understanding 2

Ray Ltd has the following four production departments:

- Machining 1
- Machining 2
- Assembly
- Packaging

The budgeted overheads relating to the four production departments for Quarter 3 20X5 are:

	£	£
Depreciation		80,000
Rent and rates		120,000
Indirect labour costs:		
Machining 1	40,500	
Machining 2	18,300	
Assembly	12,400	
Packaging	26,700	
Total		97,900
Assembly costs		15,600
Total overheads		313,500

Overheads are allocated or apportioned to the production departments on the most appropriate basis. The following information is also available:

Department	Carrying amount of non-current assets (£000)	Square metres occupied	Number of employees
Machining 1	1,280	625	8
Machining 2	320	250	4
Assembly	960	500	3
Packaging	640	1,125	7
Total	3,200	2,500	22

Complete the overhead analysis sheet below (round to the nearest £)

Overhead analysis sheet

	Basis	Machining 1	Machining 2	Assembly	Packaging	Total
Depreciation						
Rent and rates						
Indirect Labour cost						
Assembly costs						
TOTAL						

4 Reapportionment

4.1 Introduction

The next stage is to apportion the service cost centre total costs to the production cost centres that make use of the service cost centre. This process is known as **reapportionment** or secondary apportionment.

This is done because the aim is to have all the production costs identified with a **production** cost centre so that we can then work out the cost of the units that the production cost centre produces.

4.2 A single service centre

 Example 3

A business has one service centre, the canteen, which serves two production centres. The overhead costs for a period have been allocated and apportioned between the three departments as given below.

	Production A	Production B	Canteen
Overhead	£10,000	£15,000	£12,000
Number of employees	100	200	

Reapportion the canteen's overheads to the production departments on the basis of the number of employees.

Solution

Exactly the same technique is used to reapportion as is used to apportion.

	Department A £	Department B £	Canteen £
Overhead	10,000	15,000	12,000
Number of employees	12,000 ÷ 300 × 100 = 4,000	12,000 ÷ 300 × 200 = 8,000	(12,000)
Total overhead for production department	14,000	23,000	

 Test your understanding 3

The cost of the stores department and the personnel department of RFB plc are to be reapportioned across the other cost centres. What bases would you recommend for each cost?

Stores department

A   Number of employees

B   Floor space

C   Number of issues to production

D   Kilowatt hours

Personnel department

A   Number of employees

B   Floor space

C   Number of issues to production

D   Kilowatt hours

4.3 Two service centres

When there are two or more service centres that need to re-apportion costs to production cost centres there are a couple of options:

(a) The service centres only supply services to the production cost centres i.e. they do not provide services to each other.

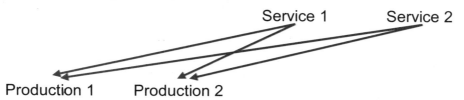

(b) One of the service centres (number 2 in diagram) provides services to the production cost centres and to the other service centre. The remaining service centre (number 1 in the diagram) only provides services to the production cost centres.

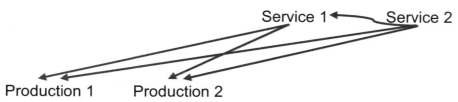

4.4 The direct method

This is used in situation (a) above i.e., where the service centres do not supply services to each other.

⋰ Example 4

A business has two production centres, departments A and B, and two service centres, a canteen and a maintenance department.

The costs allocated and apportioned to the four departments are:

	£
Production A	50,000
Production B	60,000
Canteen	8,000
Maintenance	10,000

The following information related to the service centres:

	Production A	Production B
Usage of maintenance dept	40%	60%
Usage of canteen	45%	55%

The maintenance department supplies 40% of its services to department A, 60% to department B and nothing to the canteen.

The canteen supplies 45% to department A, 55% to B and nothing to the maintenance department.

	Dept A £	Dept B £	Canteen £	Maintenance £
	50,000	60,000	8,000	10,000
Reapportionment of maintenance	(40%) 4,000	(60%) 6,000	–	(10,000)
Reapportionment of canteen	(45%) 3,600	(55%) 4,400	(8,000)	–
Total	57,600	70,400	0	0

It does not matter which service cost centre you re-apportion first when using this method.

4.5 The step down method

This is used in situation (b) above i.e., where one of the service centres supplies services to the other.

 Example 5

A business has two production centres, departments A and B, and two service centres, a canteen and a maintenance department. The costs allocated and apportioned to the four departments are:

	£
Production A	50,000
Production B	60,000
Canteen	8,000
Maintenance	10,000

The following information related to the service centres:

	Production A	Production B	Canteen
Usage of maintenance dept	40%	45%	15%
Usage of canteen	45%	55%	–

The maintenance department supplies 40% of its services to department A, 45% to department B and 15% to the canteen. The canteen supplies 45% to department A, 55% to B and nothing to the maintenance department.

Step 1: Identify the service centre whose services are used by the other service department and apportion its costs to all the departments. In this case the maintenance department services the canteen so the maintenance costs are apportioned first.

Step 2: Now apportion the new total costs of the canteen i.e. its original costs (£8,000) plus its share of the maintenance costs (£1,500) to the production departments.

	Dept A £	Dept B £	Canteen £	Maintenance £
	50,000	60,000	8,000	10,000
Reapportionment maintenance	(40%) 4,000	(45%) 4,500	(15%) 1,500	(10,000)
Reapportionment canteen	(45%) 4,275	(55%) 5,225	(9,500)	–
Total	58,275	69,725	0	0

Test your understanding 4

Adam has a factory with two production departments, machining and painting, which are serviced by the maintenance and quality control departments.

Relevant information for a particular period is as follows:

	Machining	**Painting**	**Maintenance**	**Quality Control**
Apportioned overheads	£20,000	£40,000	£10,000	£15,000
Maintenance	30%	60%		10%
Quality Control	50%	50%		

Required:

Show the reapportionment necessary using the step down method and the resulting total overheads to be attributed to each production department.

	Machining £	Painting £	Maintenance £	Quality control £
Apportioned overheads	20,000	40,000	10,000	15,000
Reapportionment of maintenance				
Reapportionment of quality control				
Total				

Absorption

5.1 Introduction

Having collected all indirect production costs in the production cost centres via overhead allocation and apportionment/reapportionment, the total overhead of each production cost centre must be charged to the **output of the production cost centres.**

🔍 Definition

Overhead absorption is the charging of a production cost centre's overhead costs to the cost units produced by the cost centre.

The **absorption rate** is calculated at the start of the period and is therefore **based on budgeted activity** and on **budgeted overheads**. Various bases for absorption exist and the most suitable one should be chosen depending on the situation.

5.2 One product business

If only one type of product is being produced it is possible to calculate the overhead absorption rate (OAR) using the planned production in units.

$$\frac{\text{Budgeted overhead}}{\text{Budgeted units produced}}$$

Once we know how much overhead each unit is absorbing we can calculate the full production cost per unit.

💡 Example 6

Henry produces one product. Each unit of the product uses £20 worth of material and £10 of labour. Henry has two production centres, assembly and finishing. The following overheads are expected to be incurred:

Rent and rates   £12,000

Light and heat   £15,000

The assembly department occupies twice the floor area of the finishing department. Production is budgeted for 1,000 units.

Calculate the assembly overhead cost per unit, the finishing overhead cost per unit and hence the total cost per unit.

Solution

Step 1

Apportion the overheads to the cost centres, on the basis of size, therefore in the ratio of 2 to 1.

Overhead £	Basis £	Total £	Assembly	Finishing
Rent and rates	Area 2:1	12,000	8,000	4,000
Light and heat	Area 2:1	15,000	10,000	5,000
27,000		18,000	9,000	

Step 2

Calculate an overhead absorption rate per unit for each department.

Overhead per unit

Assembly

$$\frac{\text{Budgeted overhead}}{\text{Budgeted units produced}} = \frac{£18,000}{1,000} = £18 \text{ per unit}$$

Finishing

$$\frac{\text{Budgeted overhead}}{\text{Budgeted units produced}} = \frac{£9,000}{1,000} = £9 \text{ per unit}$$

Step 3

Total production cost per unit:	£
Direct costs	
Materials	20
Labour	10
Overheads	
Assembly	18
Finishing	9
	57

5.3   Multi-product business

The use of an absorption rate per unit is fine for one-product businesses/cost centres, but **may be inappropriate for multi-product businesses.**

 Example 7

Sam produces pocket calculators and has one production department, incurring £15,000 overheads. Sam has planned production of 5,000 units.

Overhead absorption rate per unit = $\dfrac{£15,000}{5,000}$ = £3/unit

Suppose Sam instead makes 3,000 pocket calculators and 2,000 scientific calculators. The scientific calculators take up twice as much time to produce as the pocket calculators. The total overhead is the same as before. The overhead absorption rate per unit produced will be the same as before:

Overhead absorption rate per unit = $\dfrac{£15,000}{3000 + 2,000}$ = $\dfrac{£15,000}{5,000}$ = £3/unit

Decide whether this is a reasonable basis to absorb overheads.

Solution

This is probably not a reasonable basis. The scientific calculator takes longer to make and would involve the use of more of the indirect costs (e.g. supervisor's time). It is therefore necessary to choose an absorption basis that best reflects the demand of that product on the production department through which it passes. It may be more appropriate to calculate an overhead absorption rate per hour.

Bases commonly used as an **alternative to the rate per unit**, when more than one product is involved, are as follows.

(a)   rate per direct labour hour

(b)   rate per machine hour.

The calculation is as before but rather than dividing by budgeted units, budgeted activity it used:

$$\frac{\text{Budgeted overhead}}{\text{Budgeted activity}}$$

Whichever method is used, the result will still only be a **rough estimate** of what each product costs as it is based on budgeted figures.

Example 8

Sam makes 3,000 pocket calculators and 2,000 scientific calculators. The scientific calculators take up 2 hours to produce and the pocket calculators take only 1 hour to produce. The total overhead is the same as before. The overhead absorption rate per hour produced will be:

$$\text{Overhead absorption rate per unit} = \frac{£15,000}{3000hr + 4,000hr} = \frac{£15,000}{7,000}$$

$$= £2.14/hour$$

This then needs to be assigned on a per unit basis.

The pocket calculators take one hour to produce so will be charged with one hour's worth of overhead = £2.14

The scientific calculators take two hours to produce so will be charged with two hours' worth of overhead = £2.14 × 2 = £4.18

The difference in unit overhead charges should reflect the effort that has been made in producing the units.

 Test your understanding 5

Bertram manufactures three products, the cost of each being:

	Apple	Banana	Carrot
Direct materials	£14.40	£25.60	£36.00
Direct labour			
Machining @ £4.80 per hour	2 hours	1.5 hours	2 hours
Assembling @ £3.20 per hour	2 hours	2.5 hours	1 hour

Planned production is:

Product A   10,000 units
Product B   20,000 units
Product C   40,000 units

Production overheads for the forthcoming year are estimated at £120,000.

What would be the budgeted overhead absorption rate per product using the direct labour hour rate?

	Apple £/hr	Banana £/hr	Carrot £/hr
A	1	0.75	1
B	2	2	1.5
C	1	1.25	0.5
D	4	4	3

5.4 Service industry

One of the main difficulties in service costing is the establishment of a suitable cost unit. Service organisations may use several different cost units to measure the different kinds of service that they are providing. Examples for a hotel might include:

- Meals served for the restaurant

- Rooms occupied for the cleaning staff

- Hours worked for the reception staff.

A composite cost unit is more appropriate if a service is a function of two variables. Examples of composite cost units are as follows:

- How much is carried over what distance (tonne/miles) for haulage companies.

- How many patients are treated for how many days (patient/days) for hospitals.

- How many passengers travel how many miles (passenger/miles) for public transport companies.

Example 9

There are 60 rooms in a hotel, 60% of which were occupied last night and require cleaning and maintenance. The hotel incurs the following costs:

	£
Cleaning products	50
Repairs	250
Wages	1,500

The hotels cost unit is rooms occupied.

Required:

Calculate the average cost per room occupied.

Solution

Total hotel expenditure = £1,800

Total rooms occupied = 60 × 60% = 36 rooms

Average cost per room occupied = £1,800 ÷ 36 = £50 per room

5.5 Choosing an absorption rate

The choice of which rate to be used depends largely on the nature of the operations concerned.

There is no correct method but in order to produce useful information it will always be preferable to choose an absorption rate which is in some way related to the costs being incurred.

- if the overhead consisted mainly of depreciation of machinery then it would be sensible to use the machine hour rate.

- if the overhead consisted mainly of the salaries of supervisors who supervise the workforce then it would make sense to use the labour hour rate.

Example 10

A factory has two production departments, cutting and finishing. The budgeted overheads and production details are:

	Cutting	Finishing
Budgeted overhead	£100,000	£80,000
Budgeted direct labour hours	10,000	40,000
Budgeted machine hours	60,000	5,000

The cutting department is a machine intensive department whilst finishing is labour intensive.

The factory makes two products, the Pig and the Cow. The production details for these are:

	Pig	Cow
Direct labour hours		
Cutting	1	2
Finishing	4	6
Machine hours		
Cutting	8	6
Finishing	2	2

Calculate the overhead cost to be absorbed into each product using an appropriate absorption rate for each cost centre.

Solution

Step 1: Choose and calculate the absorption rates

It makes sense to use the machine hour rate for the machine intensive cutting department and the labour hour rate for the labour intensive finishing department.

Cutting – machine hour rate $= \dfrac{£100,000}{60,000}$

$= £1.67$ per machine hour

Finishing – labour hour rate $= \dfrac{£80,000}{40,000}$

$= £2$ per direct labour hour

Step 2 Absorption into unit costs

	£
Product Pig	
Cutting 8 hours × £1.67	13.36
Finishing 4 hours × £2	8.00
	————
	21.36
	————
Product Cow	
Cutting 6 hours × £1.67	10.02
Finishing 6 hours × £2	12.00
	————
	22.02
	————

As the cutting cost centre is machine intensive then a machine hour absorption rate will best reflect how the overhead is incurred and, as the finishing cost centre is labour intensive, a direct labour hour rate is most appropriate in this cost centre.

Which rate should be used? Possibly both – **it depends upon the nature of the overheads**.

 Test your understanding 6

Pears plc manufactures children's clothing. The General Manager is concerned about how the costs of the various garments it produces are calculated.

	Overhead cost £000	Numbers employed	Labour hours	Material issued £000	Machine hours
Production departments					
Cutting	187	10	400	180	12,000
Sewing	232	15	300	240	28,000
Finishing	106	8	12,000	90	
Service departments					
Stores	27	2		–	
Maintenance	50	3		90	
Totals	602	38	12,700	600	40,000

Using the overhead analysis sheet below, apportion:

(a) (i) stores department's costs to the production and maintenance departments

(ii) maintenance department's costs to the cutting and sewing departments only.

Select the most suitable basis for each apportionment and state the bases used on the overhead analysis sheet. (Calculations to the nearest £000.)

Overhead analysis sheet

	PRODUCTION			SERVICE		TOTAL
	Cutting	Sewing	Finishing	Stores	Maintenance	
	£000	£000	£000	£000	£000	£000
Overheads	187	232	106	27	50	602
Apportion store Basis:						
Apportion maintenance Basis:						
Total						

(b) What would be the overhead rate for the three production departments if cutting and sewing were highly mechanised and finishing required high human input:

	Cutting	Sewing	Finishing
A	17.58	10.04	9.17
B	5.55	7.39	2.89
C	5.28	7.03	2.75
D	21.10	18.73	9.17

6 Under/over absorption of overheads

6.1 Introduction

Overhead absorption rates are calculated at the start of the accounting period. They are based on **budgeted** overhead costs and the budgeted volume of activity; they are **pre-determined**.

The reason for this is that management will need to know the **budgeted cost of each unit of production** in order to be able to make decisions about the products and the sales and production. This requires not only budgeted figures for direct materials, direct labour and direct expenses, but also for overheads.

6.2 Absorption of overheads

During the accounting period the cost of each unit produced will include overheads based upon the pre-determined budgeted overhead absorption rate.

But what happens if:

(a) the **actual production levels** are different from the budgeted levels and/or

(b) the **actual overheads** for the period are different from the budgeted overheads?

If either or both of these occur, the use of the predetermined absorption rate will result in an **over- or under-absorption of overheads** (sometimes referred to as over or under recovery of overheads.)

There is a 3 step procedure for calculating an under or over absorption:

Step 1

Calculate the OAR = Budgeted overhead ÷ Budgeted activity

Step 2

Calculate how much overhead has been absorbed by actual activity

Absorbed = OAR × Actual activity

Step 3

Compare the actual overhead cost with the absorbed overhead

Absorbed > Actual = over absorbedAbsorbed < Actual = under absorbed

Example 11

A factory budgets to produce 10,000 units, its budgeted overhead is £30,000 and the budgeted direct labour hours are 4,000.

The factory actually produced only a total of 8,000 units in the coming year, due to a machine breakdown, in 3,200 labour hours. In addition, the cost of machine repairs resulted in actual factory overheads amounting to £34,000.

The factory absorbs the overhead based on labour hours.

What is the under- or over-absorbed overhead?

Solution

Step 1 – calculate the budgeted overhead absorption rate

$$\text{OAR} = \frac{\text{Budgeted overhead cost}}{\text{Budgeted activity}}$$

$$= \frac{£30,000}{4,000}$$

= £7.50 per direct labour hour

Step 2 – calculate the overhead absorbed by actual production

Absorbed   = OAR × Actual activity

               = £7.50 × 3,200 hours

               = £24,000

Step 3 – calculate the under- or over-absorption

Under- or
over-absorption   = Actual overhead cost – Absorbed overhead cost

               = £34,000 – £24,000

               = £10,000

The absorbed overhead is less than the actual overhead so there has been an under-absorption of the overhead

6.3 Under and over absorption of overheads

Over-absorbed overhead during a period is treated as an addition to profit, because it is an adjustment to allow for the fact that too much overhead cost has been charged. Under absorption is a reduction in profit as it is an adjustment to allow for the fact that the overhead charged in the period is less than the overhead costs incurred.

6.4 The significance of under or over absorption of overheads

The amount of under or over absorbed overhead should not usually be large, provided the budgeting is realistic and provided the actual results meet budgeted expectations.

If a large amount of under or over absorption occurs the reasons are usually:

- Actual overhead expenditure was higher than budgeted, possibly due to poor control over actual spending or vice versa.

- Actual overhead expenditure was much higher or lower than budgeted due to poor budgeting of overhead expenditure.

- The actual volume of activity was higher or lower than expected for operational reasons that the production manager should be able to explain.

📝 Test your understanding 7

The actual overheads for a department were £6,500 last period and the actual output was 540 machine hours. The budgeted overheads were £5,995 and the budgeted output was 550 machine hours.

(a) What is the OAR?

    A   £11.82

    B   £10.90

    C   £12.04

    D   £11.10

(b) How much overhead will be absorbed into production?

    A   £6,622

    B   £5,994

    C   £5,886

    D   £6,383

(c) What is the under- or over-absorption of the overheads?

    A   £122 over

    B   £506 under

    C   £614 under

    D   £117 under

Test your understanding 8

A company budgeted to spend fixed overheads of £5 per hour in a given month. The actual activity level for the month was 10,000 hours and the actual overhead expenditure was £48,000.

Calculate the over or under absorption of overheads for the month.

 Test your understanding 9

You have been asked to calculate the under- or over- absorption in a production division, this division is highly automated and operates with expensive machinery, which is run wherever possible on a 24-hour a day, seven days a week basis.

The following information relates to this division for July 20Y0:

Total budgeted departmental overheads	£400,000
Total actual departmental overheads	£450,000
Total budgeted direct labour hours	3,000
Total budgeted machine hours	10,000
Total actual direct labour hours	2,500
Total actual machine hours	9,000

(a) What is the budgeted fixed overhead absorption rate for the division for July 20Y0, using the most appropriate basis of absorption?

    A   £50.00

    B   £40.00

    C   £45.00

    D   £44.44

(b) What is the value of the overhead absorbed into production?

    A   £500,000

    B   £405,000

    C   £360,000

    D   £444,400

(c) What is the under- or over absorption for the division?

A   £50,000 under

B   £50,000 over

C   £90,000 over

D   £90,000 under

Test your understanding 10

R Noble and Sons are a firm of agricultural engineers based in North Yorkshire.

They have a large workshop from which they operate. The business is divided into cost centres which include:

- Machining

- Fabrication

- Canteen

- Stores

A summary of their budgeted overhead for the three months ended 31 March 20X1 showed:

	£
Depreciation of machinery	5,000
Insurance of machinery	2,100
Heat and light	800
Power	1,750
Rent and rates	2,250
	11,900

Other relevant costs and data for the period showed:

	Machining	Fabrication	Stores	Canteen
No of employees	2	2	1	0
Value of plant	£40,000	£19,000	£2,500	£1,000
Floor area (sq m)	300	350	100	50
Kilowatt hours	600	500	400	250
Material requisitions	195	99	–	–
Direct labour hours	1,600	1,067	–	–

(a) Complete the overhead analysis sheet below (round to the nearest £).

Overhead analysis sheet

	BASIS	PRODUCTION		SERVICE		TOTAL
		Machining	Fabrication	Stores	Canteen	
Dep'n of machinery						
Insurance of machinery						
Heat and light						
Power						
Rent and rates						
Sub-total						
Reapportion canteen					( )	
Reapportion stores				( )		
TOTAL						

(b) What would be the overhead rate per kilowatt hour for the production departments is:

	Machining	Fabrication
A	£12.15	£9.22
B	£4.56	£4.32
C	£37.38	£46.57
D	£24.30	£13.17

(c) Based on the OAR calculated above what would be the under or over absorption in each department if the following occurred.

The actual Kilowatt hours for the period were: machining 614 hours and fabrication 495 hours.

The actual overhead for the period was: machining £7,960 and fabrication £3,800.

	Machining	Fabrication
A	£500 over	£764 under
B	£764 over	£500 under
C	£500 under	£764 over
D	£764 under	£500 over

7 Integrated bookkeeping – overheads

7.1 Introduction

The costs of a business have to be recorded in a bookkeeping system. Many businesses use an **integrated bookkeeping system** where the ledger accounts kept provide the necessary **information for both costing and financial accounting**.

7.2 Production overheads account

The production overhead account is where the movement of the costs associated with the overheads (indirect costs) are recorded.

Example 12

Production overheads

	£		£
Actual overhead cost (1)		Absorbed overheads (2)	
Over-absorbed (3)		Under-absorbed (4)	

1   The **actual cost** of all the indirect costs is recorded as a **debit** in the production overheads account. The credit is either in the bank or payables account. The actual cost will be made up off all the indirect production costs – material, labour and expenses.

2   The overheads that are **absorbed into production** (WIP) are recorded as a **credit** in the production overhead account. This is calculated as the **budgeted OAR × actual activity**.

3   When the account is balanced at the end of the period and the **balancing amount** is required to make the **debit** side of the account match the credit side we have an **over-absorption** of overheads.

4   When the account is balanced at the end of the period and the **balancing amount** is required to make the **credit** side of the account match the debit side we have an **under-absorption** of overheads.

7.3 The adjustment for under-/over-absorption

The adjustment for an **under-absorbed overhead** is made as a **debit** to the costing **statement of profit or loss**. If the overheads have been under-absorbed we need to **decrease profit** and increase the expense in the costing statement of profit or loss.

	£
Revenue	X
Cost of sales (using budgeted overhead absorption rates)	X
Gross profit	X
Less: Under-absorption of fixed overheads	(10,000)
Adjusted gross profit	X

The accounting entry for this adjustment would be as follows.

		£	£
Debit:	Statement of profit or loss	10,000	
Credit:	Production overheads		10,000

The adjustment for an **over-absorbed overhead** is made as a **credit** to the costing **statement of profit or loss**. If the overheads have been over-absorbed we need to **increase profit** and decrease the expense in the costing statement of profit or loss.

	£
Revenue	X
Cost of sales (using budgeted overhead absorption rates)	X
Gross profit	X
Add: Over-absorption of fixed overheads	10,000
Adjusted gross profit	X

The accounting entry for this adjustment would be as follows.

		£	£
Debit:	Production overheads	10,000	
Credit:	Statement of profit or loss		10,000

Test your understanding 11

What are the correct journal entries the following accounting transactions:

1   Indirect material issued from stores:

　　A　Dr Bank, Cr Material

　　B　Dr Production overheads, Cr Material

　　C　Dr Material, Cr Bank

　　D　Dr Material, Cr Production overheads

2   Indirect wages analysed in the wages control account:

　　A　Dr Production, Cr Wages control

　　B　Dr Wages control, Cr Production

　　C　Dr Wages control, Cr Production overheads

　　D　Dr Production overheads, Cr Wages control

3   Production overheads absorbed into the cost of production:

　　A　Dr Production, Cr Production overheads

　　B　Dr Production overheads, Cr Statement of profit or loss

　　C　Dr Production overheads, Cr Production

　　D　Dr Statement of profit or loss, Cr Production overheads

4   Over-absorption of overheads

　　A　Dr Production, Cr Production overheads

　　B　Dr Production overheads, Cr Statement of profit or loss

　　C　Dr Production overheads, Cr Production

　　D　Dr Statement of profit or loss, Cr Production overheads

Test your understanding 12

During period 5, the month of May 20X1, Lester Bird's under- and over-recovery of overhead per cost centre was:

Cost centre	Overhead absorbed	Actual overhead	(under)/over-absorbed
	£	£	£
Painting	3,950	4,250	(300)
Finishing	2,950	3,150	(200)
Trimming	1,640	1,600	40
Firing	2,750	2,600	150
	£11,290	£11,600	(310)

Post the total figures to the overhead account, showing the transfer of the under-absorption to the costing statement of profit or loss.

Production overhead control account

	£		£
£		£	

 Test your understanding 13

Biscuit Making Company

The general manager has asked you to monitor the absorption of overheads for the production departments for November 20X8.

Company policy is to absorb overheads on the following basis.

Department	Basis
Mixing	Per £ of labour cost
Baking	Machine hours
Packing	Labour hours

Budgeted and actual data for November 20X8 is:

	Mixing	Baking	Packing
Budgeted overheads	£164,000	£228,900	£215,000
Actual labour hours worked			16,000
Budgeted labour hours			17,200
Actual machine hours		16,100	
Budgeted machine hours		16,350	
Actual labour costs	£63,700		
Budgeted labour costs	£65,600		

Calculate the budgeted overhead absorption rate for each department.

	Mixing £	Baking £	Packing £
Budgeted overhead absorption rate			

Complete the tables and production overhead account.

PRODUCTION OVERHEAD SCHEDULE Month:			
	Mixing £	Baking £	Packing £
Budgeted overheads			
Actual overheads	171,500	224,000	229,000
Overhead absorbed			

	Mixing £	Baking £	Packing £
Over-absorbed overheads			
Under-absorbed overheads			

Production overhead control account

	£		£
£		£	

KAPLAN PUBLISHING

8 Activity based costing

8.1 Introduction

Activity based costing (ABC) is an alternative approach to product costing. It is a form of absorption costing, but, rather than absorbing overheads on a production volume basis it firstly allocates them to cost pools before absorbing them into units using cost drivers.

- A **cost pool** is an activity that consumes resources and for which overhead costs are identified and allocated. For each cost pool there should be a cost driver.

- A **cost driver** is a unit of activity that consumes resources. An alternative definition of a cost driver is the factor influencing the level of cost.

8.2 ABC versus absorption costing

Imagine the machining department of a business that makes clothing. In a traditional absorption costing system the overhead absorption rate would be based on machine hours because many of the overheads in the machining department would relate to the machines, for example power, maintenance and machine depreciation.

Using only machine hours as the basis would seem fair, however not only does the machining department have machine related costs, but also in an absorption costing system it would have had a share of rent and rates, heating and lighting apportioned to it. These costs would also be absorbed based on machine hours and this is inappropriate as the machine hours are not directly responsible for the rent or rates.

ABC overcomes this problem by not using departments as gathering points for costs, but instead it uses activities to group the costs (cost pools) which are caused (driven) by an activity.

There would be an activity that related to each of the following: power usage, machine depreciation and machine maintenance. Machining would not pick up a share of personnel costs or rent and rates as these would be charged to another activity. For example:

- the cost of setting up machinery for a production run might be driven by the number of setups (jobs or batches produced)

- the cost of running machines might be driven by the number of machine hours for which the machines are running

- the cost of order processing might be related to the number of orders dispatched or to the weight of items dispatched

- the cost of purchasing might be related to the number of purchase orders made.

ABCs flexibility reduces the need for arbitrary apportionments.

Using ABC should lead to more accurate product and/or service costs being calculated.

8.3 Calculating the overhead recovery rate using ABC

There are five basic steps to calculating an activity based cost:

Step 1: Group production overheads into activities, according to how they are driven.

A cost pool is the grouping of costs relating to a particular activity which consumes resources and for which overhead costs are identified and allocated. For each cost pool, there should be a cost driver.

Step 2: Identify cost drivers for each activity, i.e. what causes these activity costs to be incurred.

A cost driver is a factor that influences (or drives) the level of cost.

Step 3: Calculate a cost driver rate for each activity.

The cost driver rate is calculated in the same way as the absorption costing OAR. However, a separate cost driver rate will be calculated for each activity, by taking the activity cost and dividing by the cost driver information.

Step 4: Absorb the activity costs into the product.

The activity costs should be absorbed by applying the cost driver rate into the individual products.

Step 5: Calculate the overhead cost per unit of product

Once all the overhead has been absorbed into the product it is possible to calculate an overhead cost per unit:

Overhead cost per unit = total overhead absorbed ÷ total number of units

Example 13

A manufacturing business makes a product in two models, model M1 and model M2. Details of the two products are as follows:

	Model M1	Model M2
Annual sales	8,000 units	8,000 units
Number of sales orders	60	250
Sales price per unit	£54	£73
Direct material cost per unit	£11	£21
Direct labour hours per unit	2.0 hours	2.5 hours
Direct labour rate per hour	£8	£8
Special parts per unit	2	8
Production batch size	2,000 units	100 units
Setups per batch	1	3

Step 1: Group production overheads into activities, according to how they are driven and Step 2: Identify cost drivers for each activity

	£	Cost driver
Setup costs	97,600	Number of setups
Material handling costs	42,000	Number of batches
Special part handling costs	50,000	Number of special parts
Invoicing	31,000	Number of sales orders
Other overheads	108,000	Direct labour hours
	———	
Total overheads	328,600	
	———	

Step 3: Calculate a cost driver rate for each activity.

Calculate the total of each of the drivers for the production levels

	M1	M2	Total
Number of batches	8,000/2,000 = 4	8,000/100 = 80	84
Number of setups	4 × 1 = 4	80 × 3 = 240	244
Special parts	8,000 × 2 = 16,000	8,000 × 8 = 64,000	80,000
Number of sales orders	60	250	310
Direct labour hours	8,000 × 2 = 16,000	8,000 × 2.5 = 20,000	36,000

Calculate the overhead cost per driver for each activity.

Activity	Cost	÷	Total driver	= Cost per driver
	£			£
Setups	97,600	244	setups	400
Materials handling	42,000	84	batches	500
Special parts handling	50,000	80,000	special parts	0.625
Invoicing	31,000	310	sales orders	100
Other overheads	108,000	36,000	labour hours	3

Step 4: Absorb the activity costs into the product.

Activity		M1	M2	Total
		£	£	£
Setups	£400 × 4	1,600		
	£400 × 240		96,000	97,600
Materials handling	£500 × 4	2,000		
	£500 × 240		40,000	42,000
Special parts handling	£0.625 × 16,000	10,000		
	£0.625 × 64,000		40,000	50,000
Invoicing	£100 × 60	6,000		
	£100 × 250		25,000	31,000
Other overheads	£3 ×16,000	48,000		
	£3 × 20,000		60,000	108,000
		_____	_____	_____
		67,600	261,000	328,600

Step 5: Calculate the overhead cost per unit of product

M1 = £67,600 ÷ 8,000 units = £8.45

M2 = £261,000 ÷ 8,000 units = £32.63 (rounded to 2 decimal places)

Test your understanding 14

DRP has recently introduced an Activity Based Costing system. It manufactures three products:

	Product D	Product R	Product P
Budgeted annual production (units)	100,000	100,000	50,000
Batch size (units)	100	50	25
Machine set-ups per batch	3	4	6
Purchase orders per batch	2	1	1
Processing time per unit (minutes)	2	3	3
Budgeted number of batches	1,000	2,000	2,000

Three cost pools have been identified. Their budgeted costs for 20X4 are as follows:

Machine set-up costs £150,000

Purchasing of materials £70,000

Processing £80,000

The cost per unit attributed to Product R for machine set ups is £_____

The cost per unit attributed to Product D for processing time is £_____

✎ Test your understanding 15

P operates an activity based costing (ABC) system to attribute its overhead costs to cost objects.

In its budget for the year ending 31 August 20X6, the company expected to place a total of 2,895 purchase orders at a total cost of £110,010. This activity and its related costs were budgeted to occur at a constant rate throughout the budget year, which is divided into 13 four-week periods.

During the four-week period ended 30 June 20X6, a total of 210 purchase orders were placed at a cost of £7,650.

The over-recovery of these costs for the four-week period was:

A   £330

B   £350

C   £370

D   £390

8.4   Advantages and disadvantages of activity based costing

ABC has a number of advantages:

- It provides a more accurate cost per unit. As a result, pricing, sales strategy, performance management and decision making should be improved.

- It provides much better insight into what causes (drives) overhead costs.

- ABC recognises that overhead costs are not all related to production and sales volume.

- In many businesses, overhead costs are a significant proportion of total costs, and management needs to understand the drivers of overhead costs in order to manage the business properly. Overhead costs can be controlled by managing cost drivers.

- It can be applied to calculate realistic costs in a complex business environment.

- ABC can be applied to all overhead costs, not just production overheads.

- ABC can be used just as easily in service costing as in product costing.

Disadvantages of ABC:

- ABC will be of limited benefit if the overhead costs are primarily volume related or if the overhead is a small proportion of the overall cost.

- It is impossible to allocate all overhead costs to specific activities.

- The choice of both activities and cost drivers might be inappropriate.

- ABC can be more complex to explain to the stakeholders of the costing exercise.

- The benefits obtained from ABC might not justify the costs.

Test your understanding 16

Which of the following statements are correct (*tick all that apply*)?

		Correct?
(i)	A cost driver is any factor that causes a change in the cost of an activity.	☐
(ii)	For long-term variable overhead costs, the cost driver will be the volume of activity.	☐
(iii)	Traditional absorption costing tends to under-allocate overhead costs to low-volume products.	☐

9 Summary

This chapter has considered how the overheads of a business are gathered together and traced through to the cost units to which they relate. Under the **absorption costing** approach the budgeted overheads of the business are collected together in each of the cost centres, either by **allocation**, if the overhead relates to only one cost centre or by **apportionment** on a fair basis if the overhead relates to a number of cost centres.

Once the overheads have been allocated and apportioned, the next stage is to **reapportion** any **service** cost centre overheads into the production cost centres. Care must be taken here where the service cost centres provide their service to other service cost centres. In these cases the step down method is required to reapportion the service cost centre overheads.

When all of the budgeted overheads are included in the production cost centres, an **absorption rate** must be calculated. In many cases this will be either on a direct labour hour basis or on a machine hour basis. This will depend on the nature of the business and the nature of the cost centre.

The overhead absorption rate is based upon the budgeted overheads and the budgeted production level. This rate is then used to include the overheads in the production throughout the accounting period. If the activity levels and/or the amount of the overhead are different to the budgeted figures, then the overhead will be either **over- or under-absorbed**. An adjustment is made for this when the costing statement of profit or loss is prepared.

Activity based costing (ABC) is a form of absorption costing, but, rather than absorbing overheads on a production volume basis it firstly allocates them to **cost pools** before absorbing them into units using **cost drivers**.

Test your understanding answers

Test your understanding 1

	Production		Service		Total
	Fixing £	Mending £	Stores £	Canteen £	£
Overheads allocated directly to cost centres	5,000	4,000	1,000	2,000	12,000
Overheads to be apportioned Rent Basis: floor space					32,000
32/30 × 15,000	16,000				
32/30 × 8,000		8,534			
32/30 × 5,000			5,333		
32/30 × 2,000				2,133	
Building maintenance Basis: floor space					5,000
5/30 × 15,000	2,500				
5/30 × 8,000		1,333			
5/30 × 5,000			834		
5/30 × 2,000				333	
Machinery insurance Basis: machine value					2,400
2400/250 × 140	1,344				
2400/250 × 110		1,056	–	–	
Machinery depreciation Basis: machine value					11,000
11,000/250 × 140	6,160				
11,000/250 × 110		4,840	–	–	
Machinery running expenses Basis: machine hours					6,000
6,000/80 × 50	3,750				
6,000/80 × 30		2,250	–	–	
Power Basis: power usage percentages					7,000
£7,000 × 45%	3,150				
£7,000 × 40%		2,800			
£7,000 × 5%			350		
£7,000 × 10%				700	
Allocated and apportioned costs	37,904	24,813	7,517	5,166	75,400

Test your understanding 2

Overhead analysis sheet

	Basis	Machining 1	Machining 2	Assembly	Packaging	Total
Dep'n	Carrying amount	32,000	8,000	24,000	16,000	80,000
Rent and rates	Square meters	30,000	12,000	24,000	54,000	120,000
Indirect labour cost	Allocated	40,500	18,300	12,400	26,700	97,900
Assembly costs	Allocated	–	–	15,600	–	15,600
TOTAL		102,500	38,300	76,000	96,700	313,500

Test your understanding 3

Stores – **C**

Personnel – **A**

Test your understanding 4

	Machining £	Painting £	Maintenance £	Quality control £
Apportioned overheads	20,000	40,000	10,000	15,000
Reapportionment of maintenance	3,000	6,000	(10,000)	1,000 ―――― 16,000
Reapportionment of quality control	8,000	8,000		(16,000)
Total	31,000	54,000		

Test your understanding 5

B

	Apple	Banana	Carrot	Total
Production (units)	10,000	20,000	40,000	70,000
Production hours				
Machining	20,000	30,000	80,000	130,000
Assembly	20,000	50,000	40,000	110,000
Total hours	40,000	80,000	120,000	**240,000**

Overhead per direct labour hour: $\dfrac{£120,000}{240,000} = £0.50$

	Apple	Banana	Carrot
	£	£	£
Overheads	(4 hr × £0.50)	(4 hr × £0.50)	(3 hr × £0.50)
	= 2.00/hr	= 2.00/hr	= 1.50/hr

Test your understanding 6

(a)

Overhead analysis sheet	PRODUCTION			SERVICE		TOTAL
	Cutting	Sewing	Finishing	Stores	Maintenance	
	£000	£000	£000	£000	£000	£000
Overheads	187	232	106	27	50	602
Apportion store Basis: Mat issued	8	11	4	(27)	4	
Apportion maint'nce Basis: Mach hours	16	38			(54)	
Total	211	281	110			602

(b)   **A**

	Cutting	Sewing	Finishing
Apportioned o/heads	£211,000	£281,000	£110,000
Machine hours	12,000	28,000	
Labour hours			12,000
Absorption rates	£17.58	£10.04	£9.17

✎ Test your understanding 7

(a)   **B**

   £5,995/550 hours = £10.90

(b)   **C**

   £10.90 × 540 = £5,886

(c)   **C**

   £6,500 – £5,886 = £614 under-absorbed

✎ Test your understanding 8

Step 1:   Calculate budgeted overhead absorption rate (OAR):

   OAR = £5 per hour

Step 2:   Calculate absorbed overhead

   Absorbed overhead = £5 × 10,000 hours

   = £50,000

Step 3:   Compare overhead absorbed with actual overhead incurred

   Absorbed overhead = £50,000 > actual overhead £48,000

   therefore £2,000 over-absorption

Test your understanding 9

(a) **B** £40.00

£400,000 ÷ 10,000

(b) **C** £360,000

£40 × 9,000

(c) **D** £90,000 under

£450,000 − £360,000

Test your understanding 10

(a) **Overhead analysis sheet**

	BASIS	PRODUCTION		SERVICE		TOTAL
	Value	Machining	Fabrication	Stores	Canteen	
Dep'n of machinery	Value	3,200	1,520	200	80	5,000
Insurance of machinery	Square metres	1,344	638	84	34	2,100
Heat and light	Kw	300	350	100	50	800
Power	Square metres	600	500	400	250	1,750
Rent and rates		844	984	281	141	2,250
Sub-total	Staff	6,288	3,992	1,065	555	11,900
Reapportion canteen	Requis-itions	222	222	111	(555)	
Reapportion stores		780	396	(1,176)		
TOTAL	Value	7,290	4,610			11,900

	Machining	Fabrication
(b) **A**	£12.15	£9.22

		Machining	Fabrication
(c)	**C**	£500 under	£764 over

Machining actual	=	£7,960
Machining absorbed	=	£12.15 × 614 = £7,460
Under absorption		£500
Fabrication actual	=	£3,800
Fabrication absorbed	=	£9.22 × 495 = £4,564
Over absorption		£764

Test your understanding 11

1	**B**
2	**D**
3	**A**
4	**B**

Test your understanding 12

Production overhead control account

	£		£
Actual overhead	11,600	Absorbed overhead	11,290
		Under-absorbed costing SOPL	310
	11,600		11,600

Test your understanding 13

	Mixing £	Baking £	Packing £
Budgeted overhead absorption rate	£2.50 per £1 direct labour	£14 per machine hour	£12.50 per labour hour

PRODUCTION OVERHEAD SCHEDULE
Month: November 1998

	Mixing £	Baking £	Packing £
Budgeted overheads	164,000	228,900	215,000
Actual overheads	171,500	224,000	229,000
Overhead absorbed	159,250	225,400	200,000

	Mixing £	Baking £	Packing £
Over-absorbed overheads		1,400	
Under-absorbed overheads	12,250		29,000

Production overhead control account

	£		£
Actual overhead	624,500	Absorbed overhead	584,650
		Under absorbed	39,850
	——		——
	624,500		624,500
	——		——

Test your understanding 14

Machine set up costs for Product R

Budgeted machine set-ups:

Product D (1,000 × 3)	=	3,000
Product R (2,000 × 4)	=	8,000
Product P (2,000 × 6)	=	12,000
		————
		23,000
		————

Cost per set up= 150,000 ÷ 23,000 = £6.52

Budgeted unit cost of R: = £6.52 × 4 ÷ 50= **£0.52**

Processing costs for Product D

Budgeted processing minutes:

Product D (100,000 × 2)	=	200,000
Product R (100,000 × 3)	=	300,000
Product P (50,000 × 3)	=	150,000
		————
		650,000 minutes
		————

Cost per minute = £80,000 ÷ 650,000 = £0.12

Budgeted unit cost of D = £0.12 × 2 = **£0.24**

 Test your understanding 15

A

Cost driver rate = 110,010 ÷ 2,895 = £38 for each order

	£
Cost recovered: 210 orders × £38	7,980
Actual costs incurred	7,650
	————
Over-recovery of costs for four-week period	330
	————

KAPLAN PUBLISHING

Test your understanding 16

		Correct?
(i)	A cost driver is any factor that causes a change in the cost of an activity.	☑
(ii)	For long-term variable overhead costs, the cost driver will be the volume of activity.	☑
(iii)	Traditional absorption costing tends to under-allocate overhead costs to low-volume products.	☑

Statement (i) provides a definition of a cost driver. Cost drivers for long-term variable overhead costs will be the volume of a particular activity to which the cost driver relates, so Statement (ii) is correct. Statement (iii) is also correct. In traditional absorption costing, standard high-volume products receive a higher amount of overhead costs than with ABC. ABC allows for the unusually high costs of support activities for low-volume products (such as relatively higher set-up costs, order processing costs and so on).

Basic variance analysis

7

Introduction

In this chapter we are going to look at how to produce basic budgets, why budgets differ from actual results and the variances that arise.

ASSESSMENT CRITERIA
Calculate variances (4.1)
Analyse and investigate variances (4.2)
Report on variances (4.3)

CONTENTS

1. Fixed and flexed budgets
2. Causes of variances
3. Possible solutions for variances

1 Fixed and flexed budgets

1.1 Budgets

Budgets are prepared for number of reasons:

- To forecast future activity levels
- To communicate goals and objectives
- To plan for the use of resources – materials, labour, money
- To control the different departments
- To motivate by setting achievable targets
- These are the same as the aims of management accounting.

1.2 Fixed budgets

> ### Q Definition
>
> A **fixed budget** is a budget produced for a **single** activity level.

A fixed budget is produced at the beginning of the period and is used to provide information as to the aims and objectives that the organisation is working towards in that particular period.

The simplest form of a budget report compares the original budget against actual results.

Example 1

	Fixed budget	Actual
Units produced and sold	1,000	1,200
	£	£
Sales revenue	10,000	11,500
Material costs	1,300	1,040
Labour costs	2,600	2,125
Fixed overheads	1,950	2,200
Operating profit	4,150	6,135

1.3 Analysis of a fixed budget and the actual results

The essential feature of any budgetary control system is the process of comparing budget with actual results. The difference between these figures is usually referred to as a variance.

> ### 🔍 Definition
>
> An **adverse variance** occurs when the actual costs exceed the budgeted costs or when the actual revenue is less than the budgeted revenue.
>
> A **favourable variance** occurs when the actual cost is less than the budgeted cost or when the actual revenue exceeds the budgeted revenue.

Using the information in 1.2 we are able to calculate the variances that have occurred:

> ### 💡 Example 2
>
> | | Fixed budget | Actual | Variance |
> |---|---|---|---|
> | Units produced and sold | 1,000 | 1,200 | 200 F |
> | | £ | £ | £ |
> | Sales revenue | 10,000 | 11,500 | 1,500 A |
> | Material costs | 1,300 | 1,040 | 260 F |
> | Labour costs | 2,600 | 2,125 | 475 F |
> | Fixed overheads | 1,950 | 2,200 | 250 A |
> | Operating profit | 4,150 | 6,135 | 1,985 F |

Problems can happen if actual production and/or sales levels differ from the budgeted production levels. If we consider the variances above:

- Actual revenue is greater than budgeted but is this purely because we sold more units or is it because we sold them at a higher price?

- Actual material and labour costs are lower than budget but more units were produced so is this because we were more efficient with the usage of the material or use of the employee's time?

- Actual overheads are more than expected. Is this related to production levels or the actual cost itself?

If this control process is to be valid and effective, it is important that the variances are calculated in a meaningful way. One of the major concerns here is to ensure that the budgeted and actual figures reflect the same activity level. To overcome this issue budgets are flexed to match the actual production level.

1.4 Flexed budgets

 Definition

A **flexed or flexible budget** is one which, by recognising cost behaviour patterns, is designed to change as volume of activity changes.

Flexed budgets are produced using cost behaviour and nature principles:

- **Variable costs** increase in direct proportion to activity, i.e. as activity increases so do the costs. Variable costs are constant per unit.

- **Direct costs** are assumed to be variable costs.

- **Fixed costs** are constant as activity increases. Fixed costs per unit decrease as activity increases.

- **Stepped costs** are fixed to a certain level of activity and then the cost steps up to a new fixed level.

- **Semi-variable costs** are costs that have a fixed and a variable element. The cost therefore increases as activity increases (the variable element) but will not have a zero cost at zero activity (the fixed element). The elements of the cost can be separated by using the high-low method.

- **Sales revenue** is assumed to have a variable behaviour unless stated otherwise i.e. the more units that are sold the more revenue there is and there is a constant selling price per unit.

If we flex the budget in 1.2.

Example 3

	Fixed budget	Working:	Flexed budget	Actual
Units produced and sold	1,000		1,200	1,200
	£		£	£
Sales revenue	10,000	10,000/1,000 ×1,200	12,000	11,500
Material cost	1,300	1,300/1,000 × 1,200	1,560	1,040
Labour cost	2,600	2,600/1,000 × 1,200	3,120	2,125
Fixed overheads	1,950	N/A	1,950	2,200
Operating profit	4,150		5,370	6,135

Test your understanding 1

Victor Ltd is preparing its budget for the next quarter and it needs to consider different production levels.

Complete the table below to calculate the flexed budgets for 1,500 units and 2,000 units.

Units sold and produced	1,000	1,500	2,000
Sales revenue	40,000		
Variable costs:			
Direct materials	4,000		
Direct labour	3,800		
Fixed overhead	10,700		
Total cost	18,500		
Total profit	21,500		
Profit per unit (to 2 decimal places)	21.50		

1.5 Variance analysis using flexed budgets

When completing a budgetary control report using flexed budgets the flexed budget is prepared based on the actual activity level. This ensures that any variance discovered is not due to a change in activity level i.e. the number of units produced. Any variances identified will be due to the price charged or the amount used per unit of product. For example:

- If a material variance was discovered it would be due to the number of kg used per unit or the price paid per kg.

- If a labour variance was discovered it would be due to the number of hours worked per unit or the rate paid per hour.

The sub-division of variances into price/rate and usage/efficiency are covered on the Professional Diploma in Accounting level but you need to be aware that the sub-division exists. They are used to provide a guideline for control action by individual managers. This will be covered in more detail in a later section of this chapter.

Continuing with the figures from 1.2 – the **like for like** variances are:

Example 4

	Fixed budget	Actual	Variance
Units produced and sold	1,200	1,200	0
	£	£	£
Sales revenue	12,000	11,500	500 A
Material cost	1,560	1,040	520 F
Labour cost	3,120	2,125	995 F
Fixed overheads	1,950	2,200	250 A
Operating profit	5,370	6,135	765 F

It is now possible to see:

- Actual revenue is adverse so we must have been selling at a lower price as we are now comparing using the same volume of sales.

- Actual material costs are still favourable so the usage of material or the price paid per kg of material was better than budgeted.

- Actual labour costs are still favourable so the efficiency of the staff or the rate paid per hour was better than budgeted.

- Actual fixed overheads were more than budget. Since they should not change when activity levels change this must be due an inaccurate budget or an unexpected expense occurring.

- Overall profit is more than budget – this we can be reasonably sure is because we have kept better control of the material and labour costs than planned.

Test your understanding 2

Victor Ltd is comparing its budget for the quarter with the actual revenue and costs incurred.

	Budget	Actual
Volume sold and produced	1,000	1,400
	£	£
Sales revenue	40,000	60,000
Less costs:		
Direct materials	4,000	6,000
Direct labour	3,800	5,300
Fixed overheads	10,700	13,600
Operating profit	21,500	35,100

Complete the table below to show a flexed budget and the resulting variances, indicating if it is a favourable (F) or adverse (A) in the final column.

	Flexed budget	Actual	Variance value	Favourable or Adverse
Volume sold		1,400		
	£	£	£	
Sales revenue		60,000		
Less costs:				
Direct materials		6,000		
Direct labour		5,300		
Fixed overhead		13,600		
Operating profit		35,100		

Test your understanding 3

Youssef Ltd is preparing its budget for the next quarter and it needs to consider different production levels.

Complete the table below and calculate the estimated profit per unit at the different activity levels.

Units sold and produced	1,000	1,500	2,000
Sales revenue	80,000		
Variable cost			
Direct materials	8,000		
Direct labour	7,600		
Overheads	14,400		
Fixed cost	7,000		
Total cost	37,000		
Total profit	43,000		
Profit per unit (to 2 decimal places)	43.00		

Youssef Ltd is now comparing its budget for the quarter with the actual revenue and costs incurred.

	Budget	Actual
Volume sold	1,000	1,200
	£	£
Sales revenue	80,000	100,000
Less costs:		
Direct materials	8,000	9,000
Direct labour	7,600	9,300
Overheads	14,400	17,500
Fixed cost	7,000	7,100
Operating profit	43,000	57,100

Complete the table below to show a flexed budget and the resulting variances, indicating if it is a favourable (F) or adverse (A) in the final column.

	Flexed budget	Actual	Variance value	Favourable or Adverse
Volume sold		1,200		
	£	£	£	
Sales revenue		100,000		
Less costs:				
Direct materials		9,000		
Direct labour		9,300		
Overheads		17,500		
Fixed cost		7,100		
Operating profit		57,100		

1.6 Reconciliation of actual with budget

Once the variances have been calculated it should be possible to reconcile the actual profit with the budgeted profit.

- An adverse variance will decrease the budgeted profit so this is subtracted from budgeted profit.

- A favourable variance will increase the budgeted profit so this is added to the budgeted profit.

Example 5

Flexed budget profit			5,370
		Variance	
		£	
Sales revenue	Subtract	500 A	
Material costs	Add	520 F	
Labour costs	Add	995 F	
Fixed overheads	Subtract	250 A	
Actual profit			6,135

2 Causes of variances

2.1 Investigation of variances

To be able to control aspects of the business, management will need to investigate why the variances have happened. To decide which variances to investigate management will consider:

- The **size** of the variance – is it significant compared to the cost incurred?

- The **cost** of investigating the variance – will it cost less to investigate and put it right than the variance itself?

- Whether it is **adverse or favourable** – some companies will only investigate the adverse variances?

- **Ability to correct** the variance – is the variance controllable in house (hours worked by staff) or uncontrollable (price charged by suppliers)?

2.2 Causes of variances

Differences between actual values and budgeted values can occur for a number of reasons. The original explanation for how each variance arose must come from the line manager responsible for that particular cost. The explanations for each variance will then be brought together by the management accountant when producing a variance or exception report for senior management.

One of the main reasons is that when producing a budget we are trying to predict the future. Prediction of the future is not an exact science and it is therefore extremely difficult to get it 100% correct.

This leads to the budgeted figures not being as accurate as they could be and therefore actual values are different from these.

2.3 Sales variances

A sales variance could occur for a number of reasons:

- **Price changes** – selling the product at a higher or lower price. This could happen if **discounts** are offered to the customer or discounts are removed or reduced, a price drop is required to remain **competitive** and/or an enforced price change due to **legislation**

- **Volume changes** – higher or lower volumes are sold than expected. This could be due to a successful or unsuccessful **advertising** campaign; changes in buyers' **habits**; a problem with production may reduce availability and/or changes in **market** conditions.

When comparing a flexed budget with actual results the volume changes are already accounted for by changing the volume in the budget to match actual sales volume

2.4 Material variances

When comparing a flexed budget with actual results we are looking at the material cost per unit of product. This can be broken down into the quantity of raw material that is used per unit and the price paid for the raw material.

Flexed versus actual comparisons remove the effect on cost that is due to the number of units manufactured.

A material variance can have a number of causes when we consider the raw material used to produce the product:

- **Price changes** – an increase or decrease in the price per unit of **material** purchased. This could be due to suppliers changing prices, loss or introduction of a **bulk discount**, higher delivery charges and/or a change in the **quality** of the material.

- **Usage changes** – an increase or decrease in the amount of material used. This could be due to more **efficient** or less efficient working conditions and/or a change in the **quality** of the materials purchased.

- **Quality** – if production uses a **higher quality** material then it will **cost more** to purchase. If a **lower quality** material is used it will be **cheaper** to purchase.

- **Combination of quality and quantity**. Higher quality costs more but may well lead to less wastage so use less. Lower quality costs less but may lead to more wastage so use more.

2.5 Labour variances

When comparing a flexed budget with actual results we are looking at the labour cost per unit of product. This can be broken down into the hours of labour worked and the rate paid per hour.

Flexed versus actual comparisons remove the effect on cost that is due to the number of units manufactured.

Variances in labour costs can be caused by:

- **Rate changes** – a higher or lower hourly rate is paid to the employees than expected. If a **higher grade** of labour is used then they will require **higher remuneration**. If a **lower grade** of labour is used then they will require as **lower remuneration**. There could be an increase in the basic rate of pay (minimum wage) or a bonus may have been paid.

- **Efficiency** of staff or the **hours worked** to produce output. If the actual time taken is **longer** than budgeted then this will **cost more** but if actual time taken is **shorter** than budgeted then it will **cost less**. This could be due to change in the grade of labour as the more experience the staff the more efficient they are assumed to be.

- **Overtime**. If there is extra time needed to complete the production then this may have to lead to having to pay some staff overtime. This is often paid at a **higher rate** than normal hours. This will **increase** the labour costs due to both increased hours and increased rates of pay

2.6 Fixed overheads variances

Fixed overheads should not change when activity levels change so the cause of any variance when comparing the flexed and actual figures is due to the budgeted **expenditure** being different from actual expenditure.

2.7 Interdependence between variances

In many cases the explanation for one variance might also explain why other variances occur. For example:

- Using cheaper materials would result in a drop in the price paid for materials (a favourable variance in the purchasing department) but using cheaper materials in production might increase the wastage rate (an adverse variance in the production department).

- An increase in wastage due to using cheaper material may reduce the productivity of the labour force leading to increased working hours to meet production demands (an adverse labour variance)

- Employees trying to improve productivity (work less hours) in order to win a bonus (increase in cost) might use materials wastefully in order to save time (an adverse material variance)

> **Test your understanding 4**
>
> Victor Ltd has calculated the following variances. Discuss the possible causes for the variances.
>
> | | Flexed budget | Actual | Variance value | Favourable or Adverse |
> |---|---|---|---|---|
> | Volume sold | 1,400 | 1,400 | | |
> | | £ | £ | £ | |
> | Sales revenue | 56,000 | 60,000 | 4,000 | F |
> | Less costs: | | | | |
> | Direct materials | 5,600 | 6,000 | 400 | A |
> | Direct labour | 5,320 | 5,300 | 20 | F |
> | Fixed overhead | 10,700 | 13,600 | 2,900 | A |
> | Operating profit | 34,380 | 35,100 | 720 | F |

2.8 Sub-division of variances

Variances can be sub-divided to provide more detail:

- Sales variances can be sub-divided into the variance due to the quantity sold (volume variance) and the variance due to the sales prices charged (price variance).

- Material variances can be sub-divided into the variance due to quantity of the materials used (usage variance) and the variance due to the price paid for the materials (price variance).

- Labour variance can be sub-divided into the variance due to the hours worked (efficiency variance) and the variance due to the rate paid per hour (rate variance).

Test your understanding 5

A company has a higher than expected staff turnover and as a result staff are less experienced than expected. As an indirect result of this, are the labour rate variances and material variances likely to be adverse or favourable?

	Labour rate	*Material usage*
A	Favourable	Favourable
B	Adverse	Favourable
C	Favourable	Adverse
D	Adverse	Adverse

 Test your understanding 6

A company is obliged to buy sub-standard materials at lower than standard price because nothing else is available, As an indirect result of this purchase, are the materials usage variance and labour efficiency variance likely to be adverse or favourable.

	Material usage	*Labour efficiency*
A	Favourable	Favourable
B	Adverse	Favourable
C	Favourable	Adverse
D	Adverse	Adverse

Note: You will not be asked to calculate the subdivisions, but you will be expected to answer discursive tasks that require knowledge of their subdivision.

Test your understanding 7

Which of the following could be the cause of an adverse sales volume variance for garden furniture

(i)   The company offers discounts on sales prices in order to maintain business

(ii) Poor weather leads to a reduction in sales

(iii) A strike in the factory causes a shortage of finished goods

A   (i) and (ii) only

B   (i) and (iii) only

C   (ii) and (iii) only

D   All of them

3 Possible solutions for variances

3.1 Possible courses of action for correction of variances

Each variance should be considered in turn and any interdependence should be considered before solutions can be arrived at. Following are a number of possible solutions for variances that arise:

- Lower the price of the finished goods to increase volume of sales.

- Increase advertising to improve volume of sales without impacting on price.

- A change of supplier may be an option for improving prices for materials.

- Negotiation of bulk or trade discounts for materials purchased

- Updating machinery may make the usage of materials better and may also improve the efficiency of the labour force.

- Better quality control over the materials that are used in production may reduce wastage.

- Better supervision of staff may reduce idle time and errors in production.

- Increased training may reduce errors and make the staff more efficient.

- Closer monitoring of budgets may make the budgets more accurate.

This list is not exhaustive and it would be necessary to take each variance in turn and investigate the best way to improve the situation.

4 Summary

This chapter has demonstrated how **cost behaviours** are used to predict costs at activity levels different to budget and to produce **flexed** budgets. It will be necessary to be able to identify cost behaviours and use them to produce a flexed budget to then compare with actual results or **calculate variances**.

Another important aspect of this chapter is **analysis of variances** including possible causes and solutions to these variances.

Test your understanding answers

Test your understanding 1

Units sold and produced	1,000	1,500	2,000
Sales revenue	40,000	60,000	80,000
Variable costs:			
Direct materials	4,000	6,000	8,000
Direct labour	3,800	5,700	7,600
Fixed overhead	10,700	10,700	10,700
Total cost	18,500	22,400	26,300
Total profit	21,500	37,600	53,700
Profit per unit (to 2 decimal places)	21.50	25.07	26.85

Test your understanding 2

	Flexed budget	Actual	Variance value	Favourable or Adverse
Volume sold	1,400	1,400		
	£	£	£	
Sales revenue	56,000	60,000	4,000	F
Less costs:				
Direct materials	5,600	6,000	400	A
Direct labour	5,320	5,300	20	F
Fixed overhead	10,700	13,600	2,900	A
Operating profit	34,380	35,100	720	F

Test your understanding 3

Units sold and produced	1,000	1,500	2,000
Sales revenue	80,000	120,000	160,000
Variable cost			
Direct materials	8,000	12,000	16,000
Direct labour	7,600	11,400	15,200
Overheads	14,400	21,600	28,800
Fixed cost	7,000	7,000	7,000
Total cost	37,000	52,000	67,000
Total profit	43,000	68,000	93,000
Profit per unit (to 2 decimal places)	43.00	45.33	46.50

	Flexed budget	Actual	Variance value	Favourable or Adverse
Volume sold	1,200	1,200		
	£	£	£	
Sales revenue	96,000	100,000	4,000	F
Less costs:				
Direct materials	9,600	9,000	600	F
Direct labour	9,120	9,300	180	A
Overheads	17,280	17,500	220	A
Fixed cost	7,000	7,100	100	A
Operating profit	53,000	57,100	4,100	F

Test your understanding 4

	Flexed budget	Actual	Variance value	Favourable or Adverse
Volume sold	1,400	1,400		
	£	£	£	
Sales revenue	56,000	60,000	4,000	F
Less costs:				
Direct materials	5,600	6,000	400	A
Direct labour	5,320	5,300	20	F
Fixed overhead	10,700	13,600	2,900	A
Operating profit	34,380	35,100	720	F

Sales revenue

As the budget has been flexed to match actual sales volume the variance can only be due to price. Victor must have been able to sell at a higher price than budgeted.

Direct materials

An adverse variance could be due to an increase in the price paid per unit of raw material or an increase in the volume used in production.

Direct labour

A favourable variance could be due to a decrease in the hours worked to produce the output or a decrease in the hourly rate of pay

Fixed overhead

An adverse variance could be due to understating the budget or an unknown expense occurring.

Test your understanding 5

C

Less experienced staff are likely to be paid at a lower rate and therefore the labour rate variance will be favourable

Usage of materials is likely to be adverse as the staff are less experienced, thus there will be more wastage and a higher level of rejects

 Test your understanding 6

D

Usage of materials is likely to be adverse as the materials are sub-standard, thus there will be more wastage and a higher level of rejects

Time spent by the labour force on rejected items that will not become output leads to higher than standard time being spent per unit of output, therefore efficiency will decline.

 Test your understanding 7

C

Option (i) will cause an adverse sales price variance but would hopefully lead to a favourable volume variance.

Options (ii) and (iii) will both impact on the volume of garden furniture to be sold.

Job, batch and service costing

Introduction

We are now going to turn our attention to three costing systems. **Job costing** involves individual jobs with different materials and labour requirements (for example, car repairs). **Batch costing**, on the other hand, is suitable for businesses that produce batches of identical items (for example, bars of soap) though batch costs may vary from product to product. **Service costing** is used when an organisation provides a service rather than a product.

ASSESSMENT CRITERIA	CONTENTS
Differentiate and apply different costing systems: (2.5) – Job costing – Batch costing – Service costing	1 Different types of production 2 Job costing 3 Batch costing 4 Service costing

1 Different types of production

1.1 Costing systems

There are different types of costing system that are used depending on the type of production a business uses.

- **Specific order costing** is the costing system used when the work done by an organisation consists of **separately identifiable jobs** or **batches**.

- **Continuous operation costing** is the costing method used when goods or services are produced as a direct result of a **sequence of continuous operations or processes**.

2 Job costing

2.1 Job costing

Job costing is a form of **specific order costing** and it is used in a business where the production is made up of **individual jobs.** Each job is identified to a customer's individual requirements and specifications. The costs are identified for this specific job, coded to it and recorded as job costs. The organisation will add on their required profit margin and quote their price to the customer. Effectively **the job is the cost unit**.

Typical examples of businesses that use job costing would be ship building, civil engineering, construction, aeroplane manufacture, and vehicle repairs.

2.2 Job card

Each job is given a separate identifying number and has its own job card. The job card is used to record all of the direct costs of the job and the overheads to be absorbed into the job.

A typical job card might look like this:

Example 1

JOB NO	217		
Materials requisitions	**Quantity**	**£**	**Total**
0254 G 3578	100 kg	4,200	
0261 K 3512	50 kg	3,150	
		———	7,350
Wages – employees	**Hours**	**£**	
13343	80	656	
15651	30	300	
12965	40	360	
	———	———	
	150		1,316
	———		
Overheads	**Hours**	**£**	
Absorption rate £12	150	1,800	1,800
			———
Total cost			10,466
			———

When materials are requisitioned for a job, the issue of materials will be recorded at their issue price on the job cost card.

The labour hours and relevant hourly rate will be transferred onto the card and any expenses that can be directly attributed to a particular job are then coded to the job or jobs they relate to.

When the job is completed an appropriate proportion of administration, selling and distribution overheads will also be included on the job cost card.

Test your understanding 1

Given below are the direct costs of job number 3,362.

	£
Materials requisitions:	
15,496	1,044
15,510	938
15,525	614

Wages analysis:		£
Employee 13,249	40 hours	320
Employee 12,475	33 hours	231
Employee 26,895	53 hours	312

Overheads are apportioned to jobs at the rate of £3.50 per direct labour hour.

What is the total cost of Job 3,362?

JOB NO	3,362		
Materials requisitions		£	**Total**
			____

Wages – employees	**Hours**	£
	____	____
	____	

Overheads	**Hours**	£
		____
		____

The principles behind a job costing system are exactly the same as those in a unit costing system with the **job** being treated as the **cost unit**. A job costing system needs tight controls over the coding of all materials requisitions and hours worked to ensure that each job is charged with the correct direct costs and eventually overheads.

3 Batch costing

3.1 Introduction

Batch costing is also a form of **specific order costing**. It is suitable for a business that produces **batches of identical units**. For example, a baker may produce loaves of bread in batches.

Each batch of production will have different costs but each unit within the batch should have the same cost. Therefore the total cost of the batch of production is calculated and divided by the number of units in that batch to find the cost per unit for that batch of production.

3.2 Costs included

As with any costing system the costs to be included in the batch cost are the direct costs of material, labour and any direct expenses plus the overheads that are to be absorbed into the batch. In order to find the cost of each product or cost unit the total cost of the batch must be divided by the number of products in that batch.

Example 2

A paint manufacturer is producing 1,000 litres of matt vinyl paint in 'sea blue'. The direct costs of the production run are:

	£
Materials	1,600
Labour 15 hours @ £10	150
Overheads 15 hours @ £16	240

What is the cost per litre of this batch of paint?

Batch cost	£
Materials	1,600
Labour	
Overheads 15 hours @ £16	240
	___
Total batch cost	1,990
	___
Cost per litre	£1.99

Test your understanding 2

A manufacturer of frozen meals produces a batch of 20,000 units of salmon tagliatelli. The direct costs of this batch are:

	£
Materials	15,000
Labour 1,000 hours	4,200

Overheads are to be absorbed at rate of £1.20 per direct labour hour.

The cost of each portion of salmon tagliatelli is?

A   £1.20

B   £0.96

C   £2.16

D   £1.02

 Test your understanding 3

Jetprint Limited

Jetprint Limited specialises in printing advertising leaflets and is in the process of preparing its price list. The most popular requirement is for a folded leaflet made from a single sheet of A4 paper. From past records and budgeted figures, the following data have been estimated for a typical batch of 10,000 leaflets:

Artwork (fixed cost)	£65
Machine setting (fixed cost)	4 hours @ £22 per hour
Paper	£12.50 per 1,000 sheets
Ink and consumables	£40 per 10,000 leaflets
Printers' wages	4 hours @ £8 per hour per 10,000 leaflets

General fixed overheads are £15,000 per period during which a total of 600 printers' labour hours are expected to be worked (not all, of course, on the leaflet). The overheads are recovered only on printers' hours.

Task

Calculate the cost (to the nearest pound) for batches of 10,000 and 20,000 leaflets.

4 Service costing

4.1 Service costing

Service costing is a form of **continuous operation costing**. The output from a service industry differs from manufacturing for the following four reasons:

- **Intangibility** – the output is in the form of 'performance' rather than tangible or touchable goods or products

- **Heterogeneity** – the nature and standard of the service will be variable due to the high human input

- **Simultaneous production and consumption** – the service that you require cannot be inspected in advance of receiving it

- **Perishability** – the services that you require cannot be stored

4.2 Service cost units

One of the main difficulties in service costing is the establishment of a suitable cost unit. Examples for a hotel might include:

- **Meals served** for the restaurant

- **Rooms occupied** for the cleaning staff

- **Hours worked** for the reception staff

A **composite cost unit** may be more appropriate. For example a bus company might use passenger miles or how many passengers travel how many miles.

4.3 Cost per service unit

The total cost of providing a service will include the same costs as manufacturing but overheads may make up a larger proportion of the cost than direct costs. It is also possible that labour costs would be the only direct cost incurred by a service provider.

To calculate the cost per service unit the total cost of providing the service is divided by the number of service units used to provide the service.

$$\text{Cost per service unit} = \frac{\text{Total costs for providing the service}}{\text{Number of service units used to provide the service}}$$

Test your understanding 4

The canteen of a company records the following income and expenditure for a month.

	£	£
Income		59,010
Food	17,000	
Drink	6,000	
Bottled water	750	
Fuel costs	800	
Maintenance of machinery	850	
Repairs	250	
Wages	15,500	
Depreciation	1,000	

During the month the canteen served 56,200 meals. The canteen's cost unit is one meal.

Calculate the average cost per meal served and the average income per meal served.

5 Summary

A business that produces **one-off products** for customers, each of which is different, will use a **job costing** system. This treats each individual job as a cost unit and therefore attributes the direct costs to that job, as well as the overheads according to the organisation's overhead absorption basis.

In a business which produces a number of different products in **batches of identical units** then a **batch costing** system is appropriate. Here the costs of each batch of production are gathered together as though the batch was a cost unit and the actual cost per unit is calculated by dividing the batch cost by the number of units produced in that batch.

Test your understanding answers

Test your understanding 1

JOB NO	3,362			
Materials requisitions			£	**Total**
15496			1,044	
15510			938	
15525			614	
			———	2,596

Wages – employees	**Hours**	£	
13249	40	320	
12475	33	231	
26895	53	312	
	———	———	
	126		863
	———		

Overheads	**Hours**	£	
Absorption rate £3.50	126	441	441
			———
			3,900
			———

Test your understanding 2

D

		£
Materials		15,000
Labour		4,200
Overheads	1,000 hours @ £1.2	1,200
		———
Total cost		20,400
		———
Cost per unit	£20,400 ÷ 20,000 =	£1.02

Test your understanding 3

Jetprint Limited

	10,000 leaflets £	20,000 leaflets £
Artwork	65.00	65.00
Machine setting	88.00	88.00
Paper	125.00	250.00
Ink and consumables	40.00	80.00
Printers' wages	32.00	64.00
General fixed overheads (W)	100.00	200.00
Total cost	450.00	747.00

Workings:

$$OAR = \frac{£15,000}{600} = £25 \text{ per hour}$$

10,000 leaflets £25 × 4 hours = £100

20,000 leaflets £25 × 8 hours = £200

Test your understanding 4

Total canteen expenditure = £42,150

Total meals served = 56,200

Average cost per meal served = £42,150 ÷ 56,200 = £0.75 per meal

Average income per meal served = 59,010 ÷ 56,200 = £1.05 per meal

Process costing

9

Introduction

Process costing is used when goods or services result from a **sequence of continuous** or repetitive operations or processes, for example in the manufacture of paint.

ASSESSMENT CRITERIA

Differentiate between and apply different costing systems (2.5)

– Process costing

CONTENTS

1 Process costing
2 Losses in process
3 Scrap value of losses
4 Transferring losses and gains
5 Closing work in progress (CWIP)
6 Opening work in progress (OWIP)

1 Process costing

1.1 Introduction

Process costing is the costing method applicable where goods or services result from a **sequence of continuous** or repetitive operations or **processes**. Process costing is used when a company is **mass producing** the same item and the item goes through a number of different stages.

Process costing is an example of continuous operation costing.

Examples include the chemical, cement, oil refinery, paint and textile industries.

1.2 Illustration of process costing

Here is an example of a two-process manufacturing operation:

> **Example 1**
>
> HYRA has a manufacturing operation that involves two processes. The data for the first process during a particular period is as follows:
>
> • At the beginning of the period, 2,500 kg materials are introduced to the process at a cost of £3,500.
>
> • These materials are then worked upon, using £600 of labour and incurring/absorbing £450 of overheads.
>
> The resulting output is passed to the second process.

To keep track of the costs we could prepare a process account for each process. This resembles a **T account with extra columns**. The reason for the extra columns is that we have to keep track of how many material units we are working on as well as their value.

The costs appearing in such an account are those for **materials, labour and overheads**. (Labour and overheads are often combined under the heading 'conversion costs'.) In the case of **materials we record both units and monetary amount**; in the case of conversion costs we record the monetary amount only, because they do not add any units.

With process accounts the **inputs** into the process go on the **left** (debit) side of the account and **output** on the **right** (credit) side.

Example 2

The process account for the above example might thus appear as follows.

Process 1 account

	Kg	£		Kg	£
Materials	2,500	3,500	Output		
Labour		600	materials to		
Overheads		450	Process 2	2,500	4,550
	2,500	4,550		2,500	4,550

1.3 The basic process cost per unit

Process costing is very similar to batch costing, as we calculate the total costs for the process and divide by the number of units to get a cost per unit.

The main difference is that the process is ongoing so the costs and output for a particular time period are used.

Using the example above we can calculate the cost per kg of output that will be transferred to the second process:

The calculation that needs to be done is:

$$\text{Cost per unit} = \frac{\text{Net costs of input}}{\text{Expected output}}$$

Net costs of input = £3,500 + £600 + £450 = £4,550

Expected output = 2,500 kg

Thus, the output to process 2 would be costed at:

$$\frac{£4,550}{2,500\,\text{kg}} = £1.82 \text{ per kg output}$$

Example 3

Following on from the above example the Process 2 account might appear as follows.

Process 2 account

	Kg	£		Kg	£
Input materials			Finished goods	2,500	6,350
from Process 1	2,500	4,550			
Labour		800			
Overheads		1,000			
	———	———		———	———
	2,500	6,350		2,500	6,350
	———	———		———	———

The finished goods are then valued at:

$$\text{Cost per unit} \quad = \quad \frac{\text{Net costs of input}}{\text{Expected output}}$$

Net costs of input = £4,550 + £800 + £1,000 = £6,350

Expected output = 2,500 kg

Thus, the output from process 2 (i.e. the finished goods) would be costed at:

$$\frac{£6,350}{2,500\,\text{kg}} \quad = \quad £2.54 \text{ per unit}$$

2 Losses in process

2.1 Introduction

In many industrial processes, some input is lost (through evaporation, wastage, etc.) or damaged during the production process. This will give rise to losses in the process. We will look at the concepts of normal losses and abnormal losses or gains.

Normal loss represents items that you **expect** to lose during a process, and its cost is therefore treated as part of the cost of good production. **Abnormal losses or gains** are **not expected** so are valued at the same cost as **good production**.

2.2 Normal losses

Normal losses are usually stated as a percentage of input e.g. the normal loss is expected to be 5% of the input material. Unless the normal loss can be sold as scrap the cost of the loss is absorbed into the production cost i.e. it has a nil value.

 Example 4

At the start of a heating process 1,000 kg of material costing £16 per kg is input. During the process, conversion costs of £2,000 are incurred. Normal loss (through evaporation) is expected to be 10% of input. During March 1,000 kg were input and output was 900 kg.

Compute the unit and total cost of output in March.

Solution

First we need to sort out the units. We can do this using the flow of units equation:

Input   =   Output   +   Loss
1,000 kg =   900 kg   +   100 kg (to balance)

The normal loss is 10% of input = 100 kg thus the loss was as expected.

We now need to compute the cost per unit of good output.

Total input costs:

Materials	£16 × 1,000 kg	£16,000
Conversion costs		£2,000
		————
		£18,000

These costs will be spread over the expected output units – thus the cost attributable to the normal loss units is absorbed into the good units.

Cost per unit of output:

$$= \frac{\text{Net costs of input}}{\text{Expected output}}$$

Where the expected output is the input units less the normal loss units:

$$= \frac{£18,000}{(1,000 - 100)}$$

$$= £20 \text{ per kg}$$

Total cost of output = 900 kg × £20 = £18,000.

This can be represented in a process account as follows.

Process account – March

	Kg	£		Kg	£
Input	1,000	16,000	Output	900	18,000
Conversion costs	–	2,000	Normal loss	100	–
	1,000	18,000		1,000	18,000

Notice that the units and the monetary amounts balance. Normal loss is valued at zero as its cost has been absorbed into that of good output.

2.3   Abnormal loss

Any actual **loss in excess of the normal** (expected) loss is known as **abnormal loss**. This is not treated as part of normal production cost and is separately identified and costed throughout the process.

 Example 5

In April, 1,000 kg were input (at £16 per kg) to the same process as above and actual output was 800 kg. Conversion costs were £2,000 as before.

Required:

Prepare the process account for the month of April.

Solution

Again look at the units only to start with.

Input	**=**	**Output**	**+**	**Loss**
1,000 kg	=	800 kg	+	200 kg (to balance)

The total loss is now 200 kg, when we only expected a (normal) loss of 100 kg.

Input	**=**	**Output**	**+**	**Normal loss**	**+**	**Abnormal loss**
1,000 kg	=	800 kg	+	100 kg	+	100 kg

The extra 100 kg is an abnormal loss. It represents items that we did not expect to lose. In this example it may have been that the temperature was set too high on the process, causing more of the input to evaporate.

To make the units balance we therefore need to include 100 units on the credit side of the process account to represent this abnormal loss:

Process account – April (units only)

	Kg	£		Kg	£
Input	1,000		Output	800	
Conversion costs	–		Normal loss	100	
			Abnormal loss	100	
	1,000			1,000	

Now we examine the costs:

Cost per unit of output

$$= \frac{\text{Net costs of input}}{\text{Expected output}}$$

Where the expected output is the input units less the normal loss units:

$$= \frac{£18,000}{(1,000-100)}$$

$$= £20 \text{ per kg}$$

Total cost of output = 800 kg × £20 = £16,000.

This can be represented in a process account as follows.

Input, normal loss and output are valued as before. The value for abnormal loss is the same as that of output, i.e. £20 per kg.

Process account – April

	Kg	£		Kg	£
Input	1,000	16,000	Output	800	16,000
Conversion costs	–	2,000	Normal loss	100	–
			Abnormal loss	100	2,000
	1,000	18,000		1,000	18,000

The units and values are now balanced. The £2,000 value of the abnormal loss represents lost output.

2.4 Abnormal gain

An **abnormal gain** occurs where **losses are less than expected**. Its treatment is the same as abnormal loss only the debits and credits are reversed i.e. the gain is a debit in the t-account.

 Example 6

In May 1,000 kg at £16 per kg were input to the heating process and £2,000 conversion costs incurred. This month output was 950 kg.

Required:

Prepare the process account for the month of May.

Solution

We begin by looking at the units flow.

Input = Output + Loss
1,000 kg = 950 kg + 50 kg (to balance)

The total loss is now only 50 kg, when we expected a (normal) loss of 1,000 × 10% = 100 kg. We have therefore made an abnormal gain of 50 kg.

To balance the units on the process account then, we need to put the normal loss (100 kg) on the right and the abnormal gain (50 kg) on the left.

Abnormal gain + Input = Output + Normal loss
50 kg + 1,000 kg = 950 kg + 100 kg

Now we examine the costs:

Cost per unit of output:

$$= \frac{\text{Net costs of input}}{\text{Expected output}}$$

Where the expected output is the input units less the normal loss units, we were not expecting the loss to be any different.

$$= \frac{£18,000}{(1,000 - 100)}$$

$$= £20 \text{ per kg}$$

Total cost of output = 950 kg × £20 = £19,000.

This can be represented in a process account as follows.

Input, normal loss and output are valued at the same cost per kg as before. The value for abnormal gain is the same as that of output, i.e. £20 per kg.

The completed process account is shown below.

Process account – May

	Kg	£		Kg	£
Input	1,000	16,000	Output	950	19,000
Conversion costs	–	2,000	Normal loss	100	–
Abnormal gain	50	1,000			
	1,050	19,000		1,050	19,000

The abnormal gain has to go on the debit side to avoid having negative numbers in the T account.

We have an additional 50 units to sell at £20 per unit.

 Test your understanding 1

You are given the following information about the 'mashing' process of Mushypeas Ltd during June:

Ingredients input	1,600 kg @ £2.80 per kg
Labour	100 hours @ £6 per hour
Overheads	100 hours @ £3.60 per hour

Actual Output from the process is 1,250 kg.

Water loss from the process is expected to result in a 15% loss in input volume.

Calculate the cost per kg of output and use it to complete the mashing process account overleaf.

Solution

Mashing process – June

	Kg	£		Kg	£
Ingredients	1,600		Normal loss		
Labour			Output	1,250	
Overheads					
	——	——		——	——
	——	——		——	——

Use the following phrases and numbers to complete the above T-account (some of them may be used twice, some of them will not be required at all):

Abnormal Loss	Abnormal Gain	9,600
5,760	5,000	4,480
600	440	360
240	110	4.35
4.00	5,440	0

📝 Test your understanding 2

Blake Ltd produces a soft drink. The following information relates to period 1.

Direct material	1,000 kg at £90.30 per kg
Direct labour	320 hours at £15.50 per hour
Overhead	£1,914

Normal loss allowance is 3% of input, which can be sold for £64 per kg

Finished output	990 kg

There was no opening or closing work in progress.

Prepare a process account for the above process.

Process soft drink

	Kg	£		Kg	£
Materials			Normal loss		
Labour			Output		
Overhead					
	——	——		——	——
	——	——		——	——

3 Scrap value of losses

3.1 Introduction

It may be possible to **sell** the **normal** loss that occurs in a process as a by-product of the process for example wood shavings as a by-product of making wooden tables and chairs.

 Example 7

Maine Ltd produces tables and chairs. When they are made wood shavings are produced. These wood shavings are saved and sold off for 90p/kg. Normal waste is 10% of input. Costs for batch 975D were as follows.

	£
Materials (10,000 kg @ £2 per kg)	20,000
Labour	2,000
Overheads	500
Total	22,500
Actual output	8,500 kg

Required:

Prepare the process account.

Solution

First, the units:

Input	**=**	**Output**	**+**	**Loss**
10,000 kg	=	8,500 kg	+	1,500 kg (to balance)

The total loss is 1,500 kg, when we only expected a (normal) loss of 10% × 10,000 = 1,000 kg. Thus, we have an abnormal loss of 500 kg.

Input	**=**	**Output**	**+**	**Normal Loss**	**+**	**Abnormal Loss**
10,000 kg	=	8,500 kg	+	1,000 kg	+	500 kg

In this example we would sell the normal loss at £900 (1,000 kg @ £0.90 = £900). This is entered in the process account. The same amount is then subtracted from the process costs, reducing the cost of the inputs i.e. to the net cost of inputs.

$$\text{Cost per unit} \quad = \quad \frac{\text{Net costs of input}}{\text{Expected output}}$$

$$\text{Cost per unit} \quad = \quad \frac{\pounds22,500 - \pounds900}{10,000 - 1,000} = \pounds2.40 \text{ per kg}$$

Although we actually have 1,500 loss units to sell (1,000 litres of normal loss plus 500 units of abnormal loss), we only include the sales value of the normal loss in this calculation as this is all we are **expecting** to sell.

Process account

	Kg	£		Kg	£
Input	10,000	20,000	Output @ £2.40	8,500	20,400
Material Labour	–	2,000	Normal loss		
Overheads	–	500	@ £0.90	1,000	900
			Abnormal loss		
			@ £2.40	500	1,200
	———	———		———	———
	10,000	22,500		10,000	22,500
	———	———		———	———

 Test your understanding 3

Maston Ltd produces special oil in a single process. The oil is made by introducing 10,000 litres of liquid into a process at a cost of £5 per litre.

The normal loss is 500 litres which can be sold for £1 per litre.

Each process requires £4,000 of labour. The overhead is recovered at 150% of labour.

If there are no abnormal losses or gains, produce the process account for the above.

Process 1

	Litres	£		Litres	£
Materials			Normal loss		
Labour			Output		
Overhead					
	———			———	
	———			———	

Test your understanding 4

A chemical compound is made by raw material being passed through two processes. The output of Process A is passed to Process B where further material is added to the mix. The details of the process costs for the financial period number 10 were as shown below.

Process B

Input from process A	1,400 kg @ £19 per kg
Direct material	1,400 kg @ £12 per kg
Direct labour	£4,200
Process plant time	80 hours @ £72.50 per hour

The departmental overhead for period 10 was £2,460.

Process B

Normal loss	10% of input
Actual output	2,620 kg

Normal loss is identified as all material enters process B. This is sold as scrap for £1.50 per kg from Process B.

Required:

Prepare the process accounts below (show totals to the nearest whole £):

Process B

	Kg	£		Kg	£
Input from A			Normal loss		
Material added			Output		
Labour					
Process time					
Overhead					
	___	___		___	___
	___	___		___	___

Test your understanding 5

Mike Everett Ltd produces animal feeds. 'Calfextra' is one of its products. The product is produced in a single process.

The following information relates to week ended 10 February 20X1.

Inputs: Direct material 720 tonnes at £55 per tonne.

Direct labour 40 labour hours at £7.20 per hour.

Overhead £3,240 for the period

Normal loss is based on an allowance of 5% of input and waste has a saleable value of £1 per tonne.

Output for the period was 675 tonnes.

Prepare the process account for the period:

Calfextra

	Tonnes	£		Tonnes	£
Materials			Normal loss		
Labour			Output		
Overhead					
	———	———		———	———
	———	———		———	———

 Test your understanding 6

Mike Everett Ltd produces animal feeds. A further product is 'Pigextra' and this is produced in a single process.

For the week ended 10 March 20X1 the following information was available and related to 'Pigextra' production.

Inputs: Direct material 1,000 tonnes at £17.20 per tonne.

Direct labour 280 hours at £10.50 per hour.

Overhead £32 per direct labour hour.

Normal loss allowance is 5% of input and waste is saleable at £12 per tonne.

Output for the period was 980 tonnes.

Prepare the process account.

Pigextra

	Tonnes	£		Tonnes	£
Materials			Normal loss		
Labour			Output		
Overhead					

Test your understanding 7

X plc processes a chemical. Input to a batch was as follows.

	£
Materials (10,000 litres)	10,000
Labour and overheads	800
Total	10,800

Normal loss is 10% of input.

Actual output = 8,700 litres. The remaining liquid was skimmed off and sold for 36p per litre.

Required:

Complete the process account.

Process account

	Ltr	£		Ltr	£
Materials			Normal loss		
Conversion			Output		

4 Transferring losses and gains

4.1 Introduction

Any losses or gains need to be fully accounted for in the accounts of a business. To do this we need to introduce 2 new accounts – the scrap account and the abnormal loss/gain account.

4.2 Abnormal loss

 Example 8

Abnormal loss

A business puts 1,000 units of material into a process at a cost of £30,000 and spends £10,000 converting it into output. Output from the process is expected to be 900 units but the business only gets 850 completed units out of the process. The units of normal loss can be sold for £17.50 each.

The business has completed the process account as below:

Process account

	Units	£		Units	£
Materials	1,000	30,000	Output	850	36,125
Conversion		10,000	Normal loss	100	1,750
			Abnormal loss	50	2,125
	_____	_____		_____	_____
	1,000	40,000		1,000	40,000
	_____	_____		_____	_____

Complete the transfer of the normal loss and abnormal loss.

1   Normal loss is transferred to the scrap account at the value it is sold at: Cr Process account; Dr Scrap account

Process account

	Units	£		Units	£
Materials	1,000	30,000	Output	850	36,125
Conversion		10,000	**Normal loss**	**100**	**1,750**
			Abnormal loss	50	2,125
	_____	_____		_____	_____
	1,000	40,000		1,000	40,000
	_____	_____		_____	_____

KAPLAN PUBLISHING

Scrap account

	Units	£		Units	£
Process account	**100**	**1,750**			

2   Abnormal loss is transferred to the Abnormal loss/gain account at the average cost per unit (as per the valuation in the process account): Cr Process account; Dr Abnormal loss/gain account

Process account

	Units	£		Units	£
Materials	1,000	30,000	Output	850	36,125
Conversion		10,000	Normal loss	100	1,750
			Abnormal loss	**50**	**2,125**
	1,000	40,000		1,000	40,000

Abnormal loss/gain account

	Units	£		Units	£
Process account	**50**	**2,125**			

3   Abnormal loss is then transferred to the scrap account at the sales value of the normal loss. The normal loss in this example can be sold for £17.50 so the abnormal loss can also be sold at this price, giving it a value of £875.

Abnormal loss: Dr Scrap account; Cr Abnormal loss/gain account

Abnormal loss/gain account

	Units	£		Units	£
Process account	50	2,125	**Scrap account**	**50**	**875**

Scrap account

	Units	£		Units	£
Process account	100	1,750			
Abnormal loss	**50**	**875**			

4 The balancing figure in the abnormal loss/gain account is the true cost of the loss.

Abnormal loss/gain account

	Units	£		Units	£
Process account	50	2,125	Scrap account	50	875
			SOPL		**1,250**
	50	2,125		50	2,125

5 The balancing figure in the scrap account is the total amount of cash received from the total loss made.

Scrap account

	Units	£		Units	£
Process account	100	1,750	**Cash**	**150**	**2,625**
Abnormal loss	50	875			
	150	2,625		150	2,625

Test your understanding 8

Maston Ltd produces special oil. The oil is made by introducing 10,000 litres of liquid into a process at a cost of £5 per litre.

The normal loss is 500 litres which can be sold for £1 per litre.

Each process requires £4,000 of labour. The overhead is recovered at 150% of labour.

The output of process 1 is 9,300 litres.

Produce the process account, scrap account and abnormal/loss gain account for process 1.

Process 1

	Litres	£		Litres	£
Materials			Normal loss		
Labour			Output		
Overhead					
	___	___		___	___
	___	___		___	___

Scrap account

	Litres	£		Litres	£
	___	___		___	___
	___	___		___	___

Abnormal loss/gain account

	Litres	£		Litres	£
	___	___		___	___
	___	___		___	___

4.3 Abnormal gain

 Example 9

Abnormal gain

A business puts 1,000 units of material into a process at a cost of £30,000 and spends £10,000 converting it into output. Output from the process is expected to be 900 units but the business gets 950 completed units out of the process. The units of normal loss can be sold for £17.50 each.

The business has completed the process account as below:

Process account

	Units	£		Units	£
Materials	1,000	30,000	Output	950	40,375
Conversion		10,000	Normal loss	100	1,750
Abnormal gain	50	2,125			
	1,050	42,125		1,050	42,125

Complete the transfer of the normal loss and abnormal gain.

1   Normal loss is transferred to the scrap account at the value it is sold at: Cr Process account; Dr Scrap account

Process account

	Units	£		Units	£
Materials	1,000	30,000	Output	950	40,375
Conversion	10,000		**Normal loss**	**100**	**1,750**
Abnormal gain	50	2,125			
	1,050	42,125		1,050	42,125

Scrap account

	Units	£		Units	£
Process account	**100**	**1,750**			

2   Abnormal gain is transferred to the Abnormal loss/gain account at the average cost per unit (as per the valuation in the process account): Dr Process account; Cr Abnormal loss/gain account

Process account

	Units	£		Units	£
Materials	1,000	30,000	Output	850	36,125
Conversion		10,000	Normal loss	100	1,750
Abnormal gain	**50**	**2,125**			
	1,050	40,000		1,050	40,000

Abnormal loss/gain account

	Units	£		Units	£
			Process account	**50**	**2,125**

3   Abnormal gain is then transferred to the scrap account at the sales value of the normal loss. The normal loss in this example can be sold for £17.50 so the abnormal gain should have been sold at this price, giving it a value of £875.

Abnormal gain is Cr Scrap account; Dr Abnormal loss/gain account

Abnormal loss/gain account

	Units	£		Units	£
Scrap account	**50**	**875**	Process account	50	2,125

Scrap account

	Units	£		Units	£
Process account	100	1,750	**Abnormal gain**	**50**	**875**

4   The balancing figure in the Abnormal loss/gain account is the true saving of the gain

Abnormal loss/gain account

	Units	£		Units	£
Scrap account	50	875	Process account	50	2,125
SOPL		**1,250**			
	50	2,125		50	2,125

5   The balancing figure in the scrap account is the total amount of cash received from the total remaining loss made.

Scrap account

	Units	£		Units	£
Process account	100	1,750	Abnormal gain	50	875
			Cash		**875**
	100	1,750		50	1,750

Test your understanding 9

Gair Plc produces tin cans in a single process. The cans are made by introducing 1,000 kg of metal into a process at a cost of £5 per kg.

The normal loss is 50 kg which can be sold for £0.50 per kg.

Each process requires £400 of labour and £800 of overhead.

Output for process 1 was 900 kg of cans.

Complete the process account, scrap account, abnormal loss/gain account.

Process 1

	Kg	£		Kg	£
Materials			Normal loss		
Labour			Output		
Overhead					

Scrap account

	Kg	£		Kg	£

Abnormal loss/gain account

	Kg	£		Kg	£

Test your understanding 10

Stardust Ltd produces wooden ceiling decorations. When they are produced wood shavings are also produced. These wood shavings are saved and sold off for 60p/kg. Normal loss is 5% of input. Costs for batch 13 were as follows.

	£
Materials (20,000 kg @ £2 per kg)	40,000
Labour	4,600
Overheads	1,600
Actual output	19,500 kg

Complete the process account, scrap account and abnormal loss/gain account.

Process account

	Kg	£		Kg	£
Materials			Normal loss		
Labour			Output		
Overheads					

Scrap account					
	Kg	£		Kg	£
	___	___		___	___
	___	___		___	___

Abnormal loss/gain account					
	Kg	£		Kg	£
	___	___		___	___
	___	___		___	___

5 Closing work in progress (CWIP)

5.1 Introduction

Process costing is also used when products **are not all completed at the end of a time period** (e.g. manufacturing cars). This means that the process costs are shared between finished or complete units and **closing work in progress (CWIP) or partially completed units.**

We need to decide how the costs should be split over these different categories of production.

5.2 Equivalent units

To be able to assign the correct amount of cost to finished and partially completed units of product we use a concept called **Equivalent units** or **EU**. To demonstrate this concept:

If we had 1,000 units that are 50% complete at the end of a period. How many finished units is this equivalent to?

1,000 × 50% = 500 equivalent units (EU).

In other words, we assume we could have made 500 units and finished them instead of half finishing 1,000 units.

The calculation of equivalent units:

Equivalent units = Number of physical units × percentage completion.

Example 10

Situation A – completion levels are equal

DL Ltd is a manufacturer. In Period 1 the following production occurred.

Started	=	1,400
Closing work-in-progress	=	400 units

Degree of completion for the CWIP:

Materials	25%
Conversion	25%

Solution

Started	= >	Finished		+	CWIP
1,400	= >	1,000 (to balance)		+	400

Finished units are 100% complete for both material and conversion.

				EUs
Finished	1,000	×	100%	1,000
WIP	400	×	25%	100
				‾‾‾‾
Total				1,100
				‾‾‾‾

5.3 Equivalent units for different degrees of completion

A process involves direct materials being processed by the addition of direct labour and overheads.

Usually, all the material is put in at the beginning of the process, whereas the conversion is 'added' as the product advances through the process. This means there may be a **different amount of equivalent units for conversion and materials.**

If completion levels in the closing work in progress are unequal we have to keep track of the equivalent units for materials and for conversion separately.

Example 11

Situation B – completion levels are unequal

EM Ltd is a manufacturer. In Period 1 the following production occurred.

Started = 1,400

Closing work-in-progress = 400 units

Degree of completion:

Materials 100%

Conversion 50%

Solution

Started = > Finished + CWIP

1,400 = > 1,000 (to balance) + 400

Finished units are 100% complete for both material and conversion.

		EUs
Materials	– Finished 1,000 × 100%	1,000
	– CWIP 400 × 100%	400
		———
		1,400
		———
Conversion	– Finished 1,000 × 100%	1,000
	– CWIP 400 × 50%	200
		———
		1,200
		———

5.4 Cost per equivalent unit

We need to be able to calculate the cost of an equivalent unit to ultimately be able to value the cost of finished goods and CWIP. We will first look at this when completion levels of the CWIP are equal.

Note: You will only be required to calculate the cost per equivalent unit, not calculate the valuation of finished goods or CWIP. This is shown here for completion.

KAPLAN PUBLISHING

Example 12

Situation A continued – completion levels are equal

DL Ltd is a manufacturer. In Period 1 the following production occurred.

Started	=	1,400
Closing work-in-progress	=	400 units

Degree of completion for the CWIP:

Materials	25%
Conversion	25%

Costs incurred in Period 1 = £6,600

Solution

Started	=	Finished		+	CWIP
1,400	=	1,000 (to balance)		+	400

Finished units are 100% complete for both material and conversion.

		EUs
Finished	1,000 × 100%	1,000
WIP	400 × 25%	100
		——
Total		1,100

The cost per equivalent unit is simply calculated as total cost divided by the number of EUs produced.

The cost per EU would be £6,600/1,100 = £6 per EU.

This can be used to calculate the value of the finished goods and closing WIP:

Value of finished units = 1,000 × £6 = £6,000

Value of closing WIP = 100 × £6 = £600

Test your understanding 11

Process WIP

On 1 March 20X0 a process started work on 350 units and at the end of the month there were still 75 units in the process, each 60% complete.

The total cost of materials, labour, etc. input during March was £3,696.

Required:

What is the cost per equivalent unit:

A   £8.70

B   £9.36

C   £11.55

D   £12.45

Now we need to look at calculating the cost per equivalent unit when completion levels of the CWIP are unequal.

 Example 13

Situation B continued – completion levels are unequal

EM Ltd is a manufacturer. In Period 1 the following production occurred.

Started   =   1,400

Closing work-in-progress   =   400 units

Degree of completion:

      Materials   100%

      Conversion   50%

Costs incurred in Period 1:

      Materials   £81,060

      Conversion   £71,940

Solution

Started = Finished + CWIP

1,400 = 1,000 (to balance) + 400

Finished units are 100% complete for both material and conversion.

		EUs
Materials	– Finished 1,000 × 100%	1,000
	– CWIP 400 × 100%	400
		1,400
Conversion	– Finished 1,000 × 100%	1,000
	– CWIP 400 × 50%	200
		1,200

Total costs are then divided by the total EU to get a cost per EU for each type of input cost, and a total cost for each completed unit:

Material cost per equivalent unit = £81,060/1,400 = £57.90

Conversion cost per equivalent unit = £71,940/1,200 = £59.95

The costs may now be attributed to the categories of output as follows:

		£	£
Completed units:	1,000 × (£57.90 + £59.95)		117,850
Closing WIP:	Materials 400 × £57.90	23,160	
	Conversion 200 × £59.95	11,990	
		35,150	
			153,000

Test your understanding 12

Egton Farm Supplies Ltd produces fertilisers and chemicals. One of its products 'Eg3' is produced in a single process.

The following information relates to period 5, 20X1.

Inputs:	Direct material	1,000 tonnes of 'X' at £70/tonne.
	Direct labour	60 hours at £8/hour.
	Overhead recovery rate	£4/hour.

Completed output:	800 tonnes
Closing work-in-progress:	200 tonnes

There were no losses in the process.

Work-in-progress degree of completion

Material	100%
Labour	80%
Overhead	80%

Calculate the cost per EU for period 5.

 Test your understanding 13

Taylor Ltd makes a product using a number of processes. Details for process 1 during a particular period are as follows:

Inputs	5,000 kilo at £2.47 per kilo
Labour	£1,225
Overheads	£1,862
Completed output:	4,750 kilo
Closing work-in-progress:	250 kilo

There were no losses in the process.

Work-in-progress degree of completion

Material	100%
Labour	60%
Overhead	60%

Calculate the cost per EU for period 1.

Test your understanding 14

NH Ltd

NH Ltd has two processes.

Process 1:

Material for 12,000 items was put into process 1. There were no opening inventory and no process losses. Other relevant information is:

Transfers to Process 2	9,000 items
Direct material cost	£36,000
Direct labour cost	£32,000
Overheads	£8,530

The unfinished items were complete as to materials and 50% complete as to labour and overheads.

Process 2:

Transfers from Process 1	9,000 items transferred at £61,740
Items completed	8,200 items
Labour cost	£34,596
Overheads	£15,300

There were no materials added in Process 2 other than the units transferred from process 1. There were no process losses.

The unfinished items were deemed to be 25% complete in labour and overheads

Required:

Calculate the cost per equivalent unit for each process.

6 Opening work in progress (OWIP)

6.1 Introduction

At the start of a period there may be some work in progress from a previous period (closing work in progress) that is waiting to be finished. This is the known as the **opening work in progress (OWIP)** in the new period.

The OWIP needs to be considered to be able to calculate how much of the completed output at the end of the period was completed wholly in the period and how much only required partial effort to complete it within the period.

There are 2 different methods that can be applied to OWIP – Average cost (AVCO) and First in, first out (FIFO).

6.2 Average cost (AVCO)

The average cost method would be used where it is not possible to distinguish individual units present at the start of a process from those produced during the period e.g. liquids. In this case the **costs incurred so far to complete the OWIP are included with the period costs when calculating the cost per EU.**

🔆 Example 14

Than Pele

Than Pele Ltd is a manufacturer. The details of the first process in Period 2 are as follows:

OWIP	=	400 units
Costs incurred so far:		
Materials	£19,850	
Conversion	£4,100	
Completed output	= 1,700 units	
Costs incurred in Period 2:		
Materials	£100,000	
Conversion	£86,000	

Solution

OWIP	+	Started	=	Finished
400	+	1,300 (bal fig)	=	1,700

Equivalent units	Material	Conversion
Completed output	1,700	1,700
Total EU	1,700	1,700

Costs	Material	Conversion
OWIP	19,850	4,100
Period	100,000	86,000
Total cost	119,850	90,100
Cost per EU	£70.50	£53.00

 Test your understanding 15

Yeknom

Yeknom produces a diet drink on a production line. The details of the process in Period 7 are as follows:

OWIP	=	200 units

Costs incurred so far:

Materials	£22,000
Conversion	£9,960

Completed output	=	900 units

Costs incurred in Period 7:

Materials	£97,700
Conversion	£98,940

Required:

Calculate the cost per EU using the AVCO method of valuing OWIP.

Equivalent units		Material	Conversion
	Completed output		
	Total EU		
Costs			
	OWIP		
	Period		
	Total cost		
Cost per EU			

Test your understanding 16

Ipako

Ipako produces perfume on a production line. The details of the process in Period 4 are as follows:

OWIP	=	400 units

Costs incurred so far:

Materials	£48,000
Conversion	£34,800

Completed output	=	1,200 units

Costs incurred in Period 4:

Materials	£120,000
Conversion	£78,000

Calculate the cost per EU using the AVCO method of valuing OWIP.

6.3 First in, first out (FIFO)

The first in, first out method would be used when it may be essential to complete the started goods from previous periods before new units can be started e.g. car production lines. In this case we need to consider **how much work is required to complete the OWIP in this period.** The costs incurred in the previous period for the OWIP are not included in the cost per EU calculation but are instead included within the final valuation of the completed output.

Example 15

Than Pele

Than Pele Ltd is a manufacturer. The details of the first process in Period 3 are as follows:

OWIP	=	400 units

Costs incurred so far:

Materials	£19,850
Conversion	£4,100

Degrees of completion:

Materials	100%
Conversion	25%

Completed output	=	1,700 units

Costs incurred in Period 3:

Materials	£100,100
Conversion	£86,000

Solution

OWIP	+	Started	=	Completed
400	+	1,300 (bal fig)	=	1,700

The completed units consist of 400 OWIP that were completed this period and then a further 1,300 units that were started and finished in this period.

To complete the OWIP no more material is required but 75% more conversion is needed.

Equivalent units	Material	Conversion
OWIP to complete	0 (400 – 400 × 100%)	300 (400 – 400 × 25%)
Started and finished	1,300	1,300
Total EU	1,300	1,600
Costs		
Period	100,100	86,000
Total cost	100,100	86,000
Cost per EU	£77.00	£53.75

Test your understanding 17

Effarig

Effarig is makes safari hats on a production line. The details of the process in Period 3 are as follows:

OWIP	=	200 units

Costs incurred so far:

Materials	£1,800
Conversion	£4,000

Degrees of completion:

Materials	100%
Conversion	75%

Completed output	= 2,000 units

Costs incurred in Period 3:

Materials	£18,900
Conversion	£37,925

Required:

Calculate the cost per EU using the FIFO method of valuing OWIP.

Equivalent units	Material	Conversion
OWIP to complete		
Started and finished		
Total EU		
Costs		
Period		
Total cost		
Cost per EU		

Test your understanding 18

Noil

Noil makes electric cars on a production line. The details of the process in Period 2 are as follows:

OWIP	=	250 units

Costs incurred so far:

Materials	£54,000
Conversion	£42,000

Degrees of completion:

Materials	100%
Conversion	60%

Completed output   = 3,200 units

Costs incurred in Period 2:

Materials	£135,700
Conversion	£97,600

Calculate the cost per EU using the FIFO method of valuing OWIP.

7 Summary

Process costing is used when a company is mass producing the same item and the item goes through a number of different stages. As the item goes through the different stages, **losses** may occur: normal losses, abnormal losses and abnormal gains. Losses may be scrapped or they may have a '**scrap value**' which means that they can be sold (and that the revenue generated is used to reduce the costs of the process concerned).

Sometimes, at the end of an accounting period, a process may not be finished and there may be incomplete (**work-in-progress**) units. When this happens, it is necessary to use the concept of **equivalent units** to decide how the process costs should be split over work-in-progress and finished goods.

Note: Process and job costing systems represent the extreme ends of a continuum, and many organisations need a combination of these two elements (as in batch costing).

Test your understanding answers

Test your understanding 1

Actual output = 1,250 kg

Flow of units:

Input	=	Output	+	Loss
1,600 kg	=	1,250 kg	+	350 kg (to balance)

Normal loss = 240 kg and we therefore have an abnormal loss of 110 kg.

Process costs = £5,440

$$\text{Cost per unit of output} = \frac{\text{Total process costs}}{\text{Input units} - \text{Normal loss units}}$$

$$= \frac{£5,440}{(1,600 - 240)}$$

$$= £4 \text{ per kg}$$

Mashing process – June

	Kg	£		Kg	£
Ingredients	1,600	4,480	Output	1,250	5,000
Labour		600	Normal loss	240	–
Overheads		360	Abnormal loss	110	440
	1,600	5,440		1,600	5,440

Test your understanding 2

Process soft drink

	Kg	£		Kg	£
Material		1,000	Normal loss	30	1,920
Labour		4,960	Output	990	97,218
Overhead		1,914			
Abnormal gain	20	1,964			
	1,020	99,138		1,020	99,138

$$\text{Normal cost of normal output} = \frac{97,174 - 1,920}{1,000 - 30}$$

$$= \text{£98.20 per kg}$$

Cost of output $= 990 \times £98.20 = £97,218$

Cost of abnormal gain $= 30 \times £98.20 = £1,920$

Test your understanding 3

Process 1

	Litre	£		Litre	£
Direct material	10,000	50,000	Normal loss	500	500
Direct labour		4,000	Output	9,500	59,500
Overhead		6,000			
	10,000	60,000		10,000	60,000

Test your understanding 4

Chemical compound

Process B

	Kg	£		Kg	£ per Kg	£
From Process A	1,400	26,600	Finished			
Direct material	1,400	16,800	goods (W6)	2,620	22.00	57,640
Direct labour		4,200	Normal loss			
Overhead		2,460	(W4)	280	1.50	420
Processing time		5,800				
Abnormal gain						
(W5, W6)	100	2,200				
	2,900	58,060		2,900		58,060

(W4) Normal loss = 10% × (1,400 + 1,400) = 280

(W5) Expected output = 2,800 − 280 = 2,520 units; actual output 2,620; 100 units abnormal gain

(W6) Cost per unit = £(55,860 − 420)/(2,800 − 280) = £22.00

✏️ Test your understanding 5

Mike Everett Ltd – 'Calfextra'

Determination of losses/gains:

	Tonnes
Input	720
Normal loss 5% of input	36
Normal output	684
Actual output	675
Difference = abnormal loss	9

Calfextra

	Tonnes	£		Tonnes	£
Material	720	39,600	Normal loss	36	36
Labour		288	Output	675	42,525
Overhead		3,240	Abnormal loss	9	567
	720	43,128		720	43,128

Normal cost of normal production:

$$\frac{£43,128 - £36}{720 - 36} = \frac{£43,092}{684}$$

$$= £63 \text{ per tonne}$$

Output	675 × £63	=	£42,525
Abnormal loss	9 × £63	=	£567

Test your understanding 6

Mike Everett Ltd – 'Pigextra'

Determination of losses/gains:

	Tonnes
Input	1,000
Normal loss 5% of input	50
Normal output	950
Actual output	980
Difference = abnormal gain	30

Pigextra

	Tonnes	£		Tonnes	£
Material	1,000	17,200	Normal loss	50	600
Labour		2,940	Output	980	29,400
Overhead		8,960			
Abnormal gain	30	900			
	1,030	30,000		1,030	30,000

Normal cost of normal production:

$$\frac{£29,100 - £600}{1,000 - 50} = \frac{£28,500}{950}$$

$$= £30 \text{ per tonne}$$

Output	980 tonnes × £30	=	£29,400
Abnormal gain	30 tonnes × £30	=	£900

Test your understanding 7

X plc

Process account

	Ltrs	£		Ltrs	£
Input material	10,000	10,000	Output	8,700	10,092
Labour and			Normal loss	1,000	360
overheads	–	800	Abnormal loss	300	348
	10,000	10,800		10,000	10,800

Output valued at (£10,800 – £360)/9,000 = £1.16 per litre

Test your understanding 8

Process 1

	Litres	£		Litres	£
Direct material	10,000	50,000	Normal loss	500	500
Direct labour		4,000	Output	9,300	58,247
Overhead		6,000	Abnormal loss		
			(W1)	200	1,253
	10,000	60,000		10,000	60,000

Scrap account

	Litres	£		Litres	£
Process	500	500	Cash		700
Abnormal loss	200	200			
		700			700

Abnormal loss/gain account

	Litres	£		Litres	£
Process	200	1,253	Scrap	200	200
			SOPL		1,053
		1,253			1,253

Working 1:

Normal cost of normal output = $\dfrac{59,500}{9,500}$ = £6.2631 per litre.

Therefore, output and the abnormal loss are both costed at £6.2631 per litre.

Test your understanding 9

Gair plc

Process account

	Kg	£		Kg	£
Material	1,000	5,000	Normal loss	50	25
Labour		400	Output	900	5,850
Overheads		800	Abnormal loss	50	325
	1,000	6,200		1,000	6,200

Output valued at (£6,200 – £25)/950 = £6.50 per kg

Abnormal loss/gain account

	Kg	£		Kg	£
Process account	50	325	Scrap account	50	25
			SOPL		300
	50	325		50	325

Scrap account

	Kg	£		Kg	£
Process account	50	25	Cash	100	50
Abnormal loss	50	25			
	100	50		100	50

Test your understanding 10

Stardust Ltd

Process account

	Kg	£		Kg	£
Material	20,000	40,000	Normal loss	1,000	600
Labour		4,600	Output	19,500	46,800
Overheads		1,600			
Abnormal gain	500	1,200			
	20,500	47,400		20,500	47,400

Output valued at (46,200 – 600/19,000 = £2.40 per kg.

Abnormal loss/gain account

	Kg	£		Kg	£
Scrap account	500	300	Process account	500	1,200
SOPL		900			
	500	1,200		500	1,200

Scrap account

	Kg	£		Kg	£
Process account	1,000	600	Abnormal gain	500	300
			Cash	500	300
	1,000	600		1,000	600

Test your understanding 11

C

Physical flow of units

	Units started		Units completed		Closing WIP
	350	=	275 (bal fig)	+	75

Equivalent units of production

Units started and finished	275
Closing WIP (75 × 60%)	45
	———
	320
	———

Cost per equivalent unit $= \dfrac{£3,696}{320} = £11.55$

Test your understanding 12

Egton Farm Supplies Ltd

Statement of equivalent units and statement of cost

	Completed output	CWIP	Equivalent units	Cost £	Cost per unit £
Direct materials	800	200	1,000	70,000	70.00
Direct labour	800	160	960	480	0.50
Overhead	800	160	960	240	0.25

Test your understanding 13

Work-in-progress valuation

Statement of equivalent units and statement of cost

Element of cost	Comp output	WIP	Equivalent units	Cost £	Cost per unit
Direct materials	4,750	250	5,000	12,350	£2.47
Direct labour	4,750	150	4,900	1,225	£0.25
Overhead	4,750	150	4,900	1,862	£0.38
					£3.10

 Test your understanding 14

NH Ltd

Process 1

Units started	=	Units completed	+	Closing WIP	
12,000	=	9,000	+	3,000 (bal)	

Input	Equivalent units			Costs	Costs per EU (£)
	Completed in period	CWIP	Total EU	Total costs (£)	
Materials	9,000	3,000 (100%)	12,000	36,000	3.00
Conversion	9,000	1,500 (50%)	10,500	40,530	3.86

Process 2

Units started	=	Units completed	+	Closing WIP	
9,000	=	8,200	+	800 (bal)	

Input	Equivalent units			Costs	Costs per EU (£)
	Completed in period	CWIP	Total EU	Total costs (£)	
Material from Process 1	8,200	800 (100%)	9,000	61,740	6.86
Conversion	8,200	200 (25%)	8,400	49,896	5.94

Test your understanding 15

Equivalent units		Material	Conversion
	Completed output	900	900
	Total EU	900	900
Costs			
	OWIP	22,000	9,960
	Period	97,700	98,940
	Total cost	119,700	108,900
Cost per EU		£133	£121

Test your understanding 16

Equivalent units		Material	Conversion
	Completed output	1,200	1,200
	Total EU	1,200	1,200
Costs			
	OWIP	48,000	34,800
	Period	120,000	78,000
	Total cost	168,000	112,800
Cost per EU		£140	£94

Test your understanding 17

OWIP + Started = Completed

200 + 1,800 = 2000

The completed units consist of 200 OWIP that were completed this period and then a further 1,800 units that were started and finished in this period.

To complete the OWIP no more material is required but 25% more conversion is needed.

Equivalent units	Material	Conversion
OWIP to complete	0 (200 – 200 × 100%)	50 (200 – 200 × 75%)
Started and finished	1,800	1,800
Total EU	1,800	1,850
Costs		
Period	18,900	37,925
Total cost	18,900	37,925
Cost per EU	£10.50	£20.50

🖉 Test your understanding 18

OWIP	+	Started	=	Completed
250	+	2,950	=	3,200

The completed units consist of 250 OWIP that were completed this period and then a further 2,950 units that were started and finished in this period.

To complete the OWIP no more material is required but 40% more conversion is needed.

Equivalent units	Material	Conversion
OWIP to complete	0	100
Completed output	2,950	2,950
Total EU	2,950	3,050
Costs		
Period	135,700	97,600
Total cost	135,700	97,600
Cost per EU	£46.00	£32.00

Marginal costing

Introduction

Marginal costing is used within management accounting to aid decision making. The marginal cost of a product is the **total variable production costs**. In marginal costing **fixed overheads** are treated as **period costs** and are charged in full against the profit for the period. Absorption costing assigns fixed production overheads to the inventory (see Chapter 6).

This chapter describes marginal costing and how to reconcile absorption costing and marginal costing profits.

ASSESSMENT CRITERIA	CONTENTS
Explain and demonstrate the differences between marginal and absorption costing (1.4)	1 Marginal costing 2 The concept of contribution 3 Marginal versus absorption costing 4 The impact of changing inventory levels 5 Advantages of marginal costing

1 Marginal costing

1.1 Marginal costing

Marginal costing values each unit of inventory at the **variable production cost** required to make each unit (the marginal cost). This includes direct materials, direct labour, direct expenses and variable overheads. Variable non-production costs do not form part of the product cost but are subtracted after the cost of sales to calculate **contribution**. No **fixed overheads** (production or non-production) are included in the product costs; they are treated as a **period cost** and deducted in full lower down the statement of profit and loss.

Definition

The **marginal production cost** is the cost of one unit of product or service which would be avoided if that unit were not produced, or the amount by which costs would increase if one extra unit were produced.

Marginal costing requires knowledge of cost behaviours as costs are split based on whether they are fixed or variable. Semi-variable costs would need to be separated into their fixed and variable elements by using the high-low method. See Chapter 2.

The basic layout for calculating budgeted profit or loss under marginal costing is as follows (with illustrative figures).

	£	£
Sales revenue (10,000 × £10)		100,000
Cost of sales (at **marginal/variable** cost, £6)		(60,000)
Variable non-production costs (£1)		(10,000)
Contribution		30,000
Less: **Fixed** production costs	20,000	
Fixed non-production costs	2,000	
		(22,000)
Profit for the period		8,000

Test your understanding 1

XYZ plc

XYZ plc manufactures toy horses and has produced a budget for the quarter ended 30 June 20X5 (Quarter 1) as follows.

Sales	190 units @ selling price of £12
Production	200 units
Opening inventory	20 units
Variable production cost per unit	£8
Fixed production overhead	£400
Selling and distribution costs (fixed)	£250

Required:

Draft the statement of profit or loss using marginal costing principles:

	£	£
Sales revenue		
Less: Cost of sales		
Opening inventory		
Production costs		
Closing inventory		
Contribution		
Fixed costs		
Profit for the period		

---

2 The concept of contribution

2.1 Contribution

The concept of contribution is one of the most fundamental in cost and management accounting. Contribution measures the **difference between the sales price of a unit and the variable costs of making and selling that unit**.

> Contribution = Sales revenue less all variable costs

2.2 Changes in activity level

How do contribution and profit change if we double output and sales?

	10,000 units £		20,000 units £
Sales revenue 10,000 × £10	100,000	20,000 × £10	200,000
Variable costs 10,000 × £7	(70,000)	20,000 × £7	(140,000)
Contribution	**30,000**		**60,000**
Fixed overheads	(22,000)		(22,000)
Profit for the period	**8,000**		**38,000**
Contribution per unit	£3		£3
Profit per unit	£0.80		£1.90

If sales double then the total contribution doubles but total profit does not increase at the same rate. This shows that there is a **direct relationship between** the number of **sales** made and the value of **contribution** but not level of profit. There is **no direct link between profit and output.** If output doubles, profits do not necessarily double.

The contribution per unit remains constant at £3 whereas the profit per unit increases from £0.80 to £1.90. The increase in the profit per unit is because the fixed costs are being shared over more units.

What happens to profit if sales increase by one extra unit from 10,000 to 10,001?

	£
Sales revenue 10,001 × £10	100,010
Variable costs 10,001 × £7	(70,007)
Contribution	30,003
Fixed costs	(22,000)
Profit for the period	8,003

Total contribution increases £3, but the total fixed overheads do not change so profit also goes up by £3 (i.e. the same as contribution).

The concept of **contribution** is an extremely important one in cost and management accounting. It is important to remember that since contribution measures the **difference between sales price and the variable cost of the unit**, if a product has a positive contribution it is worth making. Any amount of contribution, however small, **goes towards paying the fixed overheads**; if enough units are made and sold such that total contribution exceeds fixed overheads then profit will start to be made. Contribution is more useful for decision making than profit.

3 Marginal versus absorption costing

3.1 Comparison of absorption and marginal costing

See Chapter 6 for a recap on absorption costing.

Below is a table that compares absorption costing and marginal costing:

Absorption costing	Marginal costing
Costs are split based on **function** – production or non-production	Costs are split based on **behaviour** – variable or fixed
Inventory is valued at the **full production cost** (fixed and variable production costs)	Inventory is valued at the **variable production cost only**
Sales – cost of sales = **gross profit**	Sales – all variable costs = **contribution**
Non-production overheads are deducted after gross profit	Variable non-production overheads are excluded from the valuation of inventory but are deducted before contribution
Fixed costs are split between production and non-production costs	All fixed cost are period costs
Adheres to IAS 2 Inventory and can therefore be used for the financial accounts of the business	Does not adhere to IAS 2 Inventory so is mainly used internally for decision making processes

Test your understanding 2

Billie Millar

The following information relates to the manufacture of product Delphinium during the month of April 2005:

Direct materials per unit	£10.60
Direct labour per unit	£16.40
Variable overheads per batch	£60,000
Fixed overheads per batch	£80,000
Number of units per batch	10,000

Task

Calculate the prime cost per unit.

Calculate the marginal cost per unit.

Calculate the absorption cost per unit.

 Test your understanding 3

The following information has been provided.

	Cost per unit £
Direct material	8.50
Direct labour	27.20
Variable production overhead	11.30
Fixed production overhead	14.00
Selling price	61.50

Required:

Calculate each of the following in £/unit:

(a)   prime cost

(b)   marginal cost

(c)   absorption cost

(d)   gross profit

(e)   contribution

Test your understanding 4

Crescent Feeds Ltd have produced the following set of cost and management accounting figures for its current accounting period.

	£	
Production and sales tonnage	–	2,500 tonnes
Direct labour	102,000	
Admin overheads	16,500	
Direct materials	210,000	
Direct expenses	5,250	
Fixed production overheads	20,400	
Variable production overheads	20,000	
Selling and distribution costs (fixed)	52,300	

Calculate for the period:

- Prime cost

- Marginal cost

- Absorption cost

- Non-production cost

- Total cost

- Prime cost per tonne of product

- Marginal cost per tonne of product

- Absorption cost per tonne of product

- Total cost per tonne of product

 The impact of changing inventory levels

4.1   Cost of sales

The cost of sales calculation in the budgeted statement of profit or loss can be broken down into 3 elements – opening inventory, production and closing inventory. The units within these elements are valued either at marginal cost or absorption cost. The value of the closing inventory is subtracted from the sum of the value of the opening inventory and production to calculate the cost of making sales.

4.2 Impact on profit

When inventory levels increase or decrease over the short term i.e. a month, profits will differ under absorption and marginal costing. Over the longer term the differences in inventory will net off and not produce different profits.

Increasing inventory is when closing inventory in the cost of sales is greater than opening inventory. Decreasing inventory is when opening inventory is greater than closing inventory.

- If inventory is increasing then absorption costing will give the higher profit.

- If inventory levels are decreasing then absorption costing will give the lower profit.

- If inventory levels remain constant then the profit values will be the same.

This is because:

- under **marginal costing** all the period's fixed production overheads are charged **in full** against that period's profit, whereas

- under **absorption costing** some of the period's fixed production overheads will be **carried forward** in the closing inventory value and charged to the next period's statement of profit or loss.

This is illustrated in the following example:

Example 1

Worked example of profit differences

	£ per unit
Sales price	£15
Prime cost	£4
Variable production costs	£2
Budgeted fixed production overheads	£40,000 per month
Budgeted production	10,000 units per month
Budgeted sales	8,000 units
Opening inventory	500 units

Required:

Produce a budgeted marginal costing and an absorption costing statement of profit or loss for a month.

Solution

When calculating the profit we will need the number of units in closing inventory. This is given by:

Opening inventory units + production units − sales units

This will be 500 + 10,000 − 8,000 = 2,500 units

Marginal costing statement of profit or loss

	£	£
Sales revenue (8,000 × £15)		120,000
Opening inventory (500 × £6)	3,000	
Marginal production costs (10,000 × £6)	60,000	
Closing inventory (2,500 × £6)	(15,000)	
	———	
Marginal cost of sales		(48,000)
		———
Contribution		72,000
Fixed costs		(40,000)
		———
Profit for the period		32,000
		———

The marginal cost includes the prime cost and the variable production cost. The fixed costs are charged in full against the sales for the period.

Absorption costing statement of profit or loss

	£	£
Sales revenue (8,000 × £15)		120,000
Opening inventory (500 × £10)	5,000	
Production costs (10,000 × £10)	100,000	
Closing inventory (2,500 × £10)	(25,000)	
	———	
Absorption cost of sales		(80,000)
		———
Profit for the period		40,000
		———

The production cost includes the prime cost of production, the variable production costs plus an amount per unit for the fixed production costs.

The fixed overhead absorbed by each unit is as follows.

$$\frac{\text{Budgeted fixed overheads}}{\text{Budgeted production}} = \frac{£40,000}{10,000} = £4 \text{ per unit}$$

4.3 Reconciliation of profits

> ### ☀ Example 1 (continued)
>
> In the example above the absorption costing profit is £8,000 higher than the marginal costing profit. Why?
>
> Under absorption costing:
>
> - The opening inventory has been charged with £2,000 of fixed production cost (500 units × £4)
>
> - The £40,000 fixed production costs have been charged to production costs (10,000 units × £4)
>
> - £10,000 of this has then been deducted from the cost of sales as part of the closing inventory value (2,500 unit × £4)
>
> - This means that under absorption costing only £32,000 of fixed costs has been charged in this month's statement of profit and loss (£2,000 + £40,000 − £10,000 = £32,000)
>
> Under marginal costing:
>
> - The full £40,000 of fixed costs as been charged to this month's statement of profit or loss
>
> - The profit under marginal costing is £8,000 lower than under absorption costing as £8,000 more cost has been charged against revenue.

It may be necessary to calculate the absorption profit from the marginal profit or vice versa. Use the proforma below to do this:

Absorption costing profit	X
Less: Change in inventory × OAR	+/–X
	‾‾‾
Marginal costing profit	X

Note: The change in inventory is calculated as the opening inventory units less the closing inventory units.

Example 1 (continued)

Using the information in the example:

Absorption costing profit	£40,000
Less: Change in inventory × OAR	
(500 – 2,500) × 4	–£8,000
Marginal costing profit	£32,000

Note: It is not ethical to switch between marginal and absorption costing to improve the performance of an area of the business.

Test your understanding 5

Voliti Limited has produced the following budgeted figures for a new product it hopes to launch.

Direct material	£10 per unit
Direct labour	£5 per unit
Variable production overheads	£8 per unit
Fixed production costs	£19,500 per month
Budgeted output	6,500 units per month
Sales price	£30 per unit
Month 1	
Production	6,500
Sales	5,000

Task

Complete the statement of profit or loss for month 1 on each of the following bases, and reconcile the resulting profit figures:

(i) Marginal costing principles

	£	£
Sales revenue		
Less: Cost of sales		
Opening inventory		
Production costs		
Closing inventory	( )	
		( )
Contribution		
Fixed costs		( )
Profit for the period		

(ii) Absorption costing principles

	£	£
Sales revenue		
Cost of sales		
Opening inventory		
Production costs		
Closing inventory	( )	
		( )
Gross profit		
Non-production costs		( )
Profit for the period		

The absorption costing profit is *higher/lower** than the marginal costing profit because there are *more/less** fixed costs charged against the sales in the absorption costing statement.

delete as appropriate

Test your understanding 6

McTack

McTack manufactures PCs and has produced a budget for the quarter ended 31 March 20X4 (Quarter 1) using absorption costing as follows.

	£	£
Sales revenue (100 units @ £500 per unit)		50,000
Production cost of 120 units		
Materials	12,000	
Labour	24,000	
Variable overhead	6,000	
Fixed overhead	6,000	
	48,000	
Less: Closing inventory (20 × £400)	(8,000)	
		(40,000)
		10,000

Required:

Redraft the statement of profit or loss using marginal costing principles.

	£	£
Sales revenue		
Less Cost of sales:		
Opening inventory		
Production costs		
Closing inventory	( )	
		( )
Contribution		
Fixed costs		( )
Profit for the period		

Reconcile the profits:

5 Advantages of marginal costing

5.1 Advantages of marginal costing

1 Marginal costing avoids needing to allocate, apportion, re-apportion and absorb fixed overheads (see Chapter 7).

2 Fixed costs logically relate to time and so are charged as period costs.

3 Profit figures are more consistent with fluctuating sales.

4 Used for short term decision-making (see Chapter 11).

6 Summary

Marginal costing calculates the **contribution** per unit of a product. In marginal costing units are valued at **variable production cost** and fixed overheads are accounted for as period costs.

In **absorption costing**, units are valued at **variable cost plus fixed production overheads** absorbed using a pre-determined absorption rate.

The differences in these methods give rise to different profit figures which are usually reconciled at the end of an accounting period.

Test your understanding answers

 Test your understanding 1

There will be closing inventory of 30 units.

Opening inventory + production – sales = closing inventory

Under marginal costing, the closing inventory will be valued at the variable production cost of £8 per unit.

Marginal costing statement of profit and loss

	£	£
Sales revenue		2,280
Less: Cost of sales		
Opening inventory (20 × 8)	160	
Production costs (200 × 8)	1,600	
Closing inventory (30 × 8)	(240)	
		1,520
Contribution		760
Fixed costs		(650)
Profit for the period		110

 Test your understanding 2

Calculate the prime cost per unit.

    10.60 + 16.40 = £27.00

Calculate the marginal cost per unit.

    27.00 + (60,000 ÷ 10,000) = £33.00

Calculate the absorption cost per unit.

    33.00 + (80,000 ÷ 10,000) = £41.00

Test your understanding 3

(a)   Prime cost per unit

	£
Direct material	8.50
Direct labour	27.20
	35.70

(b)   Marginal cost per unit

	£
Prime cost	35.70
Variable production overhead	11.30
	47.00

(c)   Absorption cost per unit

	£
Prime cost	35.70
Variable production overhead	11.30
Fixed production overhead	14.00
	61.00

(d)   Gross profit per unit

	£
Selling price	61.50
Less Absorption cost	(61.00)
	0.50

(e)   Contribution per unit

	£
Selling price	61.50
Less Marginal cost	(47.00)
	14.50

Test your understanding 4

- Prime cost (210,000 + 102,000 + 5,250) — £317,250
- Marginal cost (317,250 + 20,000) — £337,250
- Absorption cost (337,250 + 20,400) — £357,650
- Non-production cost (16,500 + 52,300) — £68,800
- Total cost (357,650 + 68,800) — £426,450
- Prime cost per tonne (317,250 ÷ 2,500) — £126.90
- Marginal cost per tonne (337,250 ÷ 2,500) — £134.90
- Absorption cost per tonne (357,650 ÷ 2,500) — £143.06
- Total cost per tonne (426,450 ÷ 2,500) — £170.58

Test your understanding 5

(i) **Marginal costing principles**

	£	£
Sales revenue		150,000
Less: Cost of sales		
Opening inventory	0	
Production costs	149,500	
Closing inventory	(34,500)	
		(115,000)
Contribution		35,000
Fixed costs		(19,500)
Profit for the period		15,500

(ii)   **Absorption costing principles**

	£	£
Sales revenue		150,000
Cost of sales		
Opening inventory	0	
Production costs	169,000	
Closing inventory	(39,000)	
		(130,000)
Gross profit		20,000
Non-production costs		(0)
Profit for the period		20,000

The absorption costing profit is **higher** than the marginal costing profit because there are **less** fixed costs charged against the sales in the absorption costing statement.

The difference of £4,500 is the increase in inventory of 1,500 units × the £3 per unit OAR for fixed overheads.

Test your understanding 6

McTack – Budgeted profit statement quarter ended 31 March

Marginal costing format

Marginal costing statement of profit or loss

	£	£
Sales revenue (100 × £500)		50,000
Less: Cost of sales		
Opening inventory	0	
Production costs (12,000 + 24,000 + 6,000)	42,000	
Closing inventory (20 × £350)	(7,000)	
		(35,000)
Contribution		15,000
Fixed costs		(6,000)
Profit for the period		9,000

Calculation of marginal cost per unit.

Marginal cost/number of units produced = marginal cost per unit

42,000/120 = £350

Reconciliation of profits

	£
Absorption costing profit	10,000
Change in inventory × OAR	
(0 – 20) × £50	–1,000
	———
Absorption costing profit	9,000
	———

Short-term decision making

Introduction

There are a number of calculations that can be completed to aid decision making in the short term. Within this chapter we will consider a number of different techniques that are required in different situations.

ASSESSMENT CRITERIA
Prepare and use short-term future income and costs (5.1):
– Relevant costs
– Break-even analysis
– Margin of safety
– Target profit
– Limiting factors

CONTENTS
1 Relevant costing
2 Cost-volume-profit (CVP) analysis
3 CVP charts
4 Limiting factors analysis

1 Relevant costing

1.1 Introduction

When assisting management in making **short term** decisions only costs or revenues that are **relevant** to the decision should be considered. Any form of decision-making process involves making a choice between two or more alternatives.

For decision making, it is necessary to identify the costs and revenues that will be affected as a result of taking one course of action rather than another. The costs that would be affected by a decision are known as relevant costs.

Since relevant costs and revenues are those which are different, the term effectively means costs and revenues which change as a result of a decision.

Even though the costs and revenues are only being estimated it is important to ensure that the calculations are made knowing as much detail as possible or that any assumptions are stated. This will maintain the integrity of the information and should demonstrate professional competence.

1.2 Relevant costs and revenues

 Definition

Relevant costs and revenues are those costs and revenues that **change as a direct result of a decision that is taken**.

A relevant cost is a **future, incremental cash flow** arising as direct result of a decision being taken:

- **Future costs and revenues** – costs and revenues that are going to be incurred sometime in the future due to the decision being taken.

- **Incremental costs and revenues** – any extra cost or revenue generated by the decision that would not arise otherwise e.g. an extra amount of fixed costs due only to the decision.

- **Cash flows rather than profits** – actual cash being spent or received should be used when making the decision. Profits can be manipulated by accounting concepts like depreciation. Cash flows are more reliable.

A relevant cost or revenue could also be referred to as an avoidable cost.

 Definition

An **avoidable cost** is any cost that would only occur as a result of taking the decision. If the decision did not go ahead then the cost would not be incurred so it is avoidable.

1.3 Non-relevant costs and revenues

Costs or revenues that can be ruled out when making a decision come under the following categories:

- **Sunk costs** – past or historic costs that cannot be changed e.g. any cost incurred due to research and development that has already been carried out will not apply after the decision has been made.

- **Committed costs** – costs that are **unavoidable** and will be incurred whether or not the project is done.

- **Non-cash flow costs** – depreciation and carrying amounts are accounting concepts, not actual cash flows and are not relevant costs

---

 Test your understanding 1

Which of the following is not a relevant cost/revenue?

A Variable costs

B Research and development costs that have already been incurred

C Incremental fixed costs

D Increase in sales revenue

1.4 Fixed and variable costs

It is usually assumed that a **variable cost** will be **relevant** to a decision as when activity increases the total variable cost incurred increases. There is a direct relationship between production activity and variable costs. However there are some situations where this may not be true.

Example 1

A company is considering a short-term pricing decision for a contract that would use 1,000 kg of material A. There are 800 kg of material A in inventory, which was bought some time ago for £3 per kg. The material in inventory could be sold for £3.50 per kg. The current purchase price of material A is £4.50.

What is the relevant cost of material A for this contract?

Solution

The cost per kg of material is considered to be a variable cost but you also need to consider whether the cost is a future cost for it to be relevant.

The company has already got 800 kg in inventory so this does not need to be purchased. The £3 per kg is an old purchase price i.e. a past or historic cost so it is not relevant. The material would therefore be valued at the current re-sale value of £3.50 per kg.

The company will need to buy a further 200 kg to complete the contract. This would be valued at the current purchase price of £4.50.

The total relevant cost of material A is:

$$800 \text{ kg} \times £3.50 = £2,800$$
$$200 \text{ kg} \times £4.50 = £900$$
$$\text{Total} = £3,700$$

Unless told otherwise variable costs and the variable element of the semi-variable costs are relevant to a decision.

Fixed costs tend to come under the umbrella of committed costs so are not relevant. Be careful though because if the fixed cost were to step up as a direct result of a decision taken then the extra cost would be relevant as it is an incremental cost.

Example 2

MCL Plc absorbs overheads on a machine hour rate, currently £20 per hour, of which £7 is for variable overheads and £13 is for fixed **overheads. The company is deciding whether to undertake a contract in** the coming year. If the contract is accepted it is estimated that the fixed costs will increase by £3,200 for the duration.

What are the relevant overhead costs for this decision?

Solution

The variable cost per hour is relevant as this cost would be avoidable of the contract were not undertaken. The relevant cost is therefore £7 per machine hour.

The fixed cost per hour is an absorption rate. This is not an indication of how much actual overheads would increase by. The £3,200 extra fixed cost is relevant as it is an incremental or extra cost.

With regards short-term decision making we assume that on the whole **fixed costs** are **non-relevant** costs so we can approach decisions using the **marginal costing technique.**

2 Cost-volume-profit (CVP) analysis

2.1 Introduction

Cost volume profit analysis looks at the link between costs, levels of activity and profits generated. It is used to make short term decisions and answer questions such as:

- how many units do we need to sell to make a certain profit?

- how many units do we need to sell to cover our costs?

- by how much will profit fall if the price is lowered by £1?

- what will happen to our profits if we rent an extra factory but find that we can operate at only half capacity?

2.2 The approach to CVP analysis

CVP analysis makes a number of assumptions as follows.

- Costs are assumed to be either **fixed** or **variable**, or at least **separable into these elements**.

- Fixed costs remain fixed throughout the activity range charted.

- Variable costs change in direct proportion to volume.

- Economies or diseconomies of scale are ignored; this ensures that **the variable cost per unit is constant**.

- Selling prices do not change with volume.

- Efficiency and productivity do not change with volume.

- It is applied to a single product or static mix of products.

- We look at the effect a change in volume has on **contribution** (not profit). Therefore we use **marginal costing**.

- Volume is the only factor affecting cost.

- **Contribution per unit** = selling price per unit – total variable cost per unit.

While some of the assumptions may seem unrealistic, over the short-term considered, they are often a **reasonable approximation** of the true position.

There are a number of calculations and formulas that make up CVP analysis:

- Breakeven point
- Margin of safety
- Target profit
- Profit/volume ratio

You will need to learn these formulae for the exam.

2.3 Breakeven point

Definition

The **breakeven point** is the volume of sales at which neither a profit nor a loss is made.

When there is no profit or loss we can assume that total fixed costs equal total contribution:

Sales revenue – variable costs = total contribution – fixed costs = profit

- If profit is zero then total contribution must equal the fixed costs.
- Contribution per unit is constant therefore we can calculate the number of units required to break even as follows:

$$\text{Breakeven point (units)} = \frac{\text{Fixed cost}}{\text{Contribution/unit}}$$

When a company breaks even its total costs will equal total revenue. Calculating the breakeven point can be useful for management because it shows the minimum volume of sales which must be achieved to avoid making a loss in the period.

At break-even point, total contribution is just large enough to cover fixed costs.

Example 3

Rachel's product, the 'Steadyarm', sells for £50. It has a variable cost of £30 per unit. Rachel's total fixed costs are £40,000 per annum.

What is her breakeven point?

Solution

To break even we want just enough contribution to cover the total fixed costs of £40,000.

We therefore want total contribution of £40,000.

Each unit of sales gives contribution of £50 – £30 = £20.

Therefore the breakeven point in units:

$$= \frac{\text{Total fixed costs}}{\text{Contribution per unit}} = \frac{£40,000}{£20} = 2,000 \text{ units}$$

We can show that this calculation is correct as below.

	£
Total contribution (2,000 units × £20)	40,000
Total fixed costs	(40,000)
	————
Profit/loss	0
	————

Breakeven point can also be expressed in sales revenue terms. We know we have to sell 2,000 units to breakeven and we know the selling price is £50. The breakeven point in sales revenue is therefore £100,000.

	£
Sales revenue (2,000 units × £50)	100,000
Variable costs (2,000 units × £30)	(60,000)
	————
Total contribution	40,000
Total fixed costs	(40,000)
	————
Profit/loss	0
	————

2.4 Margin of safety

 Definition

The **margin of safety** is the amount by which the anticipated (budgeted) sales can fall before the business makes a loss.

The margin of safety is therefore the difference between budgeted sales volume and **break-even point**. It can be expressed in absolute units or relative percentage terms.

Margin of safety (units) = Budgeted sales units – Breakeven sales units

$$\text{Margin of safety (\%)} = \frac{\text{Budgeted sales units – Breakeven sales units}}{\text{Budgeted sales unit}} \times 100$$

Margin of safety is a useful analysis of business risk – look at what might happen to profit is actual sales volume is less than budgeted.

Example 4

Rachel's product, the 'Steadyarm', sells for £50. It has a variable cost of £30 per unit. Rachel's total fixed costs are £40,000 per annum. Rachel is expecting to achieve sales of 2,500 units.

What is her margin of safety?

Solution

To calculate the margin of safety we first need to know the breakeven point in units. From the previous example we know that for Rachel to breakeven she needs to sell 2,000 units.

$$= \frac{\text{Total fixed costs}}{\text{Contribution per unit}} = \frac{£40,000}{£20} = 2,000 \text{ units}$$

We can then work out the margin of safety in units:

= Budgeted sales units – Breakeven sales units

= 2,500 – 2,000 = 500 units

And then the margin of safety as a percentage of budgeted sales units

$$= \frac{\text{Budgeted sales units} - \text{Breakeven sales units}}{\text{Budgeted sales unit}} \times 100$$

$$= \frac{2,500 - 2,000}{2,500} \times 100 = 20\%$$

Margin of safety can also be expressed in sales revenue terms. In the example above we know we have a margin of safety of 500 units and the selling price for each of these units is £50. The sales revenue margin of safety is therefore £25,000.

2.5 Achieving a target profit

A similar approach to the breakeven point calculation can be used to find the **sales volume at which a particular profit is made**.

When calculating the breakeven point we wanted to find the number of units that would mean that contribution equalled fixed costs, i.e. zero profit. Now if we know the required profit we can add this to the fixed costs to find the amount of contribution we need to cover both the fixed costs and to generate the required profit.

Sales volume to achieve a particular profit:

$$= \frac{\text{Total fixed costs} + \text{required profit}}{\text{Contribution/unit}}$$

Example 5

Information as in Rachel example above but we now want to know how many units must be sold to make a profit of £12,000.

To achieve a profit of £12,000, we require sufficient contribution firstly to cover the fixed costs (£40,000) and secondly, to give a profit of £12,000. Therefore our required contribution is £52,000.

$$= \frac{\text{Total fixed costs} + \text{required profit}}{\text{Contribution/unit}}$$

$$= \frac{£40,000 + £12,000}{£20}$$

$$= 2,600 \text{ units}$$

We can show that this is the case with a summarised statement of profit or loss account.

	£
Sales revenue (2,600 × £50)	130,000
Variable cost (2,600 × £30)	(78,000)
Total fixed costs	(40,000)
Profit	12,000

A required profit could also be achieved by changing the **selling price** rather than the sales volume.

Example 6

Information as in Rachel example above but we now want to know how much the sales price needs to change to be able to make a profit of £12,000.

To achieve a profit of £12,000, we require sufficient contribution firstly to cover the fixed costs (£40,000) and secondly, to give a profit of £12,000. Therefore our required contribution is £52,000.

This means that the contribution per unit needs to be:

$$= \frac{\text{Total fixed costs} + \text{required profit}}{\text{Budgeted sales volume}}$$

$$= \frac{£40,000 + £12,000}{2,500}$$

= £20.80

This means that contribution needs to increase from £20 to £20.80 – an increase of £0.80. To do this the sales price can be increased by £0.80 to £50.80.

We can show that this is the case with a summarised statement of profit or loss account.

	£
Sales revenue (2,500 × £50.80)	127,000
Variable cost (2,500 × £30)	(75,000)
Total fixed costs	(40,000)
Profit	12,000

Test your understanding 2

Product	Batman	Robin
Budgeted sales and production	500,000	750,000
Machine hours required	1,000,000	3,750,000
Sales revenue (£)	5,000,000	9,000,000
Direct materials (£)	1,000,000	2,250,000
Direct labour (£)	1,250,000	2,625,000
Variable overheads (£)	1,500,000	1,500,000
Fixed Costs £	1,000,000	2,450,000

The latest sales forecast is that 480,000 units of Product Batman and 910,000 units of Product Robin will be sold during the year.

Complete the table below to calculate the following:

(i) budgeted breakeven sales, in units, for each of the two products

(ii) the margin of safety (in units) for each of the two products

(iii) the margin of safety as a percentage (to two decimal places)

(iv) If only Robins were made how many would be needed to make a profit of £280,000? (assume fixed costs are product specific).

Product	Batman	Robin
Fixed costs (£)		
Unit contribution (£)		
Breakeven sales (units)		
Forecast sales (units)		
Margin of safety (units)		
Margin of safety (%)		
Target profit (units)		

✍ Test your understanding 3

A business has a contract with a customer to produce 4,000 units of product.

Revenues and costs for 4,000 units are shown below.

Possible production level	4,000 units
	£
Sales revenue	50,000
Variable and semi-variable costs:	
Material	2,000
Labour	4,000
Overheads	6,000
Fixed costs:	
Indirect labour	12,000
Overheads	8,000
Target profit for contract	20,000

The labour cost is a semi-variable cost. The fixed cost is £2,000 and the variable cost is £0.50 per unit.

Use the table below to calculate the required number of units for this contract to achieve its target profit. Enter the contribution per unit to two decimal places.

Calculation of required number of units	£
Fixed costs	
Target profit	
Fixed cost and target profit	
Sales revenue	
Variable costs	
Contribution	
Contribution per unit	
Required number of units to achieve target profit	

2.6 Profit/Volume ratio

 Definition

The **P/V ratio** is a measure of the rate at which profit (or, strictly, contribution) is generated with sales volume, as measured by revenue.

An alternative name which provides a more accurate description is the **contribution/sales (C/S)** ratio.

$$\text{P/V ratio} = \frac{\text{Contribution per unit}}{\text{Selling price per unit}} \text{ or } \frac{\text{Total contribution}}{\text{Total revenue}}$$

It tells us what **proportion or percentage of the selling price is contributing to our fixed overhead and profits.**

If, for example, the P/V ratio was 40% this would mean that 40% of the selling price was contribution which means therefore that the remaining 60% is variable cost.

It can be **used in the breakeven point and the target profit** calculations to be able to calculate the answer **in terms of sales value** (rather than volume).

$$\text{Breakeven point in sales value} = \frac{\text{Total fixed costs}}{\text{P/V ratio}}$$

$$\text{Sales value giving a profit £X} = \frac{\text{Total fixed costs} + \text{required profit}}{\text{P/V ratio}}$$

When using the P/V ratio in calculations the **decimal format** is used rather than the percentage i.e. 0.4 rather than 40%.

 Example 7

We return to the 'Steadyarm' example, where the product sells for £50, has a variable cost of £30 per unit and fixed costs and £40,000 per annum.

What value of sales revenue will give a profit of £12,000?

Sales value giving profit £12,000 means that the required contribution is £52,000.

$$= \frac{\text{Total fixed costs} + \text{required profit}}{\text{P/V ratio}}$$

$$= \frac{£40,000 + £12,000}{0.4 \text{ (W)}}$$

$$= £130,000$$

This corresponds with 2,600 units (as before) at £50 sales value per unit.

Working:

$$\text{P/V ratio} = \frac{\text{Contribution}}{\text{Selling price}} = \frac{£20}{£50} = 0.4$$

 Test your understanding 4

Camilla makes a single product, the Wocket. During 20Y1 she plans to make and sell 3,500 Wockets and has estimated the following:

	Per unit £
Selling price	16
Material	4
Labour	6
Variable overhead	2

Total fixed costs are budgeted to be £12,000

Target profit £150,000

(a) Calculate the contribution per unit earned by each Wocket.

(b) Calculate the P/V ratio

(c) Calculate Camilla's breakeven point in units.

(d) Calculate Camilla's breakeven point in revenue.

(e) Calculate Camilla's margin of safety in units

(f) Calculate Camilla's margin of safety in revenue

(g) Calculate Camilla's margin of safety as a percentage of budgeted sales (2 decimal places)

(h) Calculate the sales revenue that Camilla would require to meet her target profit.

Test your understanding 5

DH is considering the purchase of a bar/restaurant which is available for £130,000. He has estimated that the weekly fixed costs will be as follows:

	£
Business rates	125
Electricity	75
Insurances	60
Gas	45
Depreciation	125
Telephone	50
Advertising	40
Postage and stationery	20
Motor expenses	20
Cleaning	10

The contribution to sales ratio is 60%.

The weekly breakeven sales value of the business is:

A   £800

B   £970

C   £850

D   £950

3 CVP charts

3.1 Breakeven charts

We can show our analysis diagrammatically in a breakeven chart.

Breakeven chart showing fixed and variable cost lines

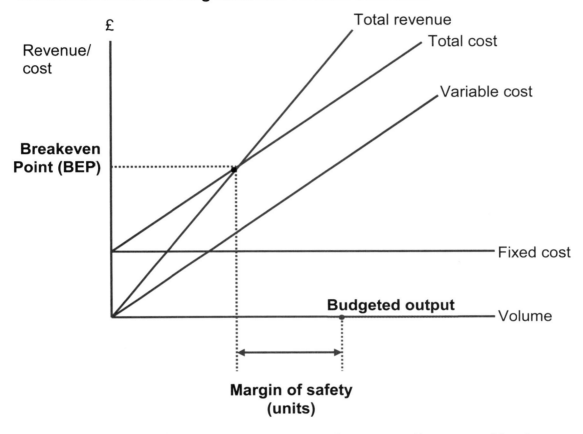

Break-even point is where total revenues and costs are the same. At sales volumes below this point there will be a loss and above this point a profit. The amount of profit or loss can be read off the chart as the difference between the total revenue and cost lines.

The margin of safety is the difference between budgeted sales volume and breakeven sales volume.

To make the diagram clearer we can show it with only the total cost line on the graph.

Breakeven chart showing total cost line

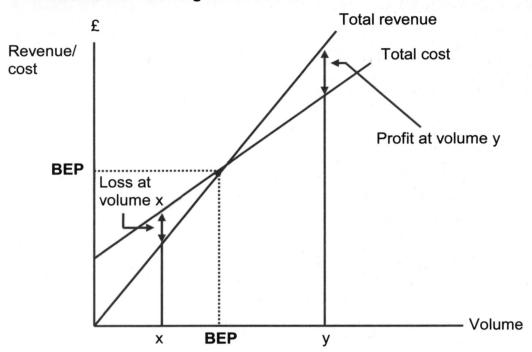

 Test your understanding 6

APSTEL Limited

The following information relates to a month's production of APSTEL Limited, a small manufacturing company mass producing a single product.

Materials per unit	£4
Labour per unit	£6
Selling price per unit	£17
Planned level of sales per month	7,000 units

Required:

(a) Read off an approximate breakeven point in sales value and units.

(b) Calculate the breakeven point in units using the formula.

(c) Calculate the margin of safety as a percentage of budgeted sales.

(d) Calculate how many units APSTEL would have to sell if they required a profit of £100,000?

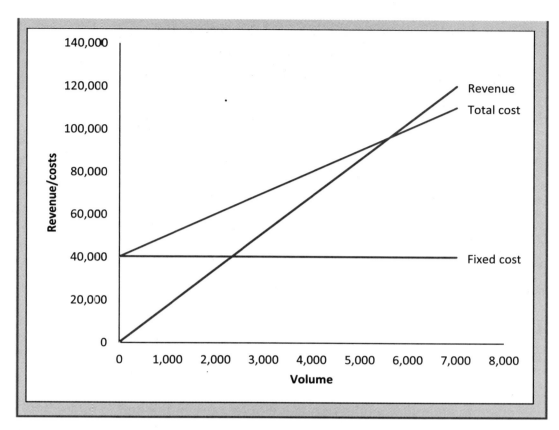

3.2 Profit-volume (P/V) chart

Break-even charts show both costs and revenues over a given range of activity but it is not easy to identify exactly what the loss or profit is at each volume of sales. A graph that shows the profit or loss at any given activity is called a profit/volume chart. Given the assumptions of constant selling price and variable unit costs at all volumes of output, the profit volume chart shows profit or loss as a straight line.

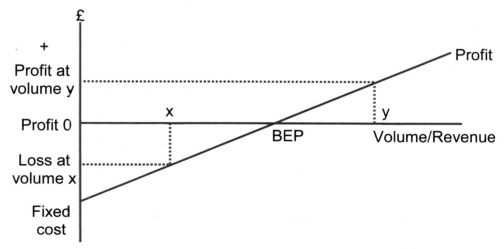

Note that at a **sales volume of nil**, the **total loss** will be the same as the business's **fixed costs**.

4 Limiting factors analysis

4.1 Introduction

Often the only factor stopping a business from increasing its profits is sales demand. However, situations sometimes arise when a resource is in short supply, and a business cannot make enough units to meet sales demand.

A resource in short supply is called a limiting factor, because it sets a limit on what can be achieved by an organisation.

Typically a scarce resource could be a limited availability of material, labour, machine time or cash may be in short supply.

4.2 Identifying a scarce resource

To identify a scarce resource, it is necessary to:

- Obtain estimates of sales demand

- Obtain estimates of the quantities of resources needed to make the units to meet the sales demand

- From these estimates, calculate how many units of each resource will be needed

- For each resource, compare the amount needed with the amount available

- If the amount needed exceeds the amount available, the resource is in short supply and so is a limiting factor.

Example 8

A company wishes to make 2,500 units in a month. Each unit requires 5 kgs of material. There is currently a shortage of material and the company can only access 10,000 kg.

How many units can the company actually make?

Maximum production would require 12,500 kg of material but there is only 10,000 kg available.

This means that production would be limited to 2,000 units (10,000 kg/ 5 kg per unit)

When a business has a limiting factor, a decision must be taken about how the available resources should be used. If more than one product is being produced then a procedure called **Limiting factor analysis** or Key factor analysis is used to calculate the **optimum product mix to maximise contribution**.

Limiting factor analysis is used if only **one** of the **resources is limited**.

4.3 Approach to limiting factor analysis

There is a step by step process to completing limiting factor analysis

- **Determine the resource that is in scarce supply** (the limiting factor), by multiplying the maximum demand for each product by the amount of the resources it requires. Compare this to what is available.

- **Calculate the contribution per unit** generated by each type of product we want to make.

- For each product divide the contribution per unit by the number of units of scarce resource needed to make one unit of that product (**contribution per limiting factor**).

- **Rank the products** from highest contribution per limiting factor to lowest contribution per limiting factor.

- **Allocate the scarce resource** to the product ranked 1 and calculate how much of the scarce resource this would use to produce the required demand.

- If there is any scarce resource remaining, follow the previous step for the product ranked 2 and so on until there is not enough scarce resource to match the demand for a product.

- Calculate how much of the remaining product can be produced with the remaining scarce resource.

- Calculate the total contribution from the new production plan and the overall profit.

Example 9

Truffle Ltd

Truffle Ltd makes 3 products the Dog, the Hound and the Canine. The money available to pay for the resources needed for next month's production is as follows:

Material £10,000
Labour £10,000
Variable overheads £15,000

Below are the details for a unit each product:

	Dog	Hound	Canine
	£	£	£
Selling price	10	12	15
Material cost	2	3	2
Labour cost	1	3	4
Other variable costs	2	4	4
Maximum monthly demand	1,000	1,500	1,250

Total fixed costs £9,000

What is Truffle's optimal production plan for the next month?

Solution

Step 1 – identify the limiting factor

To be able to meet the maximum demand for all the products the requirements would be as follows:

Material = (2 × 1000) + (3 × 1500) + (2 × 1250) = £9,000
Labour = (1 × 1000) + (3 × 1500) + (4 × 1250) = £10,500
Other variable costs = (2 × 1000) + (4 × 1500) + (4 × 1250) = £13,000

Therefore the labour cost is the limiting factor as there is enough cash available to cover the cost of materials and other variable costs.

Step 2 – calculate the contribution per unit

	Dog	Hound	Canine
	£	£	£
Selling price	10	12	15
Material cost	(2)	(3)	(2)
Labour cost	(1)	(3)	(4)
Other variable costs	(2)	(4)	(4)
Contribution per unit	5	2	5

Step 3 – calculate the contribution per limiting factor

	Dog	Hound	Canine
	£	£	£
Contribution per unit	5	2	5
Limiting factor per unit (labour cost per unit)	1	3	4
Contribution per limiting factor	5	0.66	1.25

Step 4 – rank the products

	Dog	Hound	Canine
	£	£	£
Contribution per limiting factor	5	0.66	1.25
Rank	1	3	2

Steps 5 to 8 – allocate the scarce supply

Product in rank order	Units	LF per unit	Total LF	Contribution
		£	£	£
Dog	1,000	1	1,000	5,000
Canine	1,250	4	5,000	6,250
Hound	1,333 (W)	3	4,000β	2,666
LF available			£10,000	
Total contribution				13,916
Less fixed costs				(9,000)
Profit				4,916

Working:

There is only £4,000 left to spend on labour once maximum demand is allocated to the other products (β = balancing amount). This means that Truffle will be able to make 1,333 complete Hounds (4,000/3 = 1,333.33).

Test your understanding 7

ABC

ABC makes three products with the following estimated costs and revenues.

	A	B	C
Selling price (£)	20	25	30
Variable cost per unit (£)	10	11	14
Amount of material X used per unit (kg)	2	2	4
Maximum demand (units)	250	100	200

Total fixed costs £1,250

Due to a shortage in the market, only 800 kg are available.

Using limiting factor analysis complete the table below to determine the production plan that will optimise profit

	A	**B**	**C**
Selling price (£)			
Variable cost per unit (£)			
Contribution per unit (£)			
LF per unit (kg)			
Contribution per LF (£)			
Rank			

Production plan

Product in rank order	Units	LF per unit (kg)	Total LF (kg)	Contribution (£)
1				
2				
3				
		Total LF	800 kg	
			Total Contribution	
			Fixed costs	
			Profit	

Test your understanding 8

Dunnsports

Dunnsports make a variety of sports goods. One of its product groups is cricket boots and they make a range of three styles. You are given the following data for the forthcoming quarter.

	Gower	**Boycott**	**Willis**
Selling price	£27.50	£30.00	£28.50
Direct material	£8.00	£8.50	£8.25
Direct labour at £7.50 per hour	£9.00	£9.75	£8.25
Forecast sales/production	500	510	520

Shortly after the budgeted output was agreed a machine breakdown occurred and, as parts are not available immediately, labour hours will be limited to 1,540 hours.

Required:

Complete the table below to calculate the production schedule that will optimise profit, assuming that the actual sales per product will not exceed the forecast figures quoted.

	Gower	**Boycott**	**Willis**
Selling price (£)			
Variable cost per unit (£)			
Contribution per unit (£)			
LF per unit (hours)			
Contribution per LF (£)			
Rank			

Product in rank order	**Units**	**LF per unit (hours)**	**Total LF (hours)**	**Contribution (£)**
1				
2				
3				
		Total LF	1,540	
			Total Contribution	

Test your understanding 9

Naturo

Naturo Limited can synthesise a natural plant extract called Ipethin into one of three products. Ipethin is in short supply and the company at present is able to obtain only 1,000 kgs per period at a cost of £25 per kg.

The budgeted costs and other data for a typical period are as follows:

	Product F	Product G	Product H
Kg of Ipethin per unit	1.4	0.96	2.6
Labour hours per unit (£8 per hour)	3	8	4
Selling price per unit	£110	£150	£180
Maximum demand (units)	200	400	300

Fixed costs are £25,000 per period.

Task

Determine the preferred order of manufacture in order to maximise profit.

	F	G	H
Selling price (£)			
Variable cost per unit (£)			
Contribution per unit (£)			
LF per unit (kg)			
Contribution per LF (£)			
Rank			

Production plan

Product in rank order	Units	LF per unit (kg)	Total LF (kg)	Contribution (£)
1				
2				
3				
		Total LF	1,000 kg	
			Total Contribution	
			Fixed costs	
			Profit	

Test your understanding 10

Triproduct Limited makes and sells three types of electronic security systems for which the following information is available.

Expected cost and selling prices per unit:

Product	Day scan	Night scan	Omni scan
	£	£	£
Materials	70	110	155
Manufacturing labour	40	55	70
Installation labour	24	32	44
Variable overheads	16	20	28
Selling price	250	320	460

Fixed costs for the period are £450,000 and the installation labour, which is highly skilled, is available for 25,000 hours only in a period and is paid £8 per hour.

Both manufacturing and installation labour are variable costs.

The maximum demand for the products is:

Day scan	Night scan	Omni scan
2,000 units	3,000 units	1,800 units

Determine the best production plan, assuming that Triproduct Limited wishes to maximise profit.

	Day	Night	Omni
Selling price (£)			
Variable cost per unit (£)			
Contribution per unit (£)			
LF per unit (hrs)			
Contribution per LF (£)			
Rank			

Production plan

Product in rank order	Units	LF per unit (hr)	Total LF (hr)	Contribution (£)
1				
2				
3				
		Total LF	25,000 hr	
			Total Contribution	
			Fixed costs	
			Profit	

 Test your understanding 11

Burma Limited manufactures two products: Alfie and Boris. Details about the products are as follows.

Sales price and costs per unit	Alfie	Boris
Sales price	£16.20	£22.80
Direct materials	£4.00	£6.00
Direct labour	£2.00	£4.00
Fixed production overheads per unit based on labour hour	£3.00	£6.00
Variable selling costs	£0.50	£0.50
Maximum sales units	10,000 units	15,000 units

Direct materials cost £2 per kilo, and direct labour costs £10 per hour.

In the coming year it is expected that the supply of labour will be limited to 4,000 hours.

Fixed production overhead rates have been calculated using the maximum expected number of labour hours available in the coming period.

State how many units of each product Burma Limited should produce in order to maximise profit.

	Alfie	**Boris**
Selling price (£)		
Variable cost per unit (£)		
Contribution per unit (£)		
LF per unit (hrs)		
Contribution per LF (£)		
Rank		

Production plan

Product in rank order	Units	LF per unit (hr)	Total LF (hr)	Contribution (£)
1				
2				
		Total LF	4,000 hr	
			Total Contribution	
			Fixed costs	
			Profit	

5 Summary

In this chapter we have considered the approaches required to make short-term decisions about operating levels. CVP analysis recognises that changes in profit arise from changes in contribution which, in turn, is directly related to activity levels. Thus, we can use contribution per unit to calculate the required activity level to achieve a particular profit level, including zero (breakeven point). The formulae are not provided in the exam so make sure you have learnt them.

Breakeven point in units

$$\frac{\text{Fixed cost}}{\text{Contribution/unit}}$$

Sales volume to achieve a particular profit

$$\frac{\text{Total fixed costs} + \text{required profit}}{\text{Contribution/unit}}$$

If we **know the breakeven point**, then we can also calculate the margin of safety.

Margin of safety (units)

> Budgeted sales units – Breakeven sales units

Margin of safety (%)

$$\frac{\text{Budgeted sales units} - \text{breakeven sales units}}{\text{Budgeted sales units}} \times 100\%$$

Profit/Volume ratio or C/S ratio

$$\frac{\text{Contribution per unit}}{\text{Selling price}}$$

Breakeven point in sales revenue terms (£)

$$\frac{\text{Fixed cost}}{\text{C/S ratio}}$$

Sales revenue (£) to achieve a particular profit

$$\frac{\text{Total fixed costs} + \text{required profit}}{\text{C/S ratio}}$$

Key factor analysis is a technique that we can use when we have a resource (materials, labour or machine time, for example) that is in short supply. Scarce resources should be allocated between products on the basis of the contribution that they earn per unit of scarce resource.

Test your understanding answers

 ## Test your understanding 1

B   Research and development costs that have **already been incurred.**

This is a sunk cost and not relevant to a future decision.

 ## Test your understanding 2

Product	Batman	Robin
Fixed costs (£)	1,000,000	2,450,000
Unit contribution (£)	2.50	3.50
Breakeven sales (units)	400,000	700,000
Forecast sales (units)	480,000	910,000
Margin of safety (units)	80,000	210,000
Margin of safety (%)	16.67%	23.08%
Target profit (units)		780,000

Unit contribution

Calculate the revenue and each variable cost per unit based on budget. Sales revenue less variable costs = contribution

Batman   £10 − (2 + 2.50 + 3) = £2.50

Robin   £12 − (3 + 3.5 + 2) = £3.50

Target profit

$$\frac{2,450,000 + 280,000}{£3.50} = 780,000 \text{ units of Robin}$$

Test your understanding 3

Calculation of required number of units	£
Fixed costs (12,000 + 8,000 + 2,000)	22,000
Target profit	20,000
Fixed cost and target profit	42,000
Sales revenue	50,000
Variable costs (2,000 + (4,000 × 0.5) + 6,000)	10,000
Contribution	40,000
Contribution per unit	10.00
Required number of units to achieve target profit	4,200

Test your understanding 4

(a) **Contribution per unit**

= Selling price per unit – Variable cost per unit

= £16 – £12 = **£4**

(b) **P/V ratio**

PV ratio = 4/16 = **0.25**

(c) **Breakeven point (units)**

= Total fixed costs/Contribution per unit

= £12,000/£4 = **3,000 units**

(d) **Breakeven point (revenue)**

= Breakeven point (units) × sales revenue per unit

= 3,000 units × £16 = **£48,000**

(e) **Margin of safety (units)**

= budgeted sales – breakeven point

= 3,500 – 3,000 = **500 units**

KAPLAN PUBLISHING

(f) **Margin of safety (revenue)**

= margin of safety (units) × sales revenue per unit

= 500 × £16 = **£8,000**

(g) **Margin of safety (%)**

= (budgeted sales − breakeven point)/budgeted sales × 100%

= (3,500 − 3,000)/3,500 × 100% = **14.29%**

(h) **Sales revenue to meet the target profit.**

(£12,000 + £150,000)/0.25 = **£648,000**

 Test your understanding 5

D   £950

Weekly fixed costs are £570; C/S ratio is 0.6 therefore weekly breakeven sales £570/0.6 = £950.

 Test your understanding 6

(a) **Breakeven point from graph**

Approx £97,000 sales and 5,700 units.

(b) **Breakeven point in units**

$$\frac{\text{Fixed cost}}{\text{Contribution/unit}}$$

$$= \frac{£40,000}{£7}$$

= **5,715 units (rounding up)**

(c) **Margin of safety (%)**

$$\frac{\text{Budgeted sales units} - \text{breakeven sales units}}{\text{Budgeted sales units}} \times 100$$

$$= \frac{7,000 - 5715}{7,000} \times 100$$

= **18.36%**

(d) **Target profit**

$$\frac{\text{Total fixed costs} + \text{required profit}}{\text{C/S ratio}}$$

$$= \frac{140,000}{7}$$

= 20,000 units

Test your understanding 7

	A	B	C
Selling price (£)	20	25	30
Variable cost per unit (£)	10	11	14
Contribution per unit	10	14	16
LF per unit (kg)	2	2	4
Contribution per LF (£)	5	7	4
Ranking	2	1	3

Product in rank order	Units	LF per unit (kg)	Total LF (kg)	Contribution (£)
1 B	100	2	200	1,400
2 A	250	2	500	2,500
3 C	25	4	100 β	400
		Total LF	800 kg	
			Total Contribution	4,300
			Fixed costs	(1,250)
			Profit	3,050

Test your understanding 8

	Gower	Boycott	Willis
Selling price (£)	27.50	30.00	28.50
Variable cost per unit (£)	17.00	18.25	16.50
Contribution per unit (£)	10.50	11.75	12.00
LF per unit (hours) (W)	1.2	1.3	1.1
Contribution per LF (£)	8.75	9.04	10.91
Rank	3	2	1

Product in rank order	Units	LF per unit (hours)	Total LF (hours)	Contribution (£)
1 Willis	520	1.1	572	6,240
2 Boycott	510	1.3	663	5,992.50
3 Gower	254	1.2	305 β	2,667
		Total LF	1,540	
			Total Contribution	14,899.50

Working: LF per unit

Labour charge per unit/Labour charge per hour

Gower £9.00/£7.50 = 1.2 hours per unit

Test your understanding 9

	Product		
	F	*G*	*H*
	£	£	£
Selling price	110	150	180
Ipethin (material)	(35)	(24)	(65)
Labour	(24)	(64)	(32)
Contribution	51	62	83
Limiting factor (kg of Ipethin)	1.4	0.96	2.6
Contribution per unit of limiting factor	£36.43	£64.58	£31.92
Preferred order of manufacture	2	1	3

Best production plan

	Units	kg used
G to maximum demand	400 (× 0.96)	384
F to maximum demand	200 (× 1.4)	280

This leaves (1,000 – 384 – 280) = 336 kg for H

Therefore production of C = $\dfrac{336}{2.6}$ = 129 units

	F	G	H	Total
Units	200	400	129	
	£	£	£	£
Contribution	10,200	24,800	10,707	45,707
Fixed costs				(25,000)
Maximum profit				20,707

KAPLAN PUBLISHING

Test your understanding 10

	Day scan £	Night scan £	Omni scan £
Selling price	250	320	460
Variable costs	(150)	(217)	(297)
Contribution per unit	100	103	163
Installation hours required	3	4	5.5
Contribution per installation hour	£33.33	£25.75	£29.64
Production priority	1st	3rd	2nd

Best production plan

	Units	Hours used
Day scan to maximum demand	2,000 (× 3)	6,000
Omni scan to maximum demand	1,800 (× 5.5)	9,900

This leaves (25,000 – 6,000 – 9,900) = 9,100 installation labour hours for Night scan.

Therefore production of Night scan = $\dfrac{9,100}{4}$ = 2,275 units

	Day scan	Omni scan	Night scan	Total
Units	2,000	1,800	2,275	
	£	£	£	£
Contribution	200,000	293,400	234,325	727,725
Fixed costs				(450,000)
Maximum profit				277,725

Test your understanding 11

	Alfie	Boris
Selling price (£)	16.20	22.80
Variable cost per unit (£)	6.50	10.50
Contribution per unit (£)	9.70	12.30
LF per unit (hrs)	0.2	0.4
Contribution per LF (£)	48.50	30.75
Rank	1	2

Product in rank order	Units	LF per unit (hr)	Total LF (hr)	Contribution (£)
1 Alfie	10,000	0.2	2,000	97,000
2 Boris	5,000	0.4	2,000	61,500
		Total LF	4,000 hr	
			Total Contribution	158,500
			Fixed costs	60,000 (W1)
			Profit	98,500

Working:

(W1) **Fixed production overheads**

Using (say) product A: fixed overheads per unit = £3; Labour hours per unit = 0.2.

Thus fixed overheads per hour = £3/0.2 = £15.

Maximum hours available = 4,000.

Fixed production overheads budgeted at 4,000 × £15 = £60,000.

Long-term decision making

Introduction

In this chapter the focus is on long-term investment decisions – usually lasting **more than one year**. This could vary from the decision to build a new factory to whether or not to discontinue a product range.

The investment appraisal techniques that are discussed in this chapter are payback period, net present cost, net present value and internal rate of return.

ASSESSMENT CRITERIA	CONTENTS
Use long-term future income and costs (5.3)	1 Long-term investments
	2 Investment appraisal and cash flows
– Payback	3 Payback period
– Discounted cash flow	4 Discounting
– Internal rate of return	5 Net present value/cost
	6 Internal rate of return

1 Long-term investments

1.1 Introduction

The key characteristic of a capital investment project is the tying up of capital for a number of years, or for the long term, in order to earn profits or returns over the period.

1.2 What will the capital be invested in?

The most common investment you will encounter will be in **tangible non-current assets**, such as a new machine, factory or premises from which to operate a new service business.

Other intangible forms of investment include **research and development**, **patent rights or goodwill** obtained on the purchase of an existing business.

1.3 What form will the returns take?

The purchase of a new non-current asset will often be with the intention of starting a new line of business – say the manufacturing of a new product, or the provision of a new or extended service. The returns will be the **net income** generated by the new business.

Alternatively, the investment may be to benefit the existing operations, such that **sales are increased** (where existing products/services are improved technologically or in quality) or **costs are reduced** (where production processes are updated or personnel reorganised). The returns will be measured as the **increase in net income or net reduction in costs** resulting from the investment.

1.4 Authorisation for a capital project

For projects involving a significant amount of capital investment, **authorisation** will be required. This authorisation will usually be given by the main board, or a sub-committee formed from the board for this purpose. Smaller projects (such as the replacement of an existing machine) may be within the authorisation limits of the manager of the area of business involved.

1.5   Importance of non-financial factors

Although these appraisal methods will usually give a basis for a **recommendation as to whether or not the project should be accepted,** they will only be able to take account of monetary costs and benefits. **Qualitative factors** will also need to be considered when reaching a final decision – such as possible effects on staff morale (for example, if the project involves increased automation or considerable overtime), the environment, customer satisfaction and the business's status/reputation.

2   Investment appraisal and cash flows

2.1   Introduction

Any potential investment will need to be evaluated with regards the costs and revenues that will occur i.e. the net cash flow received from the investment activity. This will involve estimating the cash flows for sales, costs, capital expenditure and disposal proceeds.

As with short term decision making it is important to ensure that the calculations are made knowing as much detail as possible or that any assumptions are stated. This will maintain the integrity of the information and should demonstrate professional competence.

2.2   The cash flows under consideration

When estimating future cash flows we want to identify what difference the project will make therefore we only consider **future incremental cash** flows to be relevant, e.g. if a new machine was to be purchased, the factory rent may be unaffected so would not need to be included when assessing the investment, but the purchase cost of the new machine is relevant so would be included.

As well as knowing what the future cash flows will be, we also need to know when they will occur. The time the investment starts is called time or year 0 or t = 0. Subsequent future cash flows are assumed to happen at year-ends, e.g. all of the sales revenues and costs for the first year are assumed to be paid at the end of the first year this is called time or year 1 or t = 1.

If we do this for all the future cash flows of the project, then we will typically end up with a table like the following:

	t = 0 £000	Year 1 (t = 1) £000	Year 2 (t = 2) £000	Year 3 (t = 3) £000	Year 4 (t = 4) £000	Year 5 (t = 5) £000
Initial Investment	(100)					
Scrap value						30
Sales revenues		40	50	60	50	40
Variable costs		(10)	(12)	(15)	(13)	(11)
Net cash flow	(100)	30	38	45	37	59

2.3 Methods of capital investment appraisal

Capital investment appraisal is an analysis of the expected financial returns from a capital project over its expected life. There are several methods of carrying out a capital expenditure appraisal such as:

- Payback
- Net present value method of discounted cash flow
- Internal rate of return method of discounted cash flow

3 Payback period

3.1 Calculation

Definition

The **payback period** is the length of time a project takes to recoup the initial money invested in it. This is the time which elapses until the invested capital is recovered.

Payback is commonly used as an initial screening method, and projects that meet the payback period are then evaluated using another investment appraisal method.

When the annual cash flows are constant, then the calculation is very straightforward e.g. if £100,000 is invested and £20,000 cash in received each year, then it will take 100/20 = 5 years to recover the investment cost.

However, if the annual cash flows vary, then we need to calculate the cumulative net position at the end of each year.

Example 1

A machine costs £100,000 now. We expect the following cash flows:

	Year 1 (t = 1) £000	Year 2 (t = 2) £000	Year 3 (t = 3) £000	Year 4 (t = 4) £000	Year 5 (t = 5) £000
Scrap value					30
Sales revenues	40	50	60	50	40
Variable costs	(10)	(12)	(15)	(13)	(11)

Calculate the payback period for the investment.

Solution

Time	Net cash flow £000	Cumulative position £000	Working to calculate the cumulative position
t = 0	(100)	(100)	
t = 1	30	(70)	(100) + 30
t = 2	38	(32)	(70) + 38
t = 3	45	13	(32) + 45
t = 4	37	50	13 + 37
t = 5	59	109	50 + 59

From this table we can see that the initial investment would be recovered sometime in the third year as this is when the cumulative position initially becomes positive.

If cash flows are assumed to occur at the end of each year the payback period would 3 years.

If we assume that cash flows accrue evenly through the year i.e. there is an equal amount of sales revenue each month and an equal amount of costs each month, we are then able to estimate at what point during the year break even occurs.

From the figures above we can see that the outstanding amount at the start of year 3 is £32,000 (*) and that during the third year there is a total of £45,000 (**) cash flow. See extract of table below:

Time	Net cash flow £000	Cumulative position £000
t = 2	38	**(32)***
t = 3	**45****	13

The payback period is therefore calculated as follows:

Calculate the cash flow per month

£45,000/12 = £3,750

Calculate how many months are needed to cover remaining investment

£32,000/£3,750 = 8.533 months

Payback is 2 years and 8½ months

This could also be calculated as follows:

$= 2 \frac{32}{45}$ or 2.71 years

0.71 of a year is 8½ months

Note: In the exam the payback period is rounded **up** to the nearest whole month. The payback period is therefore 2 years and 9 months.

The payback period is then compared with the target payback that has been set, e.g. this company may have decided only to accept projects with paybacks lower than four years, in which case this project is acceptable.

Test your understanding 1

A machine costs £100,000 now. We expect net cash flows of £30,000 in one year's time, £40,000 in two years' time, £60,000 in three years' time and £10,000 in four years' time.

Calculate the payback period for the investment by filling in the table below:

Time	Net cash flow £000	Cumulative cash flow £000
t = 0	(100)	
t = 1	30	
t = 2	40	
t = 3	60	
t = 4	10	

Payback is   years and   months.

 Test your understanding 2

Highscore Ltd manufactures cricket bats. They are considering investing £30,000 in a new delivery vehicle which will generate savings compared with sub-contracting out the delivery service. The vehicle will have a life of six years, with zero scrap value.

The accounting technician and the transport manager have prepared the following estimates relating to the savings.

The net cash flows from the project are:

Year	£
1	9,000
2	11,000
3	10,000
4	10,500
5	10,200
6	10,100

Calculate the payback period in year(s) and months.

3.2 Advantages of payback period

(a) It is simple to calculate.

(b) It is understandable for non-financial managers

(c) It is **less affected by uncertainty** as the cash flows that are being considered are earlier forecasts.

(d) It is very useful in specific circumstances such as when the company has **liquidity problems** i.e. if cash is only available for a limited length of time it provides an estimate of how long cash will be tied up in the investment for.

3.3 Disadvantages of payback period

(a) **Flows outside the payback period are ignored**. If we consider the previous example, if the cash flow in the fifth year had been £20,000 the payback period would be unaltered at 2 years 8½ months.

(b) The **timing of flows within the payback period** are ignored. If, again for the same example, the first two years' receipts had been:

1st year   £50,000

2nd year   £20,000

again the payback period would be unaltered at 2 years 8½ months.

(c) It **ignores the time value of money** i.e. the interest that capital can earn. We shall see the relevance of this in the next sections on discounted cash flow.

(d) It does not provide a monetary value for the return available from the investment.

4 Discounting

4.1 The time value of money

A key concept in long-term decision-making is that money received today is worth more than the same sum received in the future, i.e. it has a **time value.**

Suppose you were offered £100 now or £100 in one year's time. Even though the sums are the same, most people would prefer the money now. The £100 in the future is effectively worth less to us than £100 now – the timing of the cash makes a difference.

The main reasons for this are as follows:

- **Investment opportunities**: the £100 received now could be deposited into a bank account and earn interest. It would therefore grow to become worth more than £100 in one year.

- **Inflation**: the £100 now will buy more goods than £100 in one year due to inflation increasing the cost of goods.

- **Cost of capital**: the £100 received now could be used to reduce a loan or overdraft and save interest.

- **Risk**: the £100 now is more certain than the offer of money in the future.

To do calculations using the time value of money it needs to be expressed as an interest rate (often known as a cost of capital, a required return or a **discount rate**)

Suppose we felt that £100 now was worth the same to us as £110 offered in one year's time due to the factors above. We could say that our time value of money was estimated at 10% per annum.

Therefore £100 now is worth the same as £110 offered in one year. Alternatively we say that the £110 in one year has a present value of £100 now. This process of taking future cash flows and converting them into their equivalent present value now is called **discounting**.

To calculate the present value of any future cash flow we multiply the cash flow by a suitable discount factor (or present value factor):

Present value = future cash flow × discount factor

Discount factors are provided in the assessment so you do not need to be able to calculate them but you will need to know how to use them.

For example, with a 10% discount rate, the discount factor for a cash flow at t=1 is 0.909. Thus the offer of receiving £110 in one year's time is worth in today's terms

Present value = £110 × 0.909 = £99.99

The use of the discount rate enables more accurate prediction of the return an investment will give. Future incremental cash flows can be discounted to present values and the values can then be netted off against the initial investment to see what the overall return from the investment will be.

5 Net present value/cost

5.1 Net Present Value (NPV)

🔍 Definition

The net present value is the net benefit or loss of benefit in present value terms from an investment opportunity. The NPV represents the surplus funds earned on a project.

There is a step by step procedure for completing an NPV calculation:

Step 1 Calculate the future incremental net cash flows.

Step 2 Discount the net cash flows so they are in today's terms (present values).

Step 3 Add up the present values and add them to the initial investment out flow to give a net present value or NPV.

Step 4 If the NPV is positive, then it means that the cash inflows are worth more than the outflows and the project should be accepted.

💡 Example 2

A machine costs £100,000 now. We expect the following cash flows:

	Year 1 (t = 1) £000	Year 2 (t = 2) £000	Year 3 (t = 3) £000	Year 4 (t = 4) £000	Year 5 (t = 5) £000
Scrap value					30
Sales revenues	40	50	60	50	40
Variable costs	(10)	(12)	(15)	(13)	(11)

Calculate the net present value of the investment if a discount factor of 10% is used.

Solution

	t = 0 £000	Year 1 (t = 1) £000	Year 2 (t = 2) £000	Year 3 (t = 3) £000	Year 4 (t = 4) £000	Year 5 (t = 5) £000
Net cash flow	(100)	30	38	45	37	59
Discount factor at 10%	1.000	0.909	0.826	0.751	0.683	0.621
Present value	(100)	27.3	31.4	33.8	25.3	36.6

The Net Present Value = (100) + 27.3 + 31.4 + 33.8 + 25.3 + 36.6 = 54.4

The NPV = £54,400 positive, so the project should be undertaken.

📝 Test your understanding 3

A machine costs £80,000 to buy now. The predicted sales revenue and operating costs for the following 4 years are as follows:

Year	Sales revenue £	Operating cost £
1	40,000	20,000
2	70,000	20,000
3	80,000	40,000
4	90,000	80,000

The rate of interest applicable is 15%. Should we accept or reject the machine?

The relevant present value factors are:

	Year 1	Year 2	Year 3	Year 4
15%	0.870	0.756	0.658	0.572

	Year 0	Year 1	Year 2	Year 3	Year 4
Capital expenditure					
Sales revenues					
Operating costs					
Net cash flow					
PV Factor	1.000	0.870	0.756	0.658	0.572
Discounted cash flow					
Net present value					

The net present value is *positive/negative**
*delete as appropriate

 Test your understanding 4

Machine A costs £100,000, payable immediately. Machine B costs £120,000, half payable immediately and half payable in one year's time.

The net cash flows expected are as follows.

	A £	B £
at the end of 1 year	20,000	–
at the end of 2 years	60,000	60,000
at the end of 3 years	40,000	60,000
at the end of 4 years	30,000	80,000
at the end of 5 years	20,000	–

With interest at 5%, which machine should be selected?

The relevant present value factors are:

	Year 1	Year 2	Year 3	Year 4	Year 5
5%	0.952	0.907	0.864	0.823	0.784

Machine A

	Year 0	Year 1	Year 2	Year 3	Year 4	Year 5
Capital expenditure						
Net cash flow						
PV Factor	1.000	0.952	0.907	0.864	0.823	0.784
Discounted cash flow						
Net present value						

The net present value of Machine A is *positive/negative**
*delete as appropriate

Machine B

	Year 0	Year 1	Year 2	Year 3	Year 4	Year 5
Capital expenditure						
Net cash flow						
PV Factor	1.000	0.952	0.907	0.864	0.823	0.784
Discounted cash flow						
Net present value						

The net present value of machine B is *positive/negative**
*delete as appropriate

Machine *A/B** should be selected as it has the *higher/lower** NPV
*delete as appropriate

5.2 Net present cost

In some cases you may be asked to look at only the **operating costs** of an investment rather than the costs and revenues associated with the investment. In this case the step by step procedure is exactly the same but you will need to decide which investment is cheapest to run.

📝 Test your understanding 5

Machine A costs £100,000, payable immediately. Machine B costs £80,000, payable immediately. The running costs expected are as follows.

	A £	B £
at the end of 1 year	20,000	20,000
at the end of 2 years	50,000	30,000
at the end of 3 years	30,000	40,000
at the end of 4 years	20,000	50,000
at the end of 5 years	10,000	60,000

With interest at 8%, which machine should be selected?

The relevant present value factors are:

	Year 1	Year 2	Year 3	Year 4	Year 5
8%	0.926	0.857	0.794	0.735	0.681

Machine A

	Year 0	Year 1	Year 2	Year 3	Year 4	Year 5
Capital expenditure						
Net cash flow						
PV Factor	1.000	0.926	0.857	0.794	0.735	0.681
Discounted cash flow						
Net present cost						

Machine B

	Year 0	Year 1	Year 2	Year 3	Year 4	Year 5
Capital expenditure						
Net cash flow						
PV Factor	1.000	0.926	0.857	0.794	0.735	0.681
Discounted cash flow						
Net present cost						

Machine *A/B** should be selected as it has the *higher/lower** net present cost

*delete as appropriate

5.3 Advantages of NPV/NPC

(a) It considers the **time value of money**.

(b) It uses cash flows which are less subjective than profits. Profit measures rely on such things as depreciation and other policies which are to a certain extent subjective.

(c) It considers the **whole life** of the project.

(d) It provides a monetary value for the return from an investment.

5.4 Disadvantages of NPV/NPC

(a) Cash flows are future predictions and we are **unable to predict** the future with accuracy.

(b) Discounted cash flow as a concept is **more difficult** for a non-financial manager to understand.

(c) It may be difficult to **decide on which discount rate** to use when appraising a project.

Test your understanding 6

Whitby Engineering Factors are considering an investment in a new machine tool with an estimated useful life of five years.

The investment will require capital expenditure of £50,000 and the accounting technician has prepared the following estimates of cash flow over the five-year period:

Year	£
1	18,000
2	20,000
3	21,000
4	22,000
5	18,000

The firm's cost of capital is considered to be 12% and it uses this rate to appraise any future projects.

Required:

Prepare an appraisal of the project using the discounted cash flow (NPV method) technique and payback method

	Year 0	Year 1	Year 2	Year 3	Year 4	Year 5
Capital expenditure						
Net cash flow						
PV Factor	1.000	0.893	0.797	0.712	0.636	0.567
Discounted cash flow						
Net present value						

The net present value is *positive/negative**
delete as appropriate

The payback period is   Year(s) and   Months

Accept/reject* investment
delete as appropriate

KAPLAN PUBLISHING

Test your understanding 7

An investment project has the following expected cash flows over its three-year life span.

Year	Cash flow
	£
0	(285,400)
1	102,000
2	124,000
3	146,000

Task

Calculate the net present value of the project at a discount rate of 20%.

	Year 0	Year 1	Year 2	Year 3
Capital expenditure				
Net cash flow				
PV Factor	1.000	0.833	0.694	0.579
Discounted cash flow				
Net present value				

The net present value is *positive/negative**
*delete as appropriate

The payback period is   Year(s) and   Months

Accept/*reject** investment
*delete as appropriate

 Test your understanding 8

Martinez Limited makes a single product, the Angel.

Martinez Limited has a long-term contract to supply a group of customers with 10,000 units of Angel a year for the next three years.

Martinez is considering investing in a new machine to manufacture the Angel. This machine will produce 10,000 units a year, which have a profit of £8 per unit. The machine will cost £220,000 and will last for the duration of the contract. At the end of the contract the machine will be scrapped with no resale value.

Task

Calculate the present value of the machine project if a 10% discount rate is used.

	Year 0	Year 1	Year 2	Year 3
Capital expenditure				
Net cash flow				
PV Factor	1.000	0.909	0.826	0.751
Discounted cash flow				
Net present value				

The net present value is *positive/negative**
delete as appropriate

The payback period is .... Year(s) and .... Months

Accept/*reject** investment
delete as appropriate

Test your understanding 9

Loamshire County Council operates a library service.

In order to reduce operating expenses over the next four or five years, there is a proposal to introduce a major upgrade to the computer system used by the library service. Two alternative projects are under examination with different initial outlays and different estimated savings over time. The computer manager has prepared the following schedule:

	Project A £	Project B £
Initial outlay	75,000	100,000
Annual cash savings		
1st year	20,000	30,000
2nd year	30,000	45,000
3rd year	30,000	45,000
4th year	25,000	40,000
5th year	20,000	–

Assume that the cash savings occur at the end of the year, even though in practice they would be spread over the year. From a technical point of view, both systems meet the librarian's specification. It is assumed that there will be no further savings after year 5. The county uses the net present value method for evaluating projects at a 10% discount rate.

Task

Project A

	Year 0	Year 1	Year 2	Year 3	Year 4	Year 5
Capital expenditure						
Net cash flow						
PV Factor	1.000	0.909	0.826	0.751	0.683	0.621
Discounted cash flow						
Net present value						

The net present value is *positive/negative**
*delete as appropriate

The payback period is   Year(s) and   Months

Project B

	Year 0	Year 1	Year 2	Year 3	Year 4
Capital expenditure					
Net cash flow					
PV Factor	1.000	0.909	0.826	0.751	0.683
Discounted cash flow					
Net present value					

The net present value is *positive/negative**
*delete as appropriate

The payback period is   Year(s) and   Months

Invest in *A/B**
*delete as appropriate

Test your understanding 10

A transport company is considering purchasing an automatic vehicle-cleansing machine. At present, all vehicles are cleaned by hand.

The machine will cost £80,000 to purchase and install in year 0 and it will have a useful life of four years with no residual value.

The company uses a discount rate of 10% to appraise all capital projects.

The cash savings from the machine will be:

Year	£
0	–
1	29,600
2	29,200
3	28,780
4	28,339

Task

As assistant management accountant, you are asked to carry out an appraisal of the proposal to purchase the machine and prepare a report to the general manager of the company. Your report should contain the following information:

1   the net present value of the cash flows from the project

2   the payback period of the proposal

3   a recommendation as to whether or not the proposal should be accepted.

	Year 0	Year 1	Year 2	Year 3	Year 4
Capital expenditure					
Net cash flow					
PV Factor	1.000	0.909	0.826	0.751	0.683
Discounted cash flow					
Net present value					

The net present value is *positive/negative**
**delete as appropriate*

The payback period is   Year(s)

Accept/*reject** project
**delete as appropriate*

Test your understanding 11

A company is considering setting up a small in-house printing facility.

Machines costing £14,400 will be purchased in year 0. They will last for four years and will have no value at the end of this time.

The cash savings associated with the machines will be:

Year	£
0	–
1	6,920
2	6,920
3	6,920
4	6,920

Task

(a) Calculate the net present value of the cash flows from the proposal, using a 12% discount rate over four years.

Assume that all cash flows occur at the end of the year.

(b) Calculate the payback period for the proposal assuming that cash flows occur evenly through the year.

	Year 0	Year 1	Year 2	Year 3	Year 4
Capital expenditure					
Net cash flow					
PV Factor	1.000	0.893	0.797	0.712	0.636
Discounted cash flow					
Net present value					

The net present value is *positive/negative**
delete as appropriate

The payback period is   Year(s) and   Months

Accept/*reject** project
delete as appropriate

6 Internal rate of return

6.1 The internal rate of return (IRR)

> **🔍 Definition**
>
> The **IRR** calculates the **rate of return** (or discount rate) that one project is expected to achieve if it **breaks even** i.e. no profit or loss is made. The IRR is therefore the point where the **NPV of an investment is zero**.

For one investment, a graph of NPV against discount rate looks like the following:

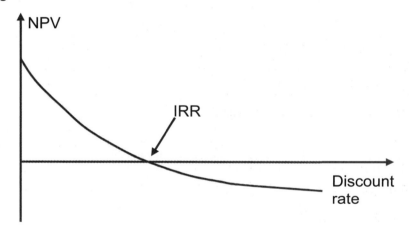

As the discount rate gets higher, the NPV gets smaller and then becomes negative. The cash flows are being discounted by a higher percentage therefore the present value of the cash flows becomes less.

The internal rate of return (IRR) is the discount rate that will cause the cash flow of a project to have a net present value equal to zero.

To decide on whether to invest using the IRR you need to compare the IRR with the discount rate that the company would like to use. If the chosen discount rate was somewhere between 10% and 15%, and the IRR of a project was 22% then we can still accept the project as our rate is less than the IRR, giving a positive NPV.

> **📝 Test your understanding 12**
>
> If the company's cost of capital is 16% and the IRR is 14% the investment should go ahead.
>
> True or false?

6.2 Calculation of the IRR

The approximate IRR of a project can be estimated by considering how close the NPVs are to zero.

The method used to estimate the IRR is as follows:

- Calculate two NPVs for the investment at different discount rates.

- Estimate the IRR with reference to the NPV values.

Example 3

A machine costs £150,000 now. We expect the following cash flows:

	Year 1 (t = 1) £000	Year 2 (t = 2) £000	Year 3 (t = 3) £000	Year 4 (t = 4) £000	Year 5 (t = 5) £000
Scrap value					30
Sales revenues	40	50	60	50	40
Variable costs	(10)	(12)	(15)	(13)	(11)

Estimate the IRR of the investment.

Solution

1   NPV with a discount rate of 10% = £4,400

2   NPV at a discount rate of 20% = -£31,000

3   Estimate the IRR.

The IRR will be closer to 10% then 20% as £4,400 is closer to zero than -£31,000. As indicated by the diagram below:

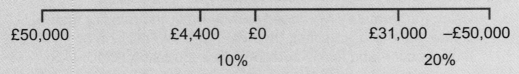

£50,000   £4,400   £0   £31,000   -£50,000

                      10%   20%

From this we could estimate the IRR as approximately 11% or 12%.

The IRR of an investment can also be calculated using linear interpolation i.e. it uses two known points on a graph and joins them with a straight line. The point where the line crosses the x-axis will be calculated to provide the IRR.

The method used to calculate the IRR is as follows:

- Calculate two NPVs for the investment at different discount rates.
- Use the following formula to find the IRR:

$$IRR\,(\%) = L + \frac{N_L}{N_L - N_H} \times (H - L)$$

Where:

L = Lower rate of interest

H = Higher rate of interest

N_L = NPV at lower rate of interest

N_H = NPV at higher rate of interest

Example 4

A machine costs £150,000 now. We expect the following cash flows:

	Year 1 (t = 1) £000	Year 2 (t = 2) £000	Year 3 (t = 3) £000	Year 4 (t = 4) £000	Year 5 (t = 5) £000
Scrap value					30
Sales revenues	40	50	60	50	40
Variable costs	(10)	(12)	(15)	(13)	(11)

Calculate the IRR of the investment.

Solution

1   NPV with a discount rate of 10% = £4,400 positive

2   NPV at a discount rate of 20% = £31,000 negative

3   Using the formula – you need to remember the rules of maths. Remove the brackets first, then deal with and division or multiplication and finally addition and subtraction (BODMAS).

$$IRR = L + \frac{N_L}{N_L - N_H} \times (H - L)$$

$$IRR = 10 + \frac{4,400}{4,400 - -31,000} \times (20 - 10)$$

$$IRR = 10 + \frac{4,400}{35,400} \times 10$$

$$IRR = 10 + 0.1243 \times 10$$

$$IRR = 10 + 1.243 = 11.24\%$$

Test your understanding 13

A business undertakes high-risk investments and requires a minimum expected rate of return of 17% per annum on its investments.
A proposed capital investment has the following expected cash flows:

	£
Year 0	(50,000)
Year 1	18,000
Year 2	25,000
Year 3	20,000
Year 4	10,000

1   Calculate the NPV using 15% cost of capital and 20% cost of capital.

The relevant present value factors are:

	Year 1	Year 2	Year 3	Year 4
15%	0.870	0.756	0.658	0.572
20%	0.833	0.694	0.579	0.482

NPV @ 15%

	Year 0	Year 1	Year 2	Year 3	Year 4
Capital expenditure					
Net cash flow					
PV Factor	1.000	0.870	0.756	0.658	0.572
Discounted cash flow					
Net present value					

NPV @ 20%

	Year 0	Year 1	Year 2	Year 3	Year 4
Capital expenditure					
Net cash flow					
PV Factor	1.000	0.833	0.694	0.579	0.482
Discounted cash flow					
Net present value					

2   Using the NPVs you have calculated, estimate the IRR of the project.

3   Should the company proceed with the investment?

6.3 Advantages of IRR

(a) It considers the **time value of money** as NPVs are used in the calculation process.

(b) It uses cash flows which are less subjective than profits. Profit measures rely on such things as depreciation and other policies which are to a certain extent subjective.

(c) It considers the **whole life** of the project.

(d) It provides a **percentage return** that is easier for non-financial managers to understand.

(e) It can be calculated without deciding on the desired cost of capital

6.4 Disadvantages of IRR

(a) Cash flows are future predictions and we are **unable to predict** the future with accuracy.

(b) It does not provide a monetary value for the return available from the investment.

6.5 Conflict between Payback, NPV and IRR

NPV is considered the most robust of the project appraisal techniques so if there is a conflict between payback, NPV and IRR then the result of the NPV should be used to make the final decision with regards investment.

 Test your understanding 14

Data

RBG plc is a large quoted company using a 25% rate of interest for appraising capital projects. One of its divisional directors has put forward plans to make a new product, the AI. This will involve buying a machine specifically for that task. The machine will cost £600,000 and have a life of 5 years. However, because of the nature of the product, the machine will have no residual value at any time.

The annual cash flows will be as follows:

	£
Sales revenues	380,000
Material costs	90,000
Labour costs	30,000
Overhead costs	20,000

Task

You are asked to appraise the divisional director's proposal by calculating:

(a)   the net present value

(b)   the payback period

	Year 0	Year 1	Year 2	Year 3	Year 4	Year 5
Capital expenditure						
Net cash flow						
PV Factor	1.000	0.800	0.640	0.512	0.410	0.328
Discounted cash flow						
Net present value						

The net present value is *positive/negative**
delete as appropriate

The payback period is   Year(s) and   Months

Further information

The IRR is 28%.

The new product *should be/should not be** purchased
delete as appropriate

 Test your understanding 15

Mickey

Mickey is considering two mutually-exclusive projects with the following details.

	A £	B £
Initial investment	450,000	100,000
Year 1	200,000	50,000
Year 2	150,000	40,000
Year 3	100,000	30,000
Year 4	100,000	20,000
Year 5	100,000	20,000

At the end of the five years each project has a scrap value. Project A's scrap value is £20,000 and Project B's scrap value is £10,000.

1   Calculate the payback period of each project.

2   Calculate the NPV of each project to the nearest £000 using a cost of capital of 10%.

The relevant present value factors are:

	Year 1	Year 2	Year 3	Year 4	Year 5
10%	0.909	0.826	0.751	0.683	0.621

Project A

	Year 0	Year 1	Year 2	Year 3	Year 4	Year 5
Capital expenditure						
Net cash flow						
PV Factor	1.000	0.909	0.826	0.751	0.683	0.621
Discounted cash flow						
Net present value						

Project B

	Year 0	Year 1	Year 2	Year 3	Year 4	Year 5
Capital expenditure						
Net cash flow						
PV Factor	1.000	0.909	0.826	0.751	0.683	0.621
Discounted cash flow						
Net present value						

If Project A is appraised using a cost of capital of 20% the NPV is £25,000 negative. If Project B is appraised using a cost of capital of 20% the NPV is £8,500 positive.

3   Calculate the IRR of each project.

4   Which project should Mickey invest in and why?

7 Summary

In this chapter we have considered the mechanics, the advantages and the disadvantages of various investment appraisal techniques. In the context of an examination, you must be able to **calculate** the **payback period, the net present value and the IRR of a project.**

The payback period ignoring discounting calculates how long it will take to recover the initial investment in a project. If this is longer than expected then the project should be rejected.

The Net Present Value is an appraisal technique that takes discounted cash flows and calculates the return from an investment in monetary terms. The project is viable if the NPV is positive,

The IRR of a project is the discount rate at which a project has a NPV equal to zero. A cost of capital (or discount rate) which is less than the IRR will give rise to a positive NPV (and is therefore considered to be an 'acceptable investment').

If there are conflicts between payback, NPV and IRR investment appraisal methods then the NPV is the strongest measure so the **NPV result will overrule the payback and IRR.**

Test your understanding answers

Test your understanding 1

Time	Cash flow £000	Cumulative position £000	Working £000
t = 0	(100)	(100)	
t = 1	30	(70)	(100) + 30
t = 2	40	(30)	(70) + 40
t = 3	60	30	(30) + 60
t = 4	10	40	30 + 10

Payback period is **2** years and **6** months.

$$= 2\,^{30}\!/_{60} \text{ or 2.5 years}$$

or

£60,000/12 = £5000

£30,000/£5000 = 6 months

Test your understanding 2

The payback period is **3** Year(s) and **0** Months

Year	Cash flow	Cumulative cash flow
0	(30,000)	(30,000)
1	9,000	(21,000)
2	11,000	(10,000)
3	10,000	0

Test your understanding 3

	Year 0	Year 1	Year 2	Year 3	Year 4
Capital expenditure	(80,000)				
Sales revenues		40,000	70,000	80,000	90,000
Operating costs		(20,000)	(20,000)	(40,000)	(80,000)
Net cash flow	(80,000)	20,000	50,000	40,000	10,000
PV Factor	1.000	0.870	0.756	0.658	0.572
Discounted cash flow	(80,000)	17,400	37,800	26,320	5,720
Net present value	7,240				

The net present value is *positive*.

Test your understanding 4

Machine A

	Year 0	Year 1	Year 2	Year 3	Year 4	Year 5
Capital expenditure	(100,000)					
Net cash flow	(100,000)	20,000	60,000	40,000	30,000	20,000
PV Factor	1.000	0.952	0.907	0.864	0.823	0.784
Discounted cash flow	(100,000)	19,040	54,420	34,560	24,690	15,680
Net present value	48,390					

The net present value of Machine A is *positive*.

Machine B

	Year 0	Year 1	Year 2	Year 3	Year 4	Year 5
Capital expenditure	(60,000)	(60,000)				
Net cash flow	(60,000)	(60,000)	60,000	60,000	80,000	0
PV Factor	1.000	0.952	0.907	0.864	0.823	0.784
Discounted cash flow	(60,000)	(57,120)	54,420	51,840	65,840	0
Net present value	54,980					

The net present value of Machine B is *positive*.

Machine *B* has the higher NPV therefore the return from using this machine is better than machine A. Machine *B* should be selected.

Test your understanding 5

Machine A

	Year 0	Year 1	Year 2	Year 3	Year 4	Year 5
Capital expenditure	100,000					
Net cash flow	100,000	20,000	50,000	30,000	20,000	10,000
PV Factor	1.000	0.926	0.857	0.794	0.735	0.681
Discounted cash flow	100,000	18,520	42,850	23,820	14,700	6,810
Net present cost	206,700					

Machine B

	Year 0	Year 1	Year 2	Year 3	Year 4	Year 5
Capital expenditure	80,000					
Net cash flow	80,000	20,000	30,000	40,000	50,000	60,000
PV Factor	1.000	0.926	0.857	0.794	0.735	0.681
Discounted cash flow	80,000	18,520	25,710	31,760	36,750	40,860
Net present cost	233,600					

Machine *A* should be selected as it has the *lower* net present cost.

✎ Test your understanding 6

	Year 0	Year 1	Year 2	Year 3	Year 4	Year 5
Capital expenditure	(50,000)					
Net cash flow	(50,000)	18,000	20,000	21,000	22,000	18,000
PV Factor	1.000	0.893	0.797	0.712	0.636	0.567
Discounted cash flow	(50,000)	16,074	15,940	14,952	13,992	10,206
Net present value	21,164					

The net present value is *positive*.

The payback period is **2** Year(s) and **7** Months

Year	Cash flow	Cumulative cash flow
0	(50,000)	(50,000)
1	18,000	(32,000)
2	20,000	(12,000)
3	21,000	9,000
4	22,000	

12,000/21,000 × 12 = 7 months

Accept.

Test your understanding 7

	Year 0	Year 1	Year 2	Year 3
Capital expenditure	(285,400)			
Net cash flow	(285,400)	102,000	124,000	146,000
PV Factor	1.000	0.833	0.694	0.579
Discounted cash flow	(285,400)	84,966	86,056	84,534
Net present value	(29,844)			

The net present value is *negative*.

The payback period is   **2**   Year(s) and   **5**   Months

Year	Cash flow	Cumulative cash flow
0	(285,400)	(285,400)
1	102,000	(183,400)
2	124,000	(59,400)
3	146,000	86,600

59,400/146,000 × 12 = 5 months

This project has a negative NPV but still pays back within the life of the project. This project should be **rejected** as when the time value of money is considered there is not a return from the investment.

Test your understanding 8

	Year 0	Year 1	Year 2	Year 3
Capital expenditure	(220,000)			
Net cash flow	(220,000)	80,000	80,000	80,000
PV Factor	1.000	0.909	0.826	0.751
Discounted cash flow	(220,000)	72,720	66,080	60,080
Net present value	(21,120)			

The net present value is *negative*.

The payback period is   **2**   Year(s) and   **9**   Months

Year	Cash flow	Cumulative cash flow
0	(220,000)	(220,000)
1	80,000	(140,000)
2	80,000	(60,000)
3	80,000	20,000

60,000/80,000 × 12 = 9 months

This project has a negative NPV but still pays back within the life of the project. This project should be rejected as when the time value of money is considered there is not a return from the investment.

 Test your understanding 9

Project A

	Year 0	Year 1	Year 2	Year 3	Year 4	Year 5
Capital expenditure	(75,000)					
Net cash flow	(75,000)	20,000	30,000	30,000	25,000	20,000
PV Factor	1.000	0.909	0.826	0.751	0.683	0.621
Discounted cash flow	(75,000)	18,180	24,780	22,530	17,075	12,420
Net present value	19,985					

The net present value is *positive*.

The payback period is **2** Year(s) and **10** Months

Year	Cash flow	Cumulative cash flow
0	(75,000)	(75,000)
1	20,000	(55,000)
2	30,000	(25,000)
3	30,000	5,000

25,000/30,000 × 12 = 10 months

Project B

	Year 0	Year 1	Year 2	Year 3	Year 4
Capital expenditure	(100,000)				
Net cash flow	(100,000)	30,000	45,000	45,000	40,000
PV Factor	1.000	0.909	0.826	0.751	0.683
Discounted cash flow	(100,000)	27,270	37,170	33,795	27,320
Net present value	25,555				

The net present value is *positive*.

The payback period is **2** Year(s) and **7** Months

Year	Cash flow	Cumulative cash flow
0	(100,000)	(100,000)
1	30,000	(70,000)
2	45,000	(25,000)
3	45,000	20,000

25,000/45,000 × 12 = 7 months

Project **B** should be invested in.

Project B should be recommended as it has the higher discounted cash flow, therefore the higher return from the investment. Payback is a cruder method of assessing future cash flows. No account is taken of flows after the payback period and equal weight given to flows within the payback period.

Test your understanding 10

	Year 0	Year 1	Year 2	Year 3	Year 4
Capital expenditure	(80,000)				
Net cash flow	(80,000)	29,600	29,200	28,780	28,339
PV Factor	1.000	0.909	0.826	0.751	0.683
Discounted cash flow	(80,000)	26,906	24,119	21,614	19,356
Net present value	11,995				

The net present value is *positive*.

The payback period is   **2**   Year(s) and   **9**   Months

Year	Cash flow	Cumulative cash flow
0	(80,000)	(80,000)
1	29,600	(50,400)
2	29,200	(21,200)
3	28,780	7,580

21,200/28,780 × 12 = 9 months

Accept.

Test your understanding 11

	Year 0	Year 1	Year 2	Year 3	Year 4
Capital expenditure	(14,400)				
Net cash flow	(14,400)	6,920	6,920	6,920	6,920
PV Factor	1.000	0.893	0.797	0.712	0.636
Discounted cash flow	(14,400)	6,180	5,515	4,927	4,401
Net present value	6,623				

The net present value is *positive*.

The payback period is   **2**   Year(s) and   **1**   Month

Year	Cash flow	Cumulative cash flow
0	(14,400)	(14,400)
1	6,920	(7480)
2	6,920	(560)
3	6,920	6,360

560/6,920 × 12 = 1 month

Accept.

Test your understanding 12

False. The IRR is lower than the cost of capital therefore the investment will have broken even at 14% and be a negative NPV at 16%.

 Test your understanding 13

1   Calculate the NPV using 15% cost of capital and 20% cost of capital.

NPV @ 15%

	Year 0	Year 1	Year 2	Year 3	Year 4
Capital expenditure	(50,000)				
Net cash flow	(50,000)	18,000	25,000	20,000	10,000
PV Factor	1.000	0.870	0.756	0.658	0.572
Discounted cash flow	(50,000)	15,660	18,900	13,160	5,720
Net present value	3,440				

NPV @ 20%

	Year 0	Year 1	Year 2	Year 3	Year 4
Capital expenditure	(50,000)				
Net cash flow	(50,000)	18,000	25,000	20,000	10,000
PV Factor	1.000	0.833	0.694	0.579	0.482
Discounted cash flow	(50,000)	14,994	17,350	11,580	4,820
Net present value	−1,256				

2   Using the NPVs you have calculated, estimate the IRR of the project.

$$IRR = L + \frac{N_L}{N_L - N_H} \times (H - L)$$

$$IRR = 15 + \frac{3,440}{3,440 - -1,256} \times (20 - 15)$$

$$IRR = 15 + \frac{3,440}{4,696} \times 5$$

$$IRR = 15 + \quad 3.663 \quad = 18.7\%$$

3   Should the company proceed with the investment?

The IRR of the project is 18.7%. The company requires a return of 17%. The IRR is higher than the required return therefore the company should invest.

 Test your understanding 14

	Year 0	Year 1	Year 2	Year 3	Year 4	Year 5
Capital expenditure	(600,000)					
Net cash flow	(600,000)	240,000	240,000	240,000	240,000	240,000
PV Factor	1.000	0.800	0.640	0.512	0.410	0.328
Discounted cash flow	(600,000)	192,000	153,600	122,880	98,400	78,720
Net present value	45,600					

The net present value is *positive*.

The payback period is   **2**   Year(s) and   **6**   Months

Year	Cash flow	Cumulative cash flow
0	(600,000)	(600,000)
1	240,000	(360,000)
2	240,000	(120,000)
3	240,000	120,000

120,000/240,000 × 12 = 6 months

The new product **should** be purchased.

Test your understanding 15

1   Calculate the payback period for each project.

Project A

	Cash flow	Cumulative cash flow
Year 0	(450,000)	(450,000)
Year 1	200,000	(250,000)
Year 2	150,000	(100,000)
Year 3	100,000	0

Payback is 3 years.

Project B

	Cash flow	Cumulative cash flow
Year 0	(100,000)	(100,000)
Year 1	50,000	(50,000)
Year 2	40,000	(10,000)
Year 3	30,000	20,000

Payback is 2 years 4 months.

2   Calculate the NPV for each project.

Project A

	Year 0	Year 1	Year 2	Year 3	Year 4	Year 5
Capital expenditure	(450)					
Net cash flow	(450)	200	150	100	100	120
PV Factor	1.000	0.909	0.826	0.751	0.683	0.621
Discounted cash flow	(450)	182	124	75	68	75
Net present value	74					

Project B

	Year 0	Year 1	Year 2	Year 3	Year 4	Year 5
Capital expenditure	(100)					
Net cash flow	(100)	50	40	30	20	30
PV Factor	1.000	0.909	0.826	0.751	0.683	0.621
Discounted cash flow	(100)	45	33	23	14	19
Net present value	34					

3　Calculate the IRR of each project.

Project A

$$IRR = 10 + \frac{74}{74 - -25} \times (20 - 10)$$

IRR = 17.5%

Project B

$$IRR = 10 + \frac{34}{34 - 8.5} \times (20 - 10)$$

IRR = 23.3%

4　Which project should Mickey invest in and why?

Project **A** should be invested in.

Project B has a shorter payback period and higher IRR but the NPV of Project A is the greater therefore providing the better return for the investment. NPV is the more robust of the investment appraisal techniques used as it considers the whole life of the project, includes the effect of the time value of money and also provides an absolute value for the return from the investment.

MOCK ASSESSMENT

1 Mock Assessment Questions

Task 1 **(16 marks)**

The following information is available for product ZYQ:

Annual demand – 1,250,000 kilograms

Annual holding cost per kilogram – £5

Fixed ordering cost – £2

(a) Calculate the Economic Order Quantity (EOQ) for ZYQ. (2 marks)

_____

The inventory record shown below for product ZYQ for the month of April has only been fully completed for the first three weeks of the month.

(b) Complete the entries in the inventory record for the two receipts on 24 and 28 April that were ordered using the EOQ method.
(2 marks)

(c) Complete ALL entries in the inventory record for the two issues in the month and for the closing balance at the end of April using the AVCO method of issuing inventory. (8 marks)

Inventory record for product ZYQ. (Show the costs per kilogram (kg) in £ to 3 decimal places, and the total costs in whole £.)

	Receipts			Issues			Balance	
Date	Quantity (kg)	Cost per kg (£)	Total cost (£)	Quantity (kg)	Cost per kg (£)	Total cost (£)	Quantity (kg)	Total cost (£)
Balance as at 22 April							900	1,125
24 April		1.275						
26 April				800				
28 April		1.475						
30 April				750				

(d) Using the LIFO method:

The issue of 800 kg to production on the 26 April would be valued at a total of _____. **(2 marks)**

(e) Which of the following costs would never be included in the valuation of inventory? **(2 marks)**

   A   Marginal costs

   B   Prime costs

   C   Product costs

   D   Period costs

Task 2 **(16 marks)**

Below are extracts from Bounce Ltd's payroll for last week.

Date	Labour cost
6 July	Stores department Employees pay £3,000 + 8% bonus
11 July	Administration department Staff salaries £4,000 + 10% bonus
13 July	Manufacturing Production employees pay 400 hours at £8.00 per hour
15 July	Assembly Production employees basic pay £4,000 + £200 overtime

The cost codes for the different accounts are:

Non-operating overheads	7000
Operating overheads	8000
Wages control account	2000
Manufacturing direct costs	1020
Assembly direct costs	1025

Complete the cost journal entries to record the four payroll payments made in July.

Date	Code	Dr £	Cr £
6 July			
6 July			
11 July			
11 July			
13 July			
13 July			
15 July			
15 July			

Task 3 (12 marks)

Information is available relating to the production of the 100,000 tins of cat food for the month of September:

Total number of labour hours worked	21,600
Overtime hours worked	4,900
Standard hours for production in September	22,400
Basic rate per hour	£8
Overtime payment per hour	£14.50

The company operates a group incentive scheme, whereby a bonus of 25% of the basic hourly rate is paid for hours saved.

(a) **Calculate the total cost of direct labour for September, assuming that overtime and the bonus are due to a specific customer request.** (5 marks)

Total basic pay (£)	
Total overtime premium (£)	
Hours saved (hours)	
Bonus (£)	
Total direct labour cost (£)	

(b) Calculate the total labour cost per tin of cat food in the month of September (to the nearest penny)   **(2 marks)**

The total labour cost of each tin in the month of September is:

£

In October the bonus was based on equivalent units. Employees will receive 20% of the basic hourly rate for every equivalent unit in excess of target. Rates of pay are not due to change in October. The target production is 90,000 units.

At the end of October 60,000 units were completed and there were 50,000 units of closing work in progress that was 100% complete for material and 70% complete for labour.

(c) Calculate the number of equivalent units with regards to labour and the bonus payable   **(3 marks)**

Equivalent units	
Excess unit	
Bonus (£)	

(d) Calculate the bonus per tin of cat food in the month of October to the nearest penny   **(2 marks)**

The bonus per equivalent unit in the month of September is:

£

Task 4 (18 marks)

Icon Ltd's budgeted overheads for the next financial year are:

	£	£
Depreciation of machinery		974,850
Power for machinery		541,000
Rent and rates		104,500
Light and heat		23,100
Indirect labour costs:		
Maintenance	101,150	
Stores	36,050	
Administration	240,100	
Total indirect labour cost		377,300

The following information is also available:

Department	Carrying amount of machinery	Machinery power usage (KwH)	Floor space (square metres)	Number of employees
Assembly	4,200,000	298,800		15
Finishing	1,800,000	199,200		10
Maintenance			18,000	4
Stores			10,800	3
Administration			7,200	8
Total	6,000,000	498,000	36,000	40

Overheads are allocated or apportioned on the most appropriate basis. The total overheads of the support cost centres are then reapportioned to the two production centres using the direct method.

- 78% of the maintenance cost centre's time is spent maintaining machinery in the Assembly and the remainder in the Finishing.

- The stores cost centre makes 70% of its issues to the Assembly, and 30% to the Finishing.

- Administration supports the two production centres equally.

- There is no reciprocal servicing between the three support cost centres.

Complete the apportionment table using the data on this page.

	Basis	Assembly £	Finishing £	Maintenance £	Stores £	Admin £	Total £
Depreciation of machinery							
Power for machinery							
Rent and rates							
Light and heat							
Indirect labour							
Totals							
Reapportion maintenance							
Reapportion stores							
Reapportion admin							
Total overheads to production centres							

Task 5 (15 marks)

Next quarter Icon Ltd's budgeted overheads and activity levels are:

	Assembly	Finishing
Budgeted overheads (£)	147,224	62,900
Budgeted direct labour hours	16,358	10,483
Budgeted machine hours	5,258	3,700

(a) **What would be the budgeted overhead absorption rate for each department if this were set based on their both being heavily automated?** (2 marks)

    A   Assembly £28/hour, Finishing £17/hour

    B   Assembly £9/hour, Finishing £17/hour

    C   Assembly £9/hour, Finishing £6/hour

    D   Assembly £28/hour, Finishing £6/hour

(b) **What would be the budgeted overhead absorption rate for each department if this were set based on their both being labour intensive?** (2 marks)

    A   Assembly £28/hour, Finishing £17/hour

    B   Assembly £9/hour, Finishing £17/hour

    C   Assembly £9/hour, Finishing £6/hour

    D   Assembly £28/hour, Finishing £6/hour

Additional data

At the end of the quarter actual overheads incurred were found to be:

	Assembly	Finishing
Actual overheads (£)	152,841	61,100

Overheads were recovered on a labour hour basis. The labour hours worked were 10% less than budget in Assembly and 5% more in Finishing (round to the nearest whole £ throughout the calculation).

(c) Calculate the overhead that was absorbed in each department and state the under or over absorption that occurred in each department (answers to the nearest £) **(8 marks)**

	Actual hours worked	Absorbed amount £	Under/over	Value £
Assembly				
Finishing				

(d) The management accountant's report shows that fixed production overheads were over-absorbed in the last accounting period. The combination that is certain to lead to this situation is: **(3 marks)**

A   production volume is lower than budget and actual expenditure is higher than budget

B   production volume is higher than budget and actual expenditure is lower than budget

C   production volume is higher than budget and actual expenditure is higher than budget

D   production volume and actual cost are as budgeted

Task 6 (25 marks)

The Finishing department of Icon Ltd uses process costing for some of its products. Following are details for the month of April.

The component requires the input of three different materials:

Material ZY1 – 400kg @ £1.66 per kilogram

Material ZY2 – 300kg @ £1.50 per kilogram

Material ZY3 – 200kg @ £0.60 per kilogram

(a) Complete the table below (to two decimal places) to show the total cost of the material input into the process. **(4 marks)**

Materials	£
Material ZY1	
Material ZY2	
Material ZY3	
Total	

Icon Ltd estimates that the process will require two employees to work 38 hours per week for 4 weeks. These employees were paid £9 per hour.

Overheads are absorbed on the basis of £14 per labour hour.

(b) **Calculate the total labour cost and total overhead cost for April.**
(4 marks)

The total labour cost is: £ _____ .

The total overhead cost is: £ _____ .

(c) **Calculate the total quantity and value of inputs into the process in April.** **(4 marks)**

The total quantity of material input into the process is: _____ kg.

The total value of inputs into the process is: £ _____ .

Icon Ltd expects a normal loss of 4% during this process, which it then sells for scrap at 50p per kg.

(d) **Calculate the total scrap value of the normal loss, state your answer to 2 decimal places.** **(2 marks)**

The total scrap value of the normal loss is £ _____ ,

(e) **Calculate the cost per kilogram of output assuming a normal loss of 4%. Your answer must be stated to four decimal places.**
(2 marks)

The cost per kilogram of output assuming a normal loss is £ _____ .

(f) **Complete the sentences below, using the options listed, to identify the correct accounting entries. Enter your answer two 2 decimal places.** **(4 marks)**

If the process results in an output of 850 kilograms there will be **an abnormal loss / an abnormal gain** of _____ kg.

This will have a total value of £ _____ .

(g) **Which of these is an example of unethical behaviour by an accounting technician?** **(2 marks)**

A   Valuing inventory so as to maximise a periods profits

B   Calculating profits objectively rather than subjectively

C   Allocating costs between products objectively

D   Treating costs as confidential

(h)   **Why might a business decide to allocate its costs between the products of different departments** **(3 marks)**

    A   To reduce its overall inventory valuation

    B   To report segmented profits/losses

    C   To speed up its internal reporting

    D   To comply with accounting standards

Task 7   (16 marks)

Product ZYQ has a selling price of £52 per unit with a total variable cost of £38 per unit. Icon Ltd estimates that the fixed costs per quarter associated with this product are £84,000.

(a)   **Calculate the budgeted breakeven, in units, for product ZYQ.**
                                        (2 marks)

	units

(b)   **Calculate the budgeted breakeven, in £, for product ZYQ.**
                                        (2 marks)

£

(c)   **Complete the table below to show the budgeted margin of safety in units, and the margin of safety percentage if Icon Ltd sells 8,000 units or 9,000 units of product ZYQ.** **(6 marks)**

Units of ZYQ sold	8,000 units	9,000 units
Margin of safety (units)		
Margin of safety percentage (to the nearest percent)		

(d)   **If Icon Ltd wishes to make a profit of £21,000, how many units of ZYQ must it sell?** **(3 marks)**

	units

(e) **If Icon Ltd increases the selling price of ZYQ by £1, what will be the impact on the breakeven point and the margin of safety, assuming no change in the number of units sold?** **(2 marks)**

- A The breakeven point will decrease and the margin of safety will increase.

- B The breakeven point will stay the same but the margin of safety will decrease.

- C The breakeven point will decrease and the margin of safety will stay the same.

- D The breakeven point will increase and the margin of safety will decrease.

Task 8 **(16 marks)**

Icon Ltd has prepared a forecast for the next quarter for one of its small wooden parts, ZYG. This component is produced in batches and the forecast is based on selling and producing 1,500 batches.

One of the customers of Icon Ltd has indicated that it may be significantly increasing its order level for component ZYG for the next quarter and it appears that activity levels of 1,800 batches and 2,000 batches are feasible.

The semi-variable costs should be calculated using the high-low method. If 3,000 batches are sold the total semi-variable cost will be £14,000, and there is a constant unit variable cost up to this volume.

Complete the table below and calculate the estimated profit per batch of ZYG at the different activity levels.

Batches produced and sold	1,500	1,800	2,000
	£	£	£
Sales revenue	45,000		
Variable costs:			
Direct materials	7,500		
Direct labour	9,000		
Overheads	6,000		
Semi-variable costs:	11,000		
Variable element			
Fixed element			
Total cost	33,500		
Profit for the period	11,500		
Profit per batch (to 2 decimal places)	7.67		

Task 9   (16 marks)

Icon Ltd has the following original budget and actual performance for product ZYG for the year ending 31 April.

(a)   **Complete the table to show a flexed budget and the resulting variances against this budget for the year. Show the actual variance amount, for sales and each cost, in the column headed 'Variance'**   **(12 marks)**

Note:

- Adverse variance must be denoted with a minus sign or brackets.

- Enter 0 where any figure is zero.

	Original budget	Flexed	Actual	Variance
Volume sold	10,000		12,000	
	£000	**£000**	**£000**	**£000**
Sales revenue	2,000		2,500	
Less costs:				
Direct materials	350		415	
Direct labour	400		435	
Fixed Overheads	980		1,180	
Profit from operations	270		470	

(b) Referring to your answer for part (a), which one of the following has had the greatest impact in decreasing the profit from operations? **(2 marks)**

    A   Sales revenue

    B   Direct materials

    C   Direct labour

    D   Fixed overheads

(c) Which of the following might have caused the variance for direct labour? **(2 marks)**

    A   An increase in units produced

    B   An increase in employees' pay

    C   Improved efficiency of employees

    D   An increase in overtime

Task 10 (20 marks)

One of the painting machines in the Finishing department is nearing the end of its working life and Icon Ltd is considering purchasing a replacement machine.

Estimates have been made for the initial capital cost, sales revenue and operating costs of the replacement machine, which is expected to have a working life of three years:

	Year 0 £000	Year 1 £000	Year 2 £000	Year 3 £000
Capital expenditure	1,900			
Other cash flows:				
Sales revenue		1,620	1,860	2,300
Operating costs		1,120	1,150	1,190

The company appraises capital investment projects using a 15% cost of capital.

(a) **Complete the table below and calculate the net present value of the proposed replacement machine (to the nearest £000).**

(14 marks)

	Year 0 £000	Year 1 £000	Year 2 £000	Year 3 £000
Capital expenditure				
Sales revenue				
Operating costs				
Net cash flows				
PV factors	1.0000	0.8696	0.7561	0.6575
Discounted cash flows				
Net present value				

The net present value is **positive / negative**.

(b) **Calculate the payback of the proposed replacement machine to the nearest whole month.** **(4 marks)**

The payback period is _____Year(s) and _____ Months

(c) **What is the approximate internal rate of return (IRR) of the project?** **(2 marks)**

A   0%

B   10%

C   15%

D   20%

2 Mock Assessment Answers

Task 1

(a) The EOQ is $\sqrt{\dfrac{2 \times 2 \times 1{,}250{,}000}{5}}$ = **1,000 kg**

(b) and (c)

Inventory record for ZYQ

Date	Receipts			Issues			Balance	
	Quantity (kg)	Cost per kg (£)	Total cost (£)	Quantity (kg)	Cost per kg (£)	Total cost (£)	Quantity (kg)	Total cost (£)
Balance as at 22 April							900	1,125
24 April	1,000	1.275	1,275				1,900	2,400
26 April				800	1.263	1,010	1,100	1,390
28 April	1,000	1.475	1,475				2,100	2,865
30 April				750	1.364	1,023	1,350	1,842

(d) 800 × 1.275 = **£1,020**

(e) **D**

Period costs

Task 2

Date	Code	Dr £	Cr £
6 July	8000	£3,000 × 1.08 = 3,240	
6 July	2000		3,240
11 July	7000	£4,000 × 1.1 = 4,400	
11 July	2000		4,400
13 July	1020	400 × £8 = 3,200	
13 July	2000		3,200
15 July	1025	£4,000 + £200 = 4,200	
15 July	2000		£4,200

Task 3

(a)

Total basic pay (£)	21,600 × £8 = £172,800
Total overtime premium (£)	4,900 × (£14.50-£8) = £31,850
Hours saved (hours)	22,400 – 21,600 = 800
Bonus (£)	800 × £8 × 25% = £1,600
Total direct labour cost (£)	£206,250

(b)   £205,250 ÷ 100,000 = **£2.06**

(c)

Equivalent units	Completed = 60,000 × 100% = 60,000
Excess unit	CWIP = 50,000 × 70% = 35,000

(d)   £8,000 ÷ 95,000 = **£0.08**

Task 4

	Basis	Assembly £	Finishing £	Maintenance £	Stores £	Admin £	Total £
Depreciation of machinery	Carrying amount	682,395	292,455				974,850
Power for machinery	KwH	324,600	216,400				541,000
Rent and rates	M²			52,250	31,350	20,900	104,500
Light and heat	M²			11,550	6,930	4,620	23,100
Indirect labour	All			101,150	36,050	240,100	377,300
Totals		1,006,995	508,855	164,950	74,330	265,620	2,020,750
Reapportion maintenance		128,661	36,289	(164,950)			
Reapportion stores		52,031	22,299		(74,330)		
Reapportion admin		132,810	132,810			(265,620)	
Total overheads to production centres		1,320,497	700,253				2,020,750

Task 5

(a)   **A**

(b)   **C**

(c)

	Actual hours worked	Absorbed amount £	Under/over	Value £
Assembly	16,358 × 0.9 = 14,722 hrs	14,722 × £9 = £132,498	Under	£152,841 – £132,498 = £20,343
Finishing	10,483 × 1.05 = 11,007 hrs	11,007 × £6 = £66,042	Over	£66,042 – £61,100 = £4,942

(d)   **B**

Fixed production overheads are over-absorbed when actual expenditure is less than budget and/or actual production volume is higher than budget.

Task 6

(a)

Materials	£
Material ZY1	664
Material ZY2	450
Material ZY3	120
Total	1,234

(b)   The total labour cost is: **£2,736**

The total overhead cost is: **£4,256**

(c)   The total quantity of material input into the process is: **900 kg**

The total value of inputs into the process is: **£8,226.**

(d)   The total scrap value of the normal loss is: **£18**

(e)   The cost per kilogram of output assuming a normal loss is: **£9.5000**

(f)   If the process results in an output of 850 kilograms there will be **an abnormal loss** of 14.00kg.

This will have a total value of **£133.00.**

(g) **A**

(h) **B**

Task 7

(a) **6,000 units**

(b) **£312,000**

(c)

Units of ZYQ sold	8,000 units	9,000 units
Margin of safety (units)	2,000	3,000
Margin of safety percentage (to the nearest percent)	25%	33%

(d) **7,500 units**

(e) **A**

Task 8

Batches produced and sold	1,500	1,800	2,000
	£	£	£
Sales revenue	45,000	54,000	60,000
Variable costs:			
Direct materials	7,500	9,000	10,000
Direct labour	9,000	10,800	12,000
Overheads	6,000	7,200	8,000
Semi-variable costs:	11,000		
Variable element		3,600	4,000
Fixed element		8,000	8,000
Total cost	33,500	38,600	42,000
Profit for the period	11,500	15,400	18,000
Profit per batch (to 2 decimal places)	7.67	8.56	9.00

Task 9

(a)

	Original budget	Flexed	Actual	Variance
Volume sold	10,000	12,000	12,000	
	£000	**£000**	**£000**	**£000**
Sales revenue	2,000	2,400	2,500	100
Less costs:				
Direct materials	350	420	415	5
Direct labour	400	480	435	45
Fixed Overheads	980	980	1,180	−200
Profit from operations	270	520	470	−50

(b) **D**

(c) **C**

Task 10

(a)

	Year 0 £000	Year 1 £000	Year 2 £000	Year 3 £000
Capital expenditure	(1,900)			
Sales revenue		1,620	1,860	2,300
Operating costs		(1,120)	(1,150)	(1,190)
Net cash flows	(1,900)	500	710	1,110
PV factors	1.0000	0.8696	0.7561	0.6575
Discounted cash flows	(1,900)	435	537	730
Net present value	(198)			

The net present value is **negative**.

(b)   The payback period is **2** years and **8** months.

Year	Cash flow	Cumulative cash flow
0	(1,900)	(1,900)
1	500	(1,400)
2	710	(690)
3	1,110	420

(690/1,110) × 12 = 7.5 months

(c)   **10%**

The NPV is negative at 15% so the IRR will be lower.

Glossary

Term	Description
Abnormal gain	The amount by which normal loss exceeds actual loss.
Abnormal loss	The amount by which actual loss exceeds normal loss.
Absorption costing	Inventory units are valued at variable cost plus fixed production overheads absorbed using a pre-determined absorption rate. Activity Based Costing is a more detailed form of Absorption costing
Batch costing	The costing system used for a business where production is made up of different product batches of identical units.
Bonus scheme	A day rate combined with a bonus based on output achieved.
Breakeven point	The level of activity required to make no profit and no loss.
Buffer inventory	Inventory held to cover variations in: – lead time, and – demand during the lead time. Sometimes defined as 'inventory held in excess of average units demanded in average lead time'.
Capital expenditure	Expenditure on the purchase or improvement of non-current assets, appearing in the statement of financial position.
Contribution	Sales revenue less variable cost of sales.
Cost absorption	The charging of overhead costs to cost units.
Cost accounting	The analysis of costs and revenues to provide useful information to assist the management accounting function.
Cost allocation	The charging of overhead costs to the specific cost centre that incurred them.
Cost apportionment	The splitting of shared overhead costs between relevant cost centres using an appropriate basis.

Term	Description
Cost centre	A location, function, activity or item of equipment in respect of which costs are accumulated.
Cost coding	The allocation of a unique code to costs, usually on the source documentation, to allow accurate and detailed analysis.
Cost unit	An individual unit of product or service for which costs can be separately ascertained.
Cost-volume-profit (CVP) analysis	Analysis of the effects of changes of volume on contribution and profit.
Depreciation	An annual internal charge to the statement of profit or loss that spreads the net cost of a non-current asset over the number of years of its useful life.
Direct costs	Costs that can be related directly to a cost unit.
Direct expenses	Expenses that can be related specifically to a cost centre.
Discounted cash flow	An investment appraisal technique which discounts future cash flows to a present value.
Economic batch quantity (EBQ)	To minimise the total of the inventory costs.
Economic order quantity (EOQ)	The quantity to be ordered/produced.
Equivalent unit	The number of whole units to which a partially completed unit is equivalent (= physical units $\times$ percentage completion).
Expenses	Items of expenditure that are not labour or materials related.
FIFO	A method of valuing issues of inventory that assumes that issues are made from the oldest inventory available (First In First Out).
Financial accounting	The production of an historic record of transactions presented in a standard format for use by parties external to the business.
Fixed costs	Costs that vary with time, not activity level.
Idle time	Paid for, but non-productive, hours.

Term	Description
Integrated bookkeeping system	A bookkeeping system whereby ledger accounts are kept that provide the necessary information for both costing and financial accounting.
Internal rate of return	The rate of interest which will cause the stream of cash flows discounted at that rate of interest to have a nil net present value.
Inventory control	The method of ensuring that the right quantity of the right quality of inventory is available at the right time and the right place.
Inventory control levels	Key inventory quantities that assist in inventory control, including re-order level, economic order quantity (EOQ), minimum and maximum inventory levels.
Job costing	The costing system used for a business where production is made up of individual, different, large jobs.
Key factor analysis	The technique of allocating resources between products according to contribution per unit of resource.
Lead time	The time between an order for goods being placed and the receipt of that order.
LIFO	A method of valuing issues of inventory that assumes that issues are made from the newest inventory available (Last In First Out).
Management accounting	The generation, presentation and interpretation of historic, budgeted and forecast information for management for the purposes of planning, control and decision-making.
Margin of safety	The amount by which the level of activity can fall below budget before a loss is made.
Marginal costing	Inventory units are valued at variable production cost; fixed overheads are accounted for as period costs.
Normal loss	The level of expected loss of input from a process.
Over/under absorption (recovery)	Where the amount of overhead absorbed into cost units, using the pre-determined absorption rate, is more/less than the overheads actually incurred.
P/V (C/S) ratio	The ratio of contribution to sales value.

Term	Description
Payback period	The amount of time it takes for an investment project to recover the cash cost of the original investment.
Piecework rates	Where a constant fixed amount is paid per unit of output.
Present value	The value at today's date of an amount of cash received/paid at some time in the future, taking account of the compound interest earned over the relevant period.
Re-order level	The quantity of inventory in hand at the time when a new order is placed.
Re-order quantity	The quantity of inventory ordered. (Be careful to distinguish between re-order level and re-order quantity.)
Revenue expenditure	Expenditure on goods and services that will be charged to the statement of profit or loss.
Secondary apportionment	The re-apportionment of service cost centres' overhead costs to production cost centres.
Semi-variable costs	Costs with both a fixed and variable element.
Stock-outs	Occasions when one or more items of inventory are needed but there are none in inventory.
Stores record card	A record kept for each inventory line, detailing receipts, issues and balance on hand, in terms of both physical quantities and monetary value.
Timesheet	A record of how an employee has spent his/her time, split between jobs/clients and non-productive time.
Usage	The quantity of items required for sale (in the case of goods for resale) or production (in the case of components or raw materials) in a given period.
Variable costs	Costs that vary in direct proportion to the level of activity.
Weighted average cost	A method of valuing issues of inventory that takes account of the relative quantities of inventory available purchased at different prices.

INDEX

A

ABC, 165

Abnormal
    gain, 216, 220, 232
    loss, 216, 218, 228
    loss/gain account, 228

Absorption, 132, 145
    cost, 8
    costing, 129, 165, 267
    rate, 145

Activity based costing, 165, 172

Administration expenses, 120

Allocation, 122, 132, 133

Annual salaries, 95

Apportionment, 132, 133

AVCO, 62, 72, 244

Average cost, 244

Avoidable cost, 285

B

Batch costing, 207

Behaviour, 16

Bonus schemes, 103

Breakeven charts, 299

Budgets, 184

C

C/S ratio, 296

Capital expenditure, 123

Causes of variances, 192

Clock cards, 93

Closing work in progress, 236

Continuous operation costing, 204, 214

Contribution, 264, 265,288

Correction of variances, 197

Cost(s)
    absorption, 8
    accounting, 3
    average, 244
    avoidable, 285
    cards, 8
    centre(s), 5, 6
    classification, 12
    direct, 15
    driver, 165
    fixed, 18, 286
    holding, 53
    indirect, 15
    marginal, 8
    net present, 330, 334
    non-relevant, 285
    object, 5
    of capital, 329
    of sales, 269
    ordering, 53
    per equivalent unit, 238
    per unit, 215
    period, 7
    pool, 165
    prime, 8, 15
    product, 7
    relevant, 284
    stepped fixed, 19, 23
    stock-out, 53
    units, 5
    variable, 17, 285

Cost-volume-profit analysis, 287

Credit note, 50

CVP, 287

CWIP, 236

D

Degrees of completion, 237

Delivery note, 47

Depreciation, 13

Diminishing (reducing) balance, 14

Direct
cost, 15
expenses, 121
labour, 106
method, 141

Discount
factors, 329
rate, 329

Discounting, 328

E

Economic order quantity, 56

Element, 12

Employee records, 90

EOQ, 56

Equivalent units (EU), 236

Ethical principles, 4

EU, 236

Expenses, 120

F

First in, first out (FIFO), 61, 62, 72, 244, 246

Fixed
budgets, 184
costs, 18, 286
overheads variances, 194

Flexed budgets, 186

Function, 13

Future incremental cash flow, 284

G

Goods
received note, 47
requisition note, 43
returned note, 49

Guaranteed minimum, 101

H

High-low method, 24

Holding costs, 53

Hourly rates, 95

I

Indirect
cost, 15
expenses, 121
labour, 106

Integrity, 4

Internal
rate of return, 342
reporting, 7

Inventory
account, 76
control, 55
valuation and profit, 72

Investment centre, *6*

J

Job
card, 204
costing, 204

L

Labour
cost account, 109
variances, *193*

Last in, first out (LIFO), 61, 62, 72

Limiting factor analysis, 302, 303

Long-term investments, 322, 323

Losses, 216

M

Management
accounting, 2
information, 3

Manufacturing expenses, 120

Marginal
cost, 8
costing, 264, 267, 276, 287

Material variances, 193

Maximum inventory, *57*

Minimum inventory, *57*

N

Nature, 15

Net present cost, 330, 334

Net present value, 330

Non-relevant costs, 285

Non-production overheads, 128

Normal loss, 216, 217

NPV, 330

O

Opening work in progress, 244

Ordering costs, 53

Over absorption, 154

Over recovery, 154

Overhead absorption rate (OAR), 145,
    147, 154

Overhead recovery rate, 166

Overheads, 15

Overtime, 95
    payment, 95
    premium, 95, 107

OWIP, 244

P

Payback period, 324

Period cost, 7

Piecework, 99

Present value, 329

Prime cost, 8, 15

Process costing, 214

Product cost, 7

Production overheads, 128
    account, 160

Profit centre, 6

Profit-volume (P/V) chart, 301

Purchase
    invoice, 48
    order, 46
    requisition, 44

Purchasing, 42

R

Reapportionment, 139

Reconciliation of profits, 272

Relevant costing, 284

Remuneration systems, 94

Re-order level, *55*

Required return, 329

Responsibility centres, 5

Revenue expenditure, 123

S

Sales variances, 192

Scrap
    account, 228
    value, 223

Selling and distribution expenses, 120

Semi-variable costs, 20, 24

Service
    cost units, 209
    costing, 209
    industry, 149

Specific order costing, 204

Step down method, 142

Stepped fixed costs, 19, 23

Stock-out costs, 53

Stores department, 51

Straight line method, 14

Sub-division of variances, 195

T

Target profit, 292

Time value of money, 328

Timesheets, 93

U

Under absorption, 154

Under recovery, 154

V

Variable cost(s), 17, 285

Variance analysis, 188

W

Weighted average, 61